LIFE IN CHRIST

Register This New Book

Benefits of Registering*

- ✓ FREE **replacements** of lost or damaged books
- ✓ FREE **audiobook** – *Pilgrim's Progress*, audiobook edition
- ✓ FREE information about new titles and other **freebies**

www.anekopress.com/new-book-registration

*See our website for requirements and limitations.

Life in Christ

Lessons from Our Lord's
Miracles and Parables

The Miracles of Our Lord
Volume 5

Charles H. Spurgeon

We love hearing from our readers. Please contact us
at www.anekopress.com/questions-comments with
any questions, comments, or suggestions.

Life in Christ, Vol. 5
© 2022 by Aneko Press
All rights reserved.
Revised edition 2022
Please do not reproduce, store in a retrieval system, or transmit in any form
or by any means – electronic, mechanical, photocopying, recording, or
otherwise, without written permission from the publisher. Please contact us
via www.AnekoPress.com for reprint and translation permissions.

Unless otherwise indicated, scripture quotations are taken from the New American
Standard Bible® (NASB), copyright © 1960, 1962, 1963, 1968, 1971, 1972, 1973, 1975,
1977, 1995 by The Lockman Foundation. Used by permission. www.Lockman.org.
Scripture quotations marked "KJV" are from The Authorized (King James) Version.
Rights in the Authorized Version in the United Kingdom are vested in the Crown.
Reproduced by permission of the Crown's patentee, Cambridge University Press.

Cover Design: Natalia Hawthorne
Cover Painting: Matt Philleo
Editors: Ruth Clark and J. Martin

Aneko Press
www.anekopress.com
Aneko Press, Life Sentence Publishing, and our logos are trademarks of
Life Sentence Publishing, Inc.
203 E. Birch Street
P.O. Box 652
Abbotsford, WI 54405
RELIGION / Christian Life / Spiritual Growth
Paperback ISBN: 978-1-62245-818-9
eBook ISBN: 978-1-62245-819-6
10 9 8 7 6 5 4 3 2 1
Available where books are sold

Contents

Ch. 1: The Problem of the Age 1

Ch. 2: The Withered Fig Tree..19

Ch. 3: Nothing but Leaves..37

Ch. 4: The Moral of a Miracle..55

Ch. 5: And Why Not Me?..73

Ch. 6: The Lord and the Leper...89

Ch. 7: First Healing and Then Service... 105

Ch. 8: The Best House-Visitation... 123

Ch. 9: Fever, and Its Cure... 141

Ch. 10: The Ministry of Gratitude 157

Ch. 11: With the Disciples on the Sea of Galilee 175

Ch. 12: Christ Asleep in the Vessel... 193

Ch. 13: Why Is Faith So Feeble?... 209

Charles H. Spurgeon – A Brief Biography.. 225

Other Similar Titles 229

Chapter 1

The Problem of the Age

And His disciples answered Him, "Where will anyone be able to find enough bread here in this desolate place to satisfy these people?" (Mark 8:4)

I have been for a while lying outside the crowd, unable either to feed the multitude or to bring the sick to the Master. Here and there one I have helped, as opportunity has occurred; but I have been called to rest rather than to serve. Yet all the while I have never ceased from constant thought about the perishing multitudes; this great city and its sad estate, this country, and Ireland, and continental nations, are all under a cloud of deep depression. One can remove his body from the turmoil, but his heart is in it still.

If ever there was a time when there was a call for the deep sympathy of all Christian people for the perishing multitudes, it is just now; if ever the church should gird herself to do her Master's service, it is today. Never forget that the church is the helpmate of Christ. She is his chosen bride, and she is, therefore, to unite with him in his great enterprise among the sons of men. The work is salvation; and that work is to be done by means of divine truth, carried to men externally by human hands, and internally through the Spirit of God. The church will be false to her heavenly Bridegroom if she does not sympathize with the tenderness of his heart, and enter into his gracious labor of love.

The question before us is certainly singular, if we remember that those who asked it had seen a former miracle of feeding the multitude. It would seem that those who had seen five thousand fed would not ask concerning the feeding of four thousand, *"Where will anyone be able to find enough bread here in this desolate place to satisfy these people?"* Inasmuch as on one memorable occasion they had seen the Master multiply loaves and fish, they might have expected him to do the same again. I grant you to the full that it was an inexcusable question. I will not offer the slightest apology for it; but it is a very *natural* question – natural, I mean, to that fallen and depraved human nature which is our daily grief. He that knows what human nature is, will be astonished at nothing evil that it produces. I do not mean human nature merely unrenewed by grace, but I mean that carnal nature which remains even in the disciples of Christ. This is of such a character that it shamefully gives way to unbelief.

> **He that knows what human nature is, will be astonished at nothing evil that it produces.**

You ask me to give an instance: I point to you. Have you not often seen the hand of God, and yet the next time you have needed divine help you have been in anxiety and doubt? Remember how Israel saw the Red Sea divided, and yet the people feared that they would die of thirst. When the split rock had relieved them, they were next afraid of hunger; and after the heavens had rained on them bread, they became alarmed at the size of the giants who dwelt in Canaan. All that God had done seemed to go for nothing with them; they relapsed into their old unbelief. Are you and I much better?

Alas, we may here see ourselves as in a mirror. Those who have a smooth path often boast of a vast amount of faith, or what they think to be faith; but those who follow a wilderness way must often confess to their shame that after receiving great mercy they still find unbelief creeping in. This is shameful to the last degree, and should cause us bitter sorrow and great fear, lest we should provoke the Lord to anger. Before us must often rise the example of those whose carcasses fell in the wilderness because of their unbelief. All this makes us fear that had we been with our Lord in the desert we would not have behaved better than Peter and James and John; we too might have forgotten the former miracle of the loaves, and might have anxiously inquired, *"Where will anyone be able to find enough bread here in this desolate place to satisfy these people?"*

The question, although it is thus surprising and inexcusable, may, however, be used today for our profit. It may at least do this good – since we shall not be able to answer it on any human lines, it will show us our inability, and that is what our Lord would make most clear before his power is revealed. I should not wonder but what he drew those people into the desert on purpose that there might be no suspicion that when they were fed, they had been supplied from fields or gardens, or by the charity of inhabitants. It was a barren spot, out of which nothing could be gotten. The disciples had to feel this, and recognize this, and state this, and then the Lord had a clear platform for working his miracle. He wants to clear you out, brother; he wants to make you see what a weak, poor, petty, miserable thing you are, and when he has brought you to that, then his own arm shall be revealed in the eyes of all the people, and all who behold it shall give to him the glory due unto his name.

Let us come, then, to our question with the hope that it may be sanctified to holy ends.

"Where will anyone be able to find enough bread here in this desolate place to satisfy these people?" First, *this is a pressing problem*: how to meet the needs of the multitude. Secondly, press as it may, *it is one of tremendous difficulty*; but thirdly, and cheeringly, *it is capable of a very glorious answer.* There is a man who, from his infinite resources, can satisfy the countless myriads of our race even in this wilderness.

First, then, it is a very pressing problem. What is to be done for the perishing multitude? What is to be done to satisfy men's souls? I confine the question to spiritual matters at this time, though I by no means make light of the dreadful social and material questions which are also specially urgent at this hour.

At this present moment myriads of *souls are in present need*. We sometimes think too exclusively of salvation as having reference to the world to come, but it has an urgent, all-important reference to this present state. A man who does not know Christ is a wretched man; a man who has never been renewed in heart, who lives in sin and loves it, is a pitiful being, a lost soul over whom angels might weep. If there were no heaven to miss, and no hell to merit, sin is a curse upon this life. It is hell to live without a Savior. If there were no poverty in London, it would be quite enough to break one's heart to think that there is sin in it, reigning over the ungodly.

That grievous side of London life which raises the bitter cry, is not after all the worst side of it; it is to a great extent the outer disease which marks a secret cancer at the heart. If drunkenness brought no consequences, if vice involved no misery, it would not be better, but far worse, for our race. It is a more horrible thing when wickedness wraps itself in scarlet and fine linen, and when vice, by the help of an abominable protectorate, is enabled to escape scot-free. Sin rampant without check would be even worse than the present woe. It is an awful thing to think that masses of our fellow men have never turned to their Creator with obedient hope, have never confessed their sin against him, and have lived without thanking him for his mercy, or trembling at his justice. Great Lord, you know better than we do what horror dwells in the ungodliness of men! Brethren, the multitudes are without the Bread of Life. Shall we not distribute it among them at once?

The multitudes are also *in awful peril as to the future.* When our Savior looked with compassion on the multitude, he not only noticed their present hunger, but he also foresaw what would come of it. *"If I send them away hungry to their homes, they will faint on the way; and some of them have come from a great distance."* Their immediate hunger touched the Savior, but he did not forget its after consequences: they would go back to their mountain dwellings, and in the attempt to climb their terraces one would fall by the hillside from lack of food, and another would drop in the sun from sheer exhaustion. Perhaps a mother carrying her babe at her bosom might find it dead for lack of nourishment, or the women themselves might faint and perish by the way. This our tender Lord could not bear to think of.

Thus, when we look into the future of a soul, we jump back aghast at the vision. In these times, my brethren, many attempts have been made to represent the condition of impenitent sinners in the world to come as less dreadful than the plain Scripture declares it to be. I cannot see what practical result can arise out of such teaching, except it be the hardening of men's hearts, and placing them more at ease than they are now in their indifference with regard to their fellow men. I know that at this hour a master argument with my heart in seeking to save my fellow men is the intolerable thought that, if they die without a Savior, they enter upon a fixed state in which they will continue in sin and in consequent misery without hope of change. I am anxious to save men from hell at once, because I see no other day of hope for them.

Since these things are so – and I am assured that they are – every man who has a spark of humanity and a grain of grace is bound to cry mightily unto God concerning the vast multitude of men who are passing away from under the sound of the gospel, rejecting it, who are living in the land of gospel light and willfully closing their eyes to it, and so are choosing endless darkness. If you are not roused to action, O Christian man, by the twofold belief that sin in this life is an intolerable evil, and that, in the world to come, it involves endless woe, what will stir you? If this does not awaken your compassion for men, if this does not bring you heartbreak, are you not hard as stones, unfeeling as savage beasts?

The case of the multitude is laid upon the church of God. The Lord Jesus Christ took up all the hungry thousands and laid them at the feet of his disciples. These were his own words, as he commissioned them: *"You give them something to eat!"* It was a great honor to them to be taken into co-partnership with their Lord – a high privilege to be workers together with him in relieving this far-spread hunger. It was a great honor, but what a responsibility it involved! If one of them had quietly stolen into the background, whispering to himself, "This is a foolishly impractical notion"; if another had hidden behind a rock and said, "I shall pray about it, but that is all I can do," – why, what a disgrace it would have been to them! Instead of which, they were found truehearted to their Master, and, the burden being laid upon them, they took up that burden in a fashion, and their Lord enabled them to carry it with joy. They had the special happiness of handing out the bread to the vast host who gratefully received the benefit. The twelve were very popular men that day, I warrant you; and they were looked upon with great envy by all who surrounded them.

Was it not a high privilege to distribute food among so many hungry men and women and children? They must have been flushed with excitement and filled with delight. I know I would have been. To go among a crowd of eager, hungry people, and to feed them to the full is a work an angel might wish for. I am sure that many generous hearts here are already devising ways of feeling this delight. Are you not? I mean literally. Will you not help to relieve the present distress by gifts of food and clothing? Returning to the spiritual aspect of the matter, the Lord has called his church in these days to this work, burdensome and indeed impossible without him; but with him, honorable, simple, and easily accomplished. He calls his church to the great task of feeding the multitudes of London, the multitudes of our empire, the multitudes throughout the whole world; and since he is present to multiply our loaves and fish, the pressing problem may not be abandoned in despair.

Brethren, we *cannot put aside this work;* we that are Christians indeed cannot escape from this service. The Master has laid it upon us, and the only way to get out of it is by renouncing his leadership altogether. To attempt to be a Christian and not to live for your fellow men is hypocrisy; to suppose that you can be faithful to Christ and let these multitudes die without an effort is a damnable delusion. He is a traitor to his Master who does not enter heart and soul into the great lifework of that Master, and his lifework was *that the world might be saved through Him* (John 3:17).

> **To attempt to be a Christian and not to live for your fellow men is hypocrisy.**

If you will say good-bye to Jesus, you may run away with your own loaf and your own little fish, and eat them in secret selfishness; but if you mean to be with Christ, you must bring to this place your loaf and your fish and contribute it; you must bring yourself, and be the personal dispenser of the multiplied bread and fish; and you must persevere in the distribution till the last man, the last woman, the last child, shall be filled. Then Jesus shall have all the glory of the feast; but to you will be the honor of having been a servant at his royal table in the dignified banquet of his love.

So you see where we are this very morning. We are called to work out a very pressing problem: *"Where will anyone be able to find enough bread here in this desolate place to satisfy these people?"* Let us not sleep, as do others; but let us rouse ourselves to work side by side with those dear and faithful brethren who are toiling fearlessly to hand out the Bread of Life to the millions in this city, the teeming myriads in this world.

But now, secondly, it is a problem of tremendous difficulty. The difficulty of feeding the four thousand was enormous; but the difficulty of saving the multitudes of the human race is as high above it as the heavens are high above the earth. After all, this miracle only gave a single meal to a few thousands who soon grew hungry again; the work needed is to feed myriads so that they shall not hunger again forever. Think of this!

For first, what a thing it is to satisfy *the needs of a single soul*! I would like those who think it must be easy to win sinners to Christ to try to convert one person. Sunday school teacher, did you ever attempt to bring one girl to Christ yourself? She shall be one of the sweetest children in the whole school; but if you have attempted her conversion without seeking divine aid in prayer, and without looking to the Spirit of God to influence that little heart for good, you have made a miserable failure of it. If you had to save a soul, where would you begin? The introduction of a holy thought into carnal minds is a miracle as great as to get a beam of light into a blind eye, or a breath of life into a dead body. How hard it is to deliver a man from brutal carelessness, and make him think of his soul, and eternity, and God! As to renewing the stony heart, as to reviving the dead soul to life, who can do it? Here we enter into the region of miracles! Can you create a fly? When you have created the most minute creature, then talk about making a new heart and a right spirit.

"*To satisfy,*" says the text – "*Where will anyone be able to . . . satisfy these people?*" To satisfy a soul is a work which only God can accomplish. Open your mouth, O man of ambition! We put the round world upon his tongue, and when he has swallowed it, he cries, like Alexander, for another. He is no more satisfied with the whole world than with a piece of bread. As to the spiritual cravings of men, how can you satisfy them? Pardon for sin, a hope of eternal life, likeness to Christ – these are necessary to satisfy; how can we give them? The world has no such food in all its stores. The work is impossible at the outset, when only one claimant appears. From what source can a man satisfy the spiritual hunger of a single soul? I would like every Christian man to be laid low with this thought, that he may be driven entirely out of conceit of himself, and may at once cry to the strong for strength, and use the simple weapon of the gospel in the power of the Holy Spirit and not in his own strength.

But, brothers and sisters, what am I talking about? One soul! What of that? *Think of the numbers who need heavenly bread.* We have not only one soul, not only one million souls, but realistically five million immortal beings in this single city. In this huge world what myriads have we? A thousand millions would not make up the countless army now encamping on the globe. Would we deliberately exempt one of these from hope? Would we desire one of these to be willfully left to perish? Must not all be fed, if possible? Shall not every man and woman and child, as far as our desire can go, partake of the feast? Well then, where are we? We are altogether at sea. Why, we have not a notion of what a million is. It will take a very, very long time even to count that number.

Think of this city of London – why, you shall ride through it, or you shall cross it on weary feet for a year, and at the end you shall only wonder more at its incalculable vastness. To supply this great metropolis with gracious influences is a labor worthy of God. The church of God is called to feed all these with the bread of heaven, and all those out yonder in the heathen world. O feebleness! What can you do alone? Yet, O feebleness, how gloriously God can use you for the accomplishment of his divine purposes! There is the problem. Did I not say truly that it is one of tremendous difficulty?

What seems to have struck the disciples was the place they were in – it was a *desolate place*. Perhaps you might see here and there a little bitter vegetation, which a goat would scorn to browse, but for the most part it was bare ground. Our Gospel writer, in describing the first miracle, is quite graphic in describing the green grass, but in this case he says that they sat *on the ground* – the ground bare of vegetation. There were no cornfields, nor fruit-bearing plants; there was literally nothing to turn to account. If the stones could have been turned into bread, the people might have been filled, but the ground itself yielded absolutely nothing. I may be supposed, perhaps, to grumble when I say that the present period is as bare of all help to the gospel as that ground was barren of help to the feast. The world has never known a period less helpful to the gospel than the present.

We read in the book of Revelation of a time when *the earth helped the woman,* but it is not so now. I see no element favorable to the conversion of the world to Christ, but everything is in array against it. The people are not so attentive to the gospel as once they were; the masses do not care even to enter the house of prayer; in London they have, to a very large extent, ceased to care about the preaching of the Word. They are to be reached; blessed be God, they shall be reached, but the tendency of the times is not towards religion, but towards unbelief, materialism, and sordid selfishness. A current, no, a torrent, of unbelief is roaring around the foundations of society, and our pulpits are reeling beneath its force. Many Christian people are only half believers now; they are almost smothered in the dense fog of doubt which is now around us. We have come into cloudland and cannot see our way. Many are sinking in the swamp, and those of us who have our feet upon the Rock of Ages have our hands full with helping our slipping friends.

Standing before God with a childlike faith, and trusting in him without question, it does not matter to us personally if the surrounding darkness should deepen into seven midnights black as hell; for we walk by faith and not by sight. Though the earth were removed, and the mountains cast into the midst of the sea, we should still hold to God and to his Christ in a death grip of unshaken confidence. But the mass of professing persons are not so. I constantly meet with brethren who are reeling to and fro, and staggering like drunken men, and are at their wits' end; and rejoicing that I have been given my sea legs, I have to cheer them and assure them that we are not shipwrecked after all. The good ship is not going down; the everlasting truth is as sure as ever; the day is not far distant when the Lord shall send us a great calm.

> The everlasting truth is as sure as ever.

It will before long come to pass that the infidel philosophies of the nineteenth century will be exhibited to little children in our Sunday schools as an instance of the monstrous folly into which wise men were allowed to plunge when they refused the word of the Lord. I am as sure of it as I am sure that I live, that the present wisdom is foolery written large, and that the doctrine which is now rejected as the decayed theory of Puritans and Calvinists will yet conquer human thought and reign supreme. As surely as the sun which sets tonight shall rise tomorrow at the predestined hour, so shall the truth of God shine forth over the whole earth. But this era is a desert place: in pulpits and out of pulpits, in social morals and in politics, it is a dreary wilderness. *"Where will anyone be able to find enough bread here in this desolate place to satisfy these people?"*

The Lord has often permitted the multitude to be in distress that he might work gracious deliverances. Take a modern instance. One hundred and fifty years ago or so, there was a general religious lethargy in England, and ungodliness was master of the situation. The devil, as he flew over England, thought that he had drugged the church so that it would never wake again. How deceived he was! A student at Oxford, who had been a tavern drink server down in Gloucester, found the Savior and began to preach him. His first sermon was said to have driven nineteen people mad, because it awakened them to true life. Certain other scholars in Oxford met together and prayed, and were dismissed from the university for the horrible iniquity of holding a prayer meeting.

Out of the same university came another mighty evangelist – John Wesley – and he, with Whitfield, became the leader of the great Methodist revival; its effects are with us to this day. The archenemy soon found that his hopes were defeated, for the church awoke again. The poor miners were listening to the gospel; their tears were making gutters down their black cheeks, while angelic men told them of pardoning love. Then respectable dissent awoke from its bed of sloth, and the Church of England began to rub her eyes and wonder where she was. An evil time brightened into a happy era. Shall it not be so again? Have no fear about it. All things shall work together for good. The Lord brings the people into the wilderness on purpose, so that there it may be seen that it is not the earth, but himself, that feeds the people.

The sting of the question before us, however, I have not quite brought out: *it was human feebleness*. His disciples answered him: *"Where will anyone be able to find enough bread here in this desolate place to satisfy these people?"* From what source can *a man* do it? We are only men. If we were angels! Oh, if we were angels! Well, what of it? If we were angels, I am sure we would be quite out of the business, *for He did not subject to angels the world to come, concerning which we are speaking.* The angels are not in the field. But from what source can a man or a woman do it? From what source shall a man feed this multitude? "Why, see," says one, "what I am! I am no great orator, I have not ten talents, I am a weak creature. From what source can I feed this multitude? What can I do?" This is the sting of it all to earnest hearts. "Ah," says one, "if I were So-and-so, what I would do!" You may thank God you are not anybody but yourself; for you are best as you are, though you are not much to speak of now. "But if I were somebody else, I could do something," which means this – that since God has chosen to make you what he has made you, you will not serve him; but if he will make you somebody else – that is, if your will may be supreme, then, of course, the house will be ordered rightly. You had better be what you are, and a little better; and get to work and serve your Master, and no longer talk about "From what source shall a man do this or that?"

The possibilities of a man are stupendous. For God with a man, nothing is impossible for that man. Give us not the power of gold, or rank, or eloquence, or wisdom, but give us a man. Our Lord thought so when he went up to heaven. He meant, as he entered the pearly gates, to scatter a divine abundance among his people down below; and he reached his hand into his Father's treasury, and he took out of it – what? He took men. *And He gave some as apostles, and some as prophets, and some as evangelists, and some as pastors and teachers.* These were his ascension gifts to the sons of men.

> **For God with a man, nothing is impossible for that man.**

Though we speak thus of what God can make of us, we are in and of ourselves poor creatures. We do meet with a perfect brother now and then, and I always feel inclined to break that bubble. The imperfections of the perfect are generally more glaring than those of ordinary believers. Alas! we are all such poor, frail creatures, that we are driven away from all confidence in ourselves, and we ask with emphasis the question, *"Where will anyone be able to find enough bread here in this desolate place to satisfy these people?"*

I am happy, therefore, to come to a blessed conclusion in the third head of our discourse, by saying that, laying the emphasis on its weakest word, "From what source can a *man*?" this question is capable of a very glorious answer.

I might almost say, as John the Baptist did, *"Among you stands One whom you do not know."* Though he has stood among us all these centuries, yet his people scarcely know him. Who knows him fully? "Oh," says one, "I know Christ." Yes, in a sense; but yet he surpasses knowledge. "I believe in God," says one; are you sure you do? I remember reading of a certain minister who spent many days in wrestling prayer because he was tempted to doubt whether there was a God, and when he came to the full conviction of it he said to his people, "You will be surprised at what I say, but it is a far greater thing to believe in God than any of you know." And so it is a greater thing to believe in Jesus than most people dream. To believe in the notion of a God is one thing, but to believe God is quite another matter. One said to me when I was troubled, "Have you not a gracious God?" I answered, "Certainly I have." He replied, "What is the good of having him, then, if you do not trust him?" I was sorely struck by that reply, and felt humbled in spirit. We do not fully know what Jesus is. He is far above our highest thought of him. He stands among us, and we know him not.

But what I want you to think of is that this wonderful Man can feed this people with bread this day, and in this wilderness. I hope to make you believe it by the power of the Spirit of God. Therefore I ask you, first, to *listen to what this Man says.* I read to you just now this narrative as we find it in the fifteenth chapter of Matthew. Turn again to the thirty-second verse: *Jesus called His disciples to Him, and said*—. Stop a moment. Prepare your ears for music. He said, *"I feel compassion for the people."* Oh, the sweetness of that word! When you are troubled about the people, troubled about Ireland, troubled about London, troubled about Africa, troubled about China, troubled about India, hear the echo of this word – *"I feel compassion for the people."* If Jesus spoke thus to his people while here, he equally says it now that he is exalted on high, for he has carried his tender human heart up to heaven with him, and out of the excellent glory we may hear him still saying, in answer to his people's prayers, *"I feel compassion for the people."* There is our hope; that heart through which the spear was thrust, and out of which there came blood and water, is the fountain of hope to our race. *"I feel compassion for the people."*

Hear him speak again, and I think you will grant that there is much sweetness in the utterance. At the end of the thirty-second verse we read, *"I do not want to send them away hungry."* We do not wish to judge Peter, and James, and John; but it seems to me that after hearing the Master say, *"I do not want to send them away hungry,"* they hardly ought to have said, *"Where will anyone be able to find enough bread here in this desolate place to satisfy these people?"* They ought quietly to have replied, "Lord, you have asked us a question which you must answer yourself, for you have distinctly made the promise, *'I do not want to send them away hungry.'*"

Do you think the Lord Jesus Christ means after all to leave this world as it is? It is written that *God did not send the Son into the world to judge the world, but that the world might be saved through Him.* Will he forego his purpose? The chronicle of time's history will not wind up with this horrible state of things. The loom of providence will not leave its piece of cloth with its edge so fearfully unraveled; it shall be finished off in due order, and yet be bordered with threads of gold. The glory of God shall yet illuminate history from the beginning even to the end. All flesh shall see the salvation of God, and all nations shall yet call the Redeemer blessed. *"I do not want to send them away hungry."* The people must therefore eat bread from the Lord's hands. Great Master, the task is far too much for us alone, but if you have said, *"I feel compassion for the people, . . . and I do not want to send them away hungry,"* then we will feed them at your command. Your humble servants are waiting to do your bidding, whatever it may be, assured that you will be with them in it all.

I beg you also to think for a moment of what the Lord did not say, because he was speaking about common bread; but of what we know to be true of him concerning his spiritual supplies for men. The greatest spiritual need of man is the pardon of sin by an atonement. Brothers, if the question were now standing, "Where shall we find an atonement?" it would indeed stagger us. Blessed be God, that question does not remain; for the atonement has been presented, completed, and fully accepted. Jesus has said, *"It is finished,"* and the real difficulty is over. The cross has rolled away the stone from the sepulcher, and hope has arisen. The application of the atonement may be difficult, but it must be a small labor compared with the making of the atonement. The well has been dug; the drawing of the water is an easier task. If Jesus died, there must be life for men. If he has prayed, *"Father, forgive them,"* there must be pardon for the guilty. If Jesus has risen into glory, our race cannot perish in shame. We argue from the cross a millennium of glory. This Man can satisfy the people because of the rich merit of his blood.

Next, remember that this glorious Man is now invested with omnipotence. His own words are, *"All authority has been given to Me in heaven and on earth. Go therefore and make disciples of all the nations, baptizing them."* Our Jesus is omnipotent. It is he who, by the infinite wisdom of God, made the world, and without him was not anything made that was made. Is anything hard for the Creator? Is anything impossible, or even difficult, to him who rules all things by the power of his word? Courage, brothers; the grand question is answered. Since there is a full atonement and there is an exalted Savior with all power in his hands, what remains to dismay us?

Listen once more. The Spirit of God has been given. Better than Christ's bodily presence among us is the presence of the Holy Spirit. It was expedient that Jesus should go away so that the Holy Spirit might abide with us as a greater blessing for the church. Is the Holy Spirit gone? Has the Holy Spirit left the church of God? Is the church appalled by her difficulties though the Spirit of God is poured out upon her? What is she about? Has she forgotten herself? Has she become insane? Brother, with Jesus himself slain as an atonement – Jesus exalted as a Prince and a Savior at the right hand of God, and with the divine Spirit abiding with us forever, what is there impossible to the church of God?

So, I close by one more point, which is this: As I have made you hear our Lord's words, and also led you to remember the infinite resources at his disposal, I now want you to *anticipate his working*. How does Christ work among men? How will he proceed when he gets to work among the masses? There are varieties of operations, but there is a continuity of law running through them all, and the divine line of action is much the same in all cases.

The way of Christ was, first of all, to find out what there was which he could use. The little supply provided by his followers consisted of a few loaves and fish. Is it not wonderful how the Lord sometimes finds out little matters which have been hidden away, and makes much of them? Scotland was once under the influence of unbelief and formalism; how was it to be delivered? Thomas Boston went into a shepherd's hut and found a book which had become extremely scarce; it was Fisher's *The Marrow of Modern Divinity*. Boston rejoiced in the light of the gospel which flashed in upon his soul, and he began to bear witness to it. A great controversy followed, and what was far better, a great awakening occurred: the lovers of the marrow of the gospel soon broke the bones of error. See what one book may do. Sweden, too, was greatly blessed by the discovery in a country house of an old copy of Luther on the Galatians. See how one voice may wake a nation.

Brethren, who knows what may come out of seven loaves and a few small fish? Yes, the enemies may do what they like; they may preach what they please; they may take away one pulpit after another from the orthodox; they may bury us under the rubbish of evolution, and false philosophy, but we shall rise again. These small clouds will soon blow over. There may not remain one single sound expounder of the gospel, but as long as God lives, the gospel will not die. Its power may slumber, but before long it shall awake out of sleep, and cry like a mighty man who shouts by reason of wine in him. As long as we have one match left, we can yet set the world on fire. As long as one Bible remains, the empire of Satan is in danger. Only barley loaves and a few small fish were in the possession of the apostolic company, but Jesus found them and began to work with them.

> **As long as one Bible remains, the empire of Satan is in danger.**

The next thing was a secret and mysterious multiplication. The bread began to grow in the disciples' hands as formerly it had grown in the ground. Peter had a loaf in his hand, and he began to break off a corner; to his amazement the loaf was just as big as before. So he broke off the other end and gave that to another hungry person, and lo, the loaf was still whole. He kept on breaking as fast as ever he could, and the loaf continued increasing till everybody had received his full. Wonderful hands they were, were they not? No, they were not; they were only the rough hands of weather-beaten fishermen. Those other hands which first took, and blessed, and broke were doing the deed all the while. It is wonderful how God works by our hands, and yet his own hand does it all.

Apart from human agency, the Lord can impress the minds of men and women, and so multiply his truth. I heard of a woman in the Isle of Skye, when there was very little gospel preaching there, who all of a sudden felt God was not working in Skye. She journeyed till she reached the ferry, and then she crossed to the mainland. She asked those she met where she could find God. At last she met with a good woman who said, "I will tell you where you will find him." She took her into a place of worship where Jesus was plainly set forth. She heard the gospel and went back to tell others about the Savior.

The devil's work is never done; it is undone again in five minutes when the grace of God is at work. Even in our ashes live our habitual fires: a breath from heaven shall kindle them into a flame. God is never at a loss for agents. He could turn the pope into an evangelist, a cardinal into a reformer, and a priest into a preacher of the gospel. The most superstitious, the most ignorant, the most infidel, the most blasphemous, the most degraded may yet be made the champions of his truth. Therefore, let no man's heart fail him; the bread shall be multiplied, and the people shall be fed.

It was done by everybody distributing his portion. Peter was dividing his loaf, and many people were especially pleased to be fed by Peter. It was quite right that they should be. If Peter fed them, let them be satisfied with Peter. Yonder was John with the same bread, breaking it with less impetuosity and more graciousness of manner; and yonder was James working away very steadily and methodically. But what of the difference of distribution? The bread was the same. So long as the people were filled, what did it matter which hand passed them their bread and fish? Dear friends, do not imagine that God will bless one preacher only, or one denomination only. He does bless some preachers more than others, for he is sovereign; but he will bless you all in your work, for he is God. I shall never forget one day, when my dear old grandfather was alive, I was to preach a sermon. There was a great crowd of people, and I did not arrive, for the train was delayed; and therefore, the venerable man commenced to preach in my stead. He was far on in his sermon when I made my appearance at the door. Looking to me, he said, "You have all come to hear my dear grandson, and therefore I will stop that you may hear him. He may preach the gospel better than I can, but he cannot preach a better gospel. Can you, Charles?" My answer from the aisle was, "I cannot preach the gospel better; but if I could, it would not be a better gospel."

So it is, brethren. Others may break the bread to more people, but they cannot break better bread than the gospel which you teach, for that is bread from our Savior's own hand. Get to work each one of you with your bread-breaking, for this is Christ's way of feeding the multitude. Let each one who has himself eaten divide his morsel with another. Today fill someone's ear with the good news of Jesus and his love. Endeavor this day, each one of you who are Christian people, to communicate to one man, woman, or child somewhat of the spiritual meat which has made your soul glad. This is my Master's way, will you not drop into it? You cannot propose a better way; none can contrive a method more likely to be successful, more honorable to your Lord, and more beneficial to yourself. Bring your barley loaf, bring your little fish, and put your provision into the common storehouse. Take it back again from the great Master's hands filled with that blessing which makes it fruitful and multiplies it, and then feed the multitude with it. So shall you go forth with joy, and be led forth with peace. So be it. Amen.

Chapter 2

The Withered Fig Tree

And He left them and went out of the city to Bethany, and spent the night there. Now in the morning, when He was returning to the city, He became hungry. Seeing a lone fig tree by the road, He came to it and found nothing on it except leaves only; and He said to it, "No longer shall there ever be any fruit from you." And at once the fig tree withered. Seeing this, the disciples were amazed and asked, "How did the fig tree wither all at once?"
(Matthew 21:17-20)

This is a miracle and a parable. We have books about the miracles, and we have an equal number of volumes about the parables; into which of these volumes shall we place this story? I would answer: put it in both. It is a singular miracle, and it is a striking parable. It is an acted parable in which our Lord gives us an object lesson. He puts truth before men's eyes, in this instance, that the lesson may make a deeper impression upon the mind and heart. I would lay great stress upon the remark that this is a parable, for, if you do not look upon it in that light, you may misunderstand it. We are not of those who come to the Word of God with the cool impertinence of the critic, thinking ourselves wiser than the Book, and therefore able to judge it.

We believe that the Holy Spirit is greater than man's spirit, and that our Lord and Master is a better judge of what is right and good than any of us can be. Our place is at his feet; we are not nitpickers, but followers. Whatever Jesus does and says, we regard with deepest reverence; our chief desire is to learn as much as we can from it. We see great mysteries in his simplest actions, and profound teaching in his plainest words. When he speaks or acts, we are like Moses at the bush, and feel that we stand on holy ground.

Flippant persons have spoken of the story before us in a very foolish manner. They have represented it as though our Lord, being hungry, thought only of his necessity, and, expecting to be refreshed by a few green figs, went up to the tree in error. Finding no fruit upon the tree, it being a season when he had no right to expect that there would be any, he was vexed, and uttered a curse against the tree, as though it had been a responsible agent. This view of the case results from the folly of the observer; it is not the truth. Our Lord desired to teach his disciples concerning the doom of Jerusalem. The reception given him in Jerusalem was full of promise, but it would come to nothing. Their loud hosannas would change to *"Crucify Him!"*

When Jerusalem was to be destroyed by Nebuchadnezzar at an earlier time, the prophets had not only spoken, but they had also used instructive signs. If you turn to the book of Ezekiel, you will there see the record of many signs and symbols which set forth the coming woe. These tokens excited curiosity, secured consideration, and brought home the prophetic warnings to the homes and hearts of the common people. Again, the judgments of God were at the gates of the guilty city. Words – the words of Jesus – had been wasted, and even tears – tears of the Savior – had been spilled in vain; it was time that the sign should be given – the sign of condemnation. Ezekiel had said, *"All the trees of the field will know that I am the Lord; I bring down the high tree, . . . dry up the green tree"*; and herein was suggested the very image which was employed by our Lord. He saw a fig tree, by a freak of nature, covered with leaves at a time when, in the ordinary course of things, it should not have been so.

Such singular things happen, here and there, in the vegetable world.

Our Lord saw that this was a fine object lesson for him, and therefore he took his disciples to see if there were figs on it as well as leaves. When he found none, he told the fig tree to remain forever fruitless, and immediately it began to wither. Our Lord would have used the fig tree to an excellent purpose had he ordered it to be used as fuel to warm cold hands, but he did better when he used it to warm cold hearts. No wrong was done to any man; it was a tree on the waste, and utterly worthless. No pain was inflicted, no anger was felt. In the object lesson, the Lord simply said to the fig tree, *"No longer shall there ever be any fruit from you,"* and it withered away. In this our Lord taught a great lesson to all ages at a small expense. The withering of a tree has been the reviving of many a soul, and if it had not been so, it was no loss to any that a tree should wither when it had proved itself barren. A great teacher may do far more than destroy a tree if he can thereby give demonstrations of truth, and scatter seeds of virtue. It is the absolute idleness of criticism to find fault with our Lord Jesus for a piece of fine poetic instruction for which, had it been spoken by any other teacher, the most lavish praise would have been awarded by these very critics.

The blighted fig tree was a singularly apt simile of the Jewish state. The nation had promised great things to God. When all the other nations were like trees without leaves, making no profession of allegiance to the true God, the Jewish nation was covered with the leafage of abundant religious profession. Scribes, Pharisees, priests, and elders of the people were all sticklers for the letter of the law, and boasters of being worshipers of the one God, and strict observers of all his laws. Their constant cry was, "The temple of the Lord, the temple of the Lord, the temple of the Lord are these." *"We have Abraham for our father"* was frequently on their lips. They were a fig tree in full leaf. But there was no fruit upon them, for the people were neither holy, nor just, nor true, nor faithful towards God, nor loving to their neighbor. The Jewish church was a mass of glittering profession, unsupported by spiritual life. Our Lord had looked into the temple and had found the house of prayer to be a den of thieves. He condemned the Jewish church to remain a lifeless, fruitless thing; and it was so. The synagogue remained open, but its teaching became a dead form. Israel had no influence upon the age. The Jewish race became, for centuries, a withered tree: it had nothing but profession when Christ came, and that profession proved powerless to save even the Holy City. Christ did not destroy the religious organization of the Jews; he left them as they were, but they withered away from the root till the Romans came, and with the axes of their legions cleared away the fruitless trunk.

What a lesson is this to nations! Nations may make a profession – a loud profession – of religion, and yet may fail to exhibit that righteousness which exalts a nation. Nations may be adorned with all the leafage of civilization, and art, and progress, and religion, but if there be no inner life of godliness, and no fruit unto righteousness, they will stand for a while, and then wither away.

What a lesson this is to churches! There have been churches which have stood prominent in numbers and in influence, but faith, and love, and holiness have not been maintained, and the Holy Spirit has left them to the vain show of a fruitless profession; and there stand those churches, with the trunk of organization, and widely extended branches, but they are dead, and every year they become more and more decayed. Brethren, such churches we have even among Nonconformists at this hour. May it never be so with this church! We may have numbers of people coming to hear the Word, and a considerable body of men and women professing to be converted, but unless vital godliness is in their midst, what are congregations and churches? We might have a valued ministry, but what would this be without the Spirit of God? We might have large public gatherings, and many outward efforts, but what are these without the spirit of prayer, the spirit of faith, and the spirit of grace and consecration? I dread lest we should ever come to be like a tree, premature with an excellent profession, but yet worthless in the sight of the Lord, because the secret life of devotion and vital union to Christ are gone. Better that the axe clears away every vestige of the tree than that it stands out against the sky an open lie, a mockery, or a delusion.

This is the lesson of the text, but I do not want you to consider it only in the sum, in its relation to nations and churches. My heart's desire is that we may learn the lesson in detail, and take it home each one to his own heart. May the Lord himself speak to each one of us today personally! In preparing the sermon, I have had great searching of heart, and I pray that the hearing of it may produce the same results. May we tremble, lest, having a profession of godliness, we should wear it conspicuously, and yet should lack the fruit-bearing which alone can warrant such a profession. The name of saintship, if it be not justified by sanctity, is an offense to honest men, and much more to a holy God. A pronounced and forward profession of Christianity without a Christian life at the back of it is a lie, abhorrent to God and man, an offense against truth, a dishonor to religion, and the forerunner of a withering curse.

May the Holy Spirit help me to preach very solemnly and powerfully at this time!

Our first observation is this: *There are in the world cases of forward, but fruitless, profession.* Our second observation will be this: *These will be inspected by King Jesus.* And our third observation will be this: *The result of that inspection will be very terrible.* Help us, O Holy Spirit!

First, then, there are in the world cases of forward, but fruitless, profession. The cases to which we refer are not so very rare. *They far excel their fellow men.* Their promise is very loud, and their exterior very impressive. They look like fruitful trees; you expect many baskets of the best figs from them. They impress us by their talk; they overpower us by their manners. We envy *them* and lash ourselves. This last thing might not harm us, but to envy hypocrites can never be otherwise than injurious in the long run, for, when their hypocrisy is discovered, we are apt to despise religion as well as the pretenders of it. Do you not know persons who are in appearance everything and in reality are nothing? O dark thought! May we not ourselves be such persons?

> A pronounced profession of Christianity without a Christian life at the back of it is a lie.

See the man, he is strong in faith, even to presumption; he is joyous in hope, even to silliness; he is loving in spirit, even to utter indifference about truth! How very glib he is in talk! How deep he is in theological speculation! How fervent he is in urging on forward movements! Yet he has never entered the kingdom by the new birth. He has never been taught of God. The gospel has come to him in word only. He is a stranger to the work of the Holy Spirit. Are there not such persons? Are there not persons who are defenders of orthodoxy, and yet are heterodox in their own conduct? Do we not know men and women whose lives deny what their lips profess? We are sure it is so. All vineyards have had in them fig trees covered with leaves which have been conspicuous from the foliage of their profession, and yet have brought forth no fruit unto the Lord.

Such persons *seem to defy the seasons.* It was not the time of figs, yet this fig tree was covered with those leaves which usually indicated ripe figs. I suppose you all know what I have often seen for myself – the fig tree puts forth its fruit before its leaves. Early in the year you see green knobs put forth at the end and points of the branches, and these, as they swell, turn out to be green figs. The leaves come forward afterwards, and by the time the tree is fully covered with leaves, the figs are ready for eating. When a fig tree is in full leaf, you expect to find figs upon it, and if you do not, it will bear no figs for that season. This tree put forth leaves abundantly before its season, and therein excelled all other fig trees. Yes, but it was a freak of nature and not a healthy result of true growth. Such freaks of nature occur in forests and in vineyards, and their kind may be met with in the moral and spiritual world. Certain men and women seem far in advance of those round about them, and astonish us by their special virtues. They are better than the best, more excellent than the most excellent – at least in appearance. They are so zealous that they are not chilled by the surrounding world; their great souls create a summer for themselves. The backwardness of saints, and the wickedness of sinners, do not hinder them; they are too vigorous to be affected by their surroundings. They are very superior persons, covered with virtues, as this fig tree with leaves.

Observe, though, that *they overleap the ordinary rule of growth.* As I have told you, the rule is, first the fig, and afterwards the fig leaves; but we have seen persons who make a profession before they have produced the slightest fruit to justify it. I like to see our young friends, when they believe in Christ, proving their faith by holiness at home, by godliness abroad, and then coming forward and confessing their faith in the Lord Jesus Christ. That looks to be the sober and normal way of proceeding, for a man first to be, and then to profess to be; first to be lit, and then to shine; first to repent and believe, and then to confess his repentance and his faith in the scriptural way, by baptism into Christ. But these people think it unnecessary to pay attention to the trifle of heart work – they dare to omit the most vital part of the matter. They attend a revival meeting, and they declare themselves saved, though they have not been renewed in heart, and possess neither repentance nor faith. They come forward to assert a mere emotion. They have nothing better than a resolve, but they flourish it as if it were the deed itself. Quick as thought, the convert sets up to be a teacher. Without test or trial of his brand-new virtues, he holds himself forth as an example to others. Now, I do not object to the rapidity of the conversion; on the contrary, I admire it, if it be true, but I cannot judge till I see the fruit and evidence in the life. If the change of conduct is distinct and true, I care not how quickly the work is done, but we must see the change. There is a heat which leads to fermentation, and a fermentation which breeds sourness and corruption.

O dear friends, never think you may skip the fruit and come at once to the leaf. Be not like a builder who would say, "It is all nonsense to spend labor and material on works underground. Foundations are never seen; I can run up a house in no time, four walls and a roof will not take long." Yes, but how long will such a house last? Is it worthwhile building a house without a foundation? If you omit the foundation, why not omit the house altogether? Is there not a tendency, especially in these days, when men are either skeptical or fanatical, to cultivate a mushroom godliness, which comes up in a night and perishes in a night? Will it not be ruinous if conviction of sin is slighted, repentance slurred, faith imitated, the new birth counterfeited, and godliness feigned? Beloved, this will never do. We must have figs before leaves, acts before declarations, faith before baptism, and union with Christ before union with the church. You cannot leap over the processes of nature, neither may you omit the processes of grace, lest by chance your foliage without fruit becomes a curse without cure.

These people usually catch the eye of others. According to the Gospel of Mark, our Lord saw this tree *from a distance.* The other trees were not in leaf, and consequently, when he began to go up the hill toward Jerusalem, he saw this one tree quite a long way before he reached it. A fig tree dressed in its clothing of lovely green would be a striking object, and would be observable at a distance. It stood also near the track from Bethany to the city gate. It stood where every traveler would observe it, and probably speak with wonder of its singular leafage for the season.

Persons whose religion is false are frequently prominent because they have not grace enough to be modest and reserved. They seek the highest room, aspire to office, and push themselves into leadership. They do not walk in secret with God, they have little concern about private godliness, and so they are all the more eager to be seen of men. This is both their weakness and their peril. Though least of all able to bear the wear and tear of publicity, they are covetous for it and are, therefore, all the more watched. This is the evil of the whole matter, for it makes their spiritual failure to be known by so many, and their sin brings all the greater dishonor upon the name of the Lord whom they profess to serve. Better far to be fruitless in a corner of the woods than on the public way which leads to the temple.

Such people not only catch the eye, but *they often also attract the company of good men*. Who blames us for drawing near to a tree which is in leaf long before its fellows? Is it not right to cultivate the acquaintance of the eminently good? Our Savior and his disciples went up to the leafy fig tree. Not merely did it win their eye, but it also drew them to itself. Have we not been fascinated by the charming conduct of one who seemed to be a brother in the Lord, more devout than usual, fearing God above many? Like Jehu, he has said, *"Come with me and see my zeal for the Lord"*; and we have been glad enough to ride in the chariot with him. He seemed so godly, so generous, so humble, and so useful, that we looked up to him and wished that we were more worthy to be associated with him. Young converts and seekers are naturally apt to do this; and therefore it is a sad calamity when their confidence turns out to have been misplaced.

Whenever we see any persons standing out prominently and making a bold profession, what should be our thoughts about them? I answer, do not judge them; do not fall into habitual mistrust. Your Lord did not stand at a distance and say, "That tree is worthless." No, he went up to it, with his disciples, and carefully inspected it. These prominent persons may be wonders of divine grace; let us hope and pray that they may be. Let the Lord and his love be magnified in them! God has his fig trees that bear figs in winter; God has his saints who are filled with good works when the love of others has grown cold. The Lord raises some up to be as standards for the truth, rallying points in the battle. The Lord can make young men mature, and new converts useful.

It has been said, by way of proverbial expression, that "some men are born with beards." The Lord can give great grace so as to make spiritual growth rapid and yet solid. He does this so often that we have no right to doubt but what the prominent brother before us is one of these growths of grace. Unless we are forced to see with bitter regret that there are no marks of grace or no evidences of faith, let us hope for the best, and be glad at the sight of God's grace. If we are inclined to be suspicious, let us turn the point of that sword towards our own bosoms. Self-suspicion will be healthy, suspicion of others may be cruel. We are not judges; and even if we were, we would do better to keep to our own court and sit on our own judgment seat, dispensing the law within the little kingdom of our own selves.

When those who are prominent turn out to be all they profess to be, they are a great blessing. It would have been well if that morning there had been figs upon that fig tree. It would have been a great refreshment to the Savior if he had been fed by the green fruit. When the Lord makes the first in position to be first in holiness, it is a blessing to the church, to the family, and to the neighborhood; indeed, it may prove to be a blessing to the whole world. We ought, therefore, to pray the Lord to water with his own hand those trees which he has planted, or, in other words, to uphold by his grace those men of his right hand whom he has made strong for himself.

> Self-suspicion will be healthy, suspicion of others may be cruel.

But when we take the text and lay it home to our own hearts, we need not be so gentle with it as in the cases of others. We have, many of us, for long years been like this fig tree, as to prominence and profession. And in this matter, so far, there is nothing of which to be ashamed. Yet it is evidently to ourselves that the parable speaks, for we have stood in open declaration and distinct service by the wayside, and we have been seen *from a distance.* Certain ones of us have made a very bold profession, and we are not ashamed to repeat that profession before men and angels, hence the question: Are we truthful in it? What if we should turn out to be contending for a faith in which we have no share? What if in us there should be none of the life of love, and consequently our profession should be as *a noisy gong or a clanging cymbal*? What if there should be talk, and no work; doctrine, and no practice? What if we are without holiness? Then we shall never see the Lord.

Whatever terrible aspect this parable miracle may have, it bears upon many of us. I, the preacher, feel how much it bears upon me. In that spirit have I thought it over, anxiously trusting that every deacon and every elder of this church, and every member and every worker among you, may have great searching of heart. May every minister of Christ who may have dropped in here today say to himself, "Yes, I have been like that fig tree in prominence and in profession; God grant that I be not like it in being devoid of fruit!"

Secondly, it is time that we remembered the solemn truth of our second observation: forward and fruitless cases will be inspected by King Jesus.

He will draw near to them, and when he comes up to them, *he will look for fruit.* The first Adam came to the fig tree for leaves, but the second Adam looks for figs. He searches our character through and through, to see whether there is any real faith, any true love, any living hope, any joy which is the fruit of the Spirit, any patience, any self-denial, any fervor in prayer, any walking with God, any indwelling of the Holy Spirit; and if he does not see these things, he is not satisfied with chapel-going, churchgoing, prayer meetings, communions, sermons, or Bible readings, for all these may be no more than leafage. If our Lord does not see the fruit of the Spirit upon us, he is not satisfied with us, and his inspection will lead to severe measures. Notice that what Jesus looks for is not your words, not your resolves, and not your declarations, but your sincerity, your inward faith, and your being indeed worked upon by the Spirit of God to bring forth fruits fit for his kingdom.

Our Lord has a right to expect fruit when he looks for it. When he went up to that fig tree, he had a right to expect fruit, because the fruit, according to nature, comes before the leaf. If, then, the leaf has come, there should be fruit. True, it was not the time for figs, but then, if it was not the time for figs, it certainly was not the season for leaves, for the figs are first. This tree, by putting forth leaves, which are the signs and tokens of ripe figs, virtually advertised itself as bearing fruit. So, however bad the times may be, some of us profess that we will not follow the times, but will follow the one immutable truth.

As Christians, we confess that we are redeemed from among men, and have been delivered from this perverse generation. Christ may not expect fruit of men who acknowledge the world and its changing ages as their supreme guide, but he may well look for it from the believer in his own Word. He looks for fruit from the preacher, from the Sunday school teacher, from the church officer, from the sister who conducts a Bible class, from that brother who has a band of young men around him to whom he is a guide in the gospel. He does expect it of all who submit to his gospel rule. As Christ had a right to expect fruit of a leaf-bearing fig tree, so he has a right to expect great things from those who declare themselves as his trustful followers. Ah me! How this fact should move the preacher with trembling! Should it not totally affect many of you in the same manner?

Fruit is what the Lord earnestly desires. The Savior, when he came under the fig tree, did not desire leaves, for we read that he was hungry, and human hunger cannot be removed by leaves of a fig tree. He desired to eat a fig or two, and he longs to have fruit from us also. He hungers for our holiness; he longs that his joy may be in us, that our joy may be full. He comes up to each of you who are members of his church, and especially to each of you who are leaders of his people, and he looks to see in you the things in which his soul is well pleased. He wants to see in us love for himself, love for our fellow men, strong faith in revelation, earnest contention for the once-delivered faith, urgent pleading in prayer, and careful living in every part of our course. He expects from us actions such as are according to the law of God and the mind of the Spirit of God, and if he does not see these, he does not receive his due. What did he die for but to make his people holy? What did he give himself for but that he might sanctify unto himself a people zealous for good works? What is the reward of the bloody sweat and the five wounds and the death agony, but that by all these we should be bought with a price? We rob him of his reward if we do not glorify him, and therefore the Spirit of God is grieved at our conduct if we do not show forth his praises by our godly and zealous lives.

And mark here, that when Christ comes to a soul, *he surveys it with keen discernment.* He is not mocked. It is not possible to deceive him. I have thought something was a fig which turned out to be only a leaf;

but our Lord makes no such mistake. Neither will he overlook the little figs just breaking forth. He knows the fruit of the Spirit in whatever stage it may be. He never mistakes fluent expression for hearty possession, nor real grace for mere emotion. Beloved, you are in good hands as to the trial of your condition when the Lord Jesus comes to deal with you. Your fellow men are quick in their judgments, and they may be either critical or partial; but the King gives forth a righteous sentence. He knows just where we are, and what we are; and he judges not after appearance, but according to truth.

Oh, that our prayer might today rise to heaven: "Jesus, Master, come and cast your searching eyes upon me, and judge whether I am living unto you or not! Give me to see myself as you see me, that I may have my errors corrected, and my graces nourished. Lord, make me to be indeed what I profess to be; and if I am not so already, convince me of my false state, and begin a true work in my soul. If I am yours, and am right in your sight, grant me a kind, assuring word to sink my fears again, and I will gladly rejoice in you as the God of my salvation."

I come, thirdly, by the help of the Spirit of God, to consider the truth that the result of the coming of Christ to the forward, but fruitless, professor will be very terrible.

The searcher finds nothing but leaves where fruit might have been expected. Nothing but leaves means nothing but lies. Is that a harsh expression? If I profess faith, and have no faith, is that not a lie? If I profess repentance, and have not repented, is that not a lie? If I unite with the people of the living God, and yet have no fear of God in my heart, is that not a lie? If I come to the communion table, and partake of the bread and wine, and yet never discern the Lord's body, is that not a lie? If I profess to defend the doctrines of grace, and yet am not assured of the truth of them, is that not a lie? If I have never felt my depravity; if I have never been effectually called, never known my election of God, never rested in the redeeming blood, and never been renewed by the Spirit, is not my defense of the doctrines of grace a lie? If there is nothing but leaves, there is nothing but lies, and the Savior sees that it is so. All the vegetation of green leaf to him without fruit is only so much deceit.

Profession without grace is the funeral pageantry of a dead soul. Religion without holiness is the light which comes from rotten wood

– the phosphorescence of decay. I speak dread words, but how can I speak less dreadfully than I do? If you and I have but a name to live, and are dead, what a state we are in! Ours is something worse than corruption: it is the corruption of corruption. To profess religion and live in sin is to sprinkle rose water upon a dunghill, and leave it a dunghill still. To give a spirit an angel's name when it bears the devil's character is almost to sin against the Holy Spirit. If we remain unconverted, of what use can it be to have our name written among the godly?

Our Lord discovered that there was no fruit, and that was a dreadful thing; but next, *he condemned the tree.* Was it not right that he should condemn it? Did he curse it? It was already a curse. It was calculated to tantalize the hungry, and take them out of their way to deceive them. God will not have the poor and needy made a jest of. An empty profession is a practical curse, and should it not receive the censure of the Lord of truth? The tree was of no use where it was; it ministered to no man's refreshment. So, the barren professor occupies a position in which he ought to be a blessing, but, in truth, an evil influence streams forth from him. If he has not the grace of God in him, he is utterly useless, and in all probability he is a curse; he is an Achan in the camp, grieving the Lord, and causing him to refuse success to his people.

Our Lord did, however, use the fig tree for a good purpose, when he caused it to wither away; for it became, henceforth, a beacon and a warning to all others who put forth vain pretenses. So, when the ungodly man, who has exhibited a flourishing profession, is allowed to fade away in his ways, some moral effect is produced upon others. They are compelled to see the peril of an unsound profession, and if they are wise, they will no longer be guilty of it. I wish to God it might be so in every case whenever a notable religionist withers away!

After that, when the Savior had condemned it, *he pronounced sentence upon it;* and what was the sentence? It was simply, "As you were." It was nothing more than a confirmation of its state. This tree has borne no fruit, it shall never bear fruit. If a man chooses to be without the grace of God, and yet makes a profession of having it, it is only just that the great Judge should say, "Continue without grace." When the great Judge at last shall speak to those who depart from God, he will simply say to them, "Depart!" Throughout life they always were departing, and after death their character is stamped with perpetuity. If you choose to be graceless, to be graceless shall be your doom. "He that is filthy, let him be filthy still." May the Lord Jesus never have to sentence any of you in this way; but may he turn us, that we may be turned, and work in us eternal life to his praise and glory!

Then there came a change over the tree. It began at once to wither. I do not know whether the disciples saw a quiver run through it at once; but on the next morning, when they passed that way, according to Mark, it had dried up from the roots. Not only did the leaves hang down, like flags when there is no wind; not only did the bark seem to have lost every token of vitality, but the whole fabric was also blighted fatally. Have you ever seen a fig tree with its strange, weird branches? It is a very extraordinary sight when bare of leaves. In this case I see its skeleton arms! It is twice dead, dead from the very roots.

Thus have I seen the fair professing person undergo a blight. He has looked like a thing that has felt the breath of a furnace, and has had its moisture dried up. The man is no longer himself; his glory and his beauty are hopelessly gone. No axe was lifted, no fire was kindled; a word did it, and the tree withered from the root. So, without thunderbolt or pestilence, the once-brave professing person is stricken as with the judgment of Cain. It is an awful fate. Better far to have the vinedresser come to you with the axe in his hand, and strike you with the head of it, and say to you, "Tree, you must bear fruit, or be hewn down." Such a warning would be terrible, but it would be infinitely better than to be left in one's place untouched, quietly to wither to destruction.

Now I have delivered my heavy burden, laying it far more upon myself than upon any one of you, for I stand more prominent than you. I have made a louder profession than most of you; and if I have not his grace in me, then I shall stand before the multitude that have seen me in my greenness, and I shall wither away to the very roots, a terrible example of what God does with those who bear no fruit to his glory.

But now I desire to conclude with tenderer words. Let no man say, "This is very hard." Brother, it is not hard, is it, that if we profess a thing, we should be expected to be true to it? Besides, I pray you not to think that anything my Lord can do is hard. He is all gentleness and tenderness. The only thing he ever did destroy was this fig tree. He destroyed no men, as Elijah did when he brought fire from heaven upon them; nor as Elisha did when the bears came out of the woods. It is only a barren tree that he causes to wither away. He is all love and tenderness. He does not want to wither you, nor will he, if you be but true. The very least he may expect is that you be true to what you profess. Are you rebellious because he asks you to not play the hypocrite? If you begin to kick against his admonition, it will look as if you were yourself untrue at heart. Instead of that, come and bow humbly at his feet and say, "Lord, if anything in this solemn truth bears upon me, I implore you so to apply it to my conscience that I may feel its power and flee to you for salvation." Many men are converted in this way – these hard but honest things drive them from false refuges, and bring them to be true to Christ and to their own souls.

"But," says one, "I know what I will do; I will never make any profession, I will bear no leaves." My friend, that also is a sullen, rebellious spirit. Instead of talking so, you should say, "Lord, I do not ask you to take away my leaves, but let me have fruit." The fruit is not likely to ripen well without leaves, as leaves are essential to the health of the tree, and the health of the tree is essential to the ripening of the fruit. Open confession of faith is good and must not be refused. Lord, I would not drop a leaf.

> I'm not ashamed to own my Lord,
>   Or to defend his cause;
> Maintain the honor of his word,
>   The glory of his cross.

Lord, I do not want to be set away in a corner; I am satisfied to stand where men may see my good works and glorify my Father who is in heaven. I do not ask to be observed, but I am not ashamed to be observed; only, Lord, make me fit for observation. If a commander said to a soldier, "Stand firm, but mind you have your cartridges ready so that you may not lift an empty gun," suppose that soldier answered, "I cannot be so particular. I would rather run to the rear." Would that be a proper reply? Coward! Because your captain warns you that you must not be a sham, you would, therefore, run off altogether! Surely, you are of an evil sort. You are not truly one of the Lord's if you cannot bear his rebuke. Let not these solemn truths drive us away, but let them draw us on to say, "Lord, I pray you, help me to make my calling and election sure. I implore you, help me to bring forth the expected fruit. Your grace can do it."

I would suggest to everyone that we cry to the Lord to make us conscious of our natural barrenness. Gracious ones, may the Lord make us mourn over our comparative barrenness, even if we do bear some fruit. To feel quite satisfied with yourself is perilous; to feel that you are holy, and indeed that you are perfect, is to be on the brink of the pit of pride. If you hold your head so high, I am afraid you will strike it against the top of the doorway. If you walk on stilts, I fear you will fall. It is a safer thing to feel, "Lord, I do serve you, and I am no deceiver. I do love you; you have worked the works of the Spirit in me. But alas! I am not what I want to be, I am not what I ought to be. I aspire to holiness; help me attain it. Lord, I would lie in the very dust before you to think that after being dug about and fertilized, as I have been, I should bear such little fruit. I feel myself less than nothing. My cry is, 'God be merciful to me.' If I had done all, I should still have been an unprofitable servant; but having done so little, Lord, where shall I hide my guilty head?"

Lastly, when you have made this confession, and the Lord has heard you, there is one emblem in Scripture I would like you to copy. Suppose today you feel so dry, and dead, and barren that you cannot serve God as you would, nor even pray for more grace as you wish to do. Then you are something like these twelve rods. They are very dead and dry, for they have been held in the hands of twelve chiefs, who have used them as their official sticks. These twelve rods are to be laid before the Lord. This one is Aaron's rod, but it is quite as dead and dry as any of the rest. The whole twelve are laid in the place where the Lord dwells. We see them the next morning. Eleven are dry rods still, but see this rod of Aaron! What has happened? It was dry as death. See, it has budded!

This is wonderful! But look, it has blossomed! There are almond flowers upon it. You know their rosy pink and white. This is marvelous! But look again, it has brought forth almonds! Here, you have them! See these green fruits which look like peaches. Take off the flesh, and here is an almond whose shell you may break and find the kernel. The heavenly power has come upon the dry stick, and it has budded, and blossomed, and even brought forth almonds. Fruit-bearing is the proof of life and favor.

Lord, take these poor sticks, and make them bud. Lord, here we are, in a bundle; perform that ancient miracle in a thousand of us. Make us bud, and blossom, and bear fruit! Come with divine power, and turn this congregation from a bundle of sticks into a grove. Oh, that our blessed Lord may get a fig from some dry stick today! At least, such a fig as this: *"God be merciful to me, the sinner"*; there is sweetness in that prayer. Our Lord Jesus likes the taste of such a fig as this: "Lord, *I do believe; help my unbelief.*" Here is another: *"Though He slay me, I will hope in Him"* – that is a whole basketful of the first ripe figs, and the Lord rejoices in their sweetness. Come, Holy Spirit, produce fruit in us this day, through faith in Jesus Christ our Lord! Amen, and Amen.

Chapter 3

Nothing but Leaves

He found nothing but leaves. (Mark 11:13)

Most of the miracles of Moses were grand displays of divine justice. What were the first ten wonders but ten plagues? The same may be said of the prophets, especially of Elijah and Elisha. Was it not significant both of the character and mission of Elijah when he called fire from heaven upon the captains of fifties? Nor was he upon whom his mantle descended less terrible when the female bears avenged him upon the mockers. It remained for our incarnate Lord to reveal the heart of God. The Only Begotten was full of grace and truth, and in his miracles preeminently God is set forth to us as love. With the exception of the miracle before us, and perhaps, a part of another, all the miracles of Jesus were entirely benevolent in their character; indeed, this one is no exception in reality, but only in appearance. The raising of the dead, the feeding of the multitude, the stilling of the storm, the healing of diseases – what were all these but displays of the loving-kindness of God? What was this to teach us but that Jesus Christ came forth from his Father on an errand of grace?

> Thine hands, dear Jesus, were not armed
>   With an avenging rod,
> No hard commission to perform
>   The vengeance of a God.

> But all was mercy, all was mild,
> And wrath forsook the throne,
> When Christ on his kind errand came
> And brought salvation down.

Let us rejoice that God commends his *love* towards us, because *at the right time Christ died for the ungodly.*

Yet, as if to show that Jesus the Savior is also Jesus the judge, a gleam of justice must dart forth. Where shall mercy direct its fall? See, my brethren, it glances not upon a man, but it lights upon an unconscious, unsuffering thing – a tree. The curse, if we may call it a curse at all, did not fall on man or beast, or even on the smallest insect; its bolt falls harmlessly upon a fig tree by the wayside. It bore upon itself the signs of barrenness, and perhaps was no one's property; little, therefore, was the loss which any man sustained by the withering of that leafy mockery, while instruction more precious than a thousand acres of fig trees has been left for the benefit of all ages. The only other instance at which I hinted just now was the permission given to the devils to enter into the swine, and the whole herd ran violently down a steep place into the sea, and perished in the waters.

In that case, again, what a mercy it was that the Savior did not permit a band of men to become the victims of the Evil One. It was infinitely better that the whole herd of swine should perish than that one poor man should be rendered a maniac through their influence. The creatures choked in the abyss were nothing but swine – swine which their Jewish owners had no right to keep; and even then they did not perish through Jesus Christ's agency, but through the malice of the devils, for of necessity must even swine run when the devil drives.

Observe, then, with attention, this solitary instance of stern judgment worked by the Savior's hand. Consider seriously that if only once in his whole life Christ works a miracle of pure judgment, the lesson so unique must be very full of meaning. If there be but one curse, where does it fall? What is its symbolic teaching? I do not know that I ever felt more solemnly the need for true fruitfulness before God than when I was looking over this miracle-parable – for such it may justly be called.

The curse, you at once perceive, falls in its metaphorical and spiritual meaning upon those high professing Christians who are destitute of true holiness; upon those who manifest a great show of leaves, but who bring forth no fruit unto God. Only one thunderbolt, and that for boasting pretenders; only one curse, and that for hypocrites. O blessed Spirit, write this heart-searching truth upon our hearts!

First of all, we will commence our exposition with the remark that there were many trees with only leaves upon them, and yet none of these were cursed by the Savior, except only this fig tree. It is the nature of many trees to yield to man nothing but their shade. The hungering Savior did not resort to the oak or to the elm to look for food, nor could the fir tree, nor the pine tree, nor the box tree offer him any hope of refreshment; nor did he breathe one hard word concerning them, for he knew what was in them, and that they neither were, nor pretended to be, fruit-bearing trees. So, dear friends, there are many men whose lives bear leaves, but no fruit – and yet, thanks be unto God, almighty patience bears with them. They are allowed to live out their time, and then it is true that they are cut down and cast into the fire; but while they are permitted to stand, no curse withers them: the longsuffering God waits to be gracious to them. Here are some of the characters who have leaves but no fruit.

There are thousands who ignorantly follow *the sign and know nothing of the substance.* In England, we think ourselves far in advance of Roman Catholic countries; but how much of the essence of Roman Catholicism peeps out in the worship of very many! They go to church or chapel, and they think that the mere going into the place and sitting for a certain time and coming out again is an acceptable act to God: mere formality, you see, is mistaken for spiritual worship! They are careful to have their infants sprinkled, but what the ceremony means they know not; and without looking into the Bible to see whether the Lord commands any such ordinance, they offer him their ignorant will-worship either in obedience to custom, or in the superstition of ignorance. What the thing is, or why it is, they do not inquire, but go through a performance as certain parrots say their prayers. They know nothing about the inward and spiritual grace which the catechism talks about, if indeed, inward spiritual grace could ever be connected with an unscriptural outward and visible sign.

When these poor souls come to the Lord's Supper, their thoughts go no farther than the bread and wine, or the hands which break the one and pour out the other; they know nothing whatever of communion with Jesus, of eating his flesh and drinking his blood; their souls have proceeded as far as the shell, but they have never broken into the kernel to taste the sweetness thereof. They have a name to live, and are dead; their religion is a mere show; a signboard without an inn; a well-set table without meat; a pretty pageant where nothing is gold, but everything is the color of gold; nothing is real, but all is pasteboard, paint, plaster, and pretense.

Nonconformists, your chapels swarm with such, and the houses of the Establishment are full of the same! Multitudes live and die satisfied with the outward trappings of religion, and are utter strangers to internal vital godliness. Yet such persons are not cursed in this life! No, they are to be pitied, to be prayed for, to be sought after with words of love and honest truth; they are to be hoped for still, for who knows but that God may call them to repentance, and they may yet receive the life of God into their souls?

Another very numerous class have *opinion but not faith,* creed but not credence. We meet them everywhere. How zealous they are for Protestantism! They would not only die for orthodoxy, but would kill others as well. Perhaps it is the Calvinistic doctrine which they have received, and then the five points are as dear to them as their five senses. These men will contend, not to say earnestly, but savagely, for the faith. They very vehemently denounce all those who differ from them in the smallest degree, and deal damnation around the land with amazing liberality to all who are not full weight according to the balance of their little Zoar, Rehoboth, or Jireh, while all the while the spirit of Christ, the love of the Spirit, the bowels of compassion, and the holiness of character are no more to be expected from them than grapes from thorns, or figs from thistles.

Doctrine, my brethren, is to be prized above all price! Woe to the church of God when error shall be thought a trifle, for truth will be lightly esteemed; and when truth is gone, what is left? But, at the same time, we are grossly mistaken if we think that orthodoxy of creed will save us. I am sick of those cries of "the truth," "the truth," "the truth" from men of rotten lives and unholy tempers. There is an orthodox as well as a heterodox road to hell, and the devil knows how to handle Calvinists quite as well as Arminians. No privileged area of any church can ensure salvation, no form of doctrine can guarantee us eternal life. *"You must be born again." "You must bring forth fruits fit for repentance." "Every tree that does not bear good fruit is cut down and thrown into the fire."* Stopping short of vital union with the Lord Jesus by real faith, we miss the great qualification for entering heaven. Yet the time is not come when these mere head-knowers are cursed. These trees have leaves only, but no fatal curse has withered them hopelessly. No; they are to be sought after. They may yet know the Lord in their hearts, and the Holy Spirit may yet make them humble followers of the Lamb. O that it may be so!

A third class have *talk without feeling*. Mr. Talkative, in *Pilgrim's Progress,* is the representative of a very numerous host. They speak very glibly concerning divine things. Whether the topic be doctrinal, experimental, or practical, they talk fluently upon everything. But evidently, the whole thing comes from the throat and the lip; there is no welling up from the heart. If the thing came from the heart it would be boiling, but now it hangs like an icicle from their lips. You know them – you may learn something from them, but all the while you are yourself aware that if they bless others by their words, they themselves remain unblessed. Ah! let us be very anxious lest this should be our own case. Let the preacher feel the anxiety of the apostle Paul, lest, after having preached to others, he himself should be a castaway; and let my hearers feel the same concern, lest, after talking about the things of God, they should prove to be mere lip servers, and not accepted children of the Most High.

Another tribe springs up just now before my eyes – those who have *regrets without repentance.* Many of you under a heart-searching sermon feel grieved on account of your sins, and yet never have the strength of mind to give them up. You say you are sorry, but yet go on in the same course. You do really feel, when death and judgment press upon you, a certain sort of regret that you could have been so foolish, but the next day the strength of temptation is such that you fall prey to the very same infatuation. It is easy to bring a man to the river of regret, but you cannot make him drink the water of repentance. If Agag could be killed with words, no Amalekite would live. If men's transient sorrows for sin were real repentance on account of it, there is not a man living who would not, sometime or other, have been a true penitent. Here, however, are leaves only, and no fruit.

We have yet again another class of persons who have *resolves without action*. They *will*! Ah! that they *will*! But it is always in the future tense. They are hearers, and they are even feelers, but they are not *doers* of the Word; it never comes to that. They would be free, but they have not patience to file their restraints, nor grace to submit their chains to the hammer. They see the right, but they permit the wrong to rule them. They are charmed with the beauties of holiness, and yet deluded with the unruliness of sin. They would run in the ways of God's commandments, but the road is too rough, and running is weary work. They would fight for God, but victory is hardly won, and so they turn back almost as soon as they have set out; they put their hand to the plow, and then prove utterly unworthy of the kingdom.

The great majority of persons who have any sort of religion at all, bear leaves, but they produce no fruit. I know there are some such here, and I solemnly warn you though no curse falls upon you, though we do not think that the miracle now under consideration has any relation to you whatever; yet remember, there is nothing to be done with trees which bring forth only leaves, but in due time to use the axe upon them, and to cast them into the fire: and *this must be your doom*. As sure as you live under the sound of the gospel, and yet are not converted by it, so surely will you be cast into outer darkness. As certainly as Jesus Christ invites you, and you will not come, so certainly will he send his angels to gather the dead branches together, and you among them, to cast them into the fire. Beware! Beware! you fruitless tree! You shall not stand forever! Mercy waters you with her tears now; God's lovingkindness digs around you still; and still the husbandman comes, seeking fruit upon you year after year. Beware! The edge of the axe is sharp, and the arm which wields it is nothing less than almighty. Beware! lest you fall into the fire!

Secondly, there were other trees with neither leaves nor fruit, and none of these were cursed!

The time of figs was not yet come. Now, as the fig tree either brings forth the fig before the leaf, or else produces figs and leaves at the same time, the major part of the trees, perhaps all of them, without exception of this one, were entirely without figs and without leaves, and yet Jesus did not curse any one of them, for the time of figs was not yet come.

What multitudes are destitute of anything like religion. They make no profession of it; they not only have no fruits of godliness, but they also have no leaves even of outward respect to it. They do not frequent the court of the Lord's house; they use no form of prayer; they never observe the ordinances. The great outlying mass of this huge city – how does religion affect it? It is a very sad thing to think that there are people living in total darkness next door to the light, and that you may find in the very street where the gospel is preached persons who have never heard a sermon. Are there not, throughout this city, tens and hundreds of thousands who know not their right hand from their left in matters of godliness? Their children go to Sunday school, but they themselves spend the whole Sabbath day in anything except the worship of God! In our country parishes, very often neither the religion of the Establishment nor of Dissent affects the population at all.

Take, for instance, that village which will be disgracefully remembered as long as Essex endures – the village of Hedingham. There are in that place not only parish churches, but also Dissenting meetinghouses, and yet the persons who foully murdered the poor wretch supposed to be a wizard must have been as ignorant and indifferent to common sense, let alone religion, as even Hottentots or Kaffirs, to whom the light of religion has never come. Why was this? Is it not because there is not enough of missionary spirit among Christian people to seek out those who are in the lowest strata of society, so that multitudes escape without ever coming into contact with godliness at all?

In London, the city missionaries will bear witness that while they can sometimes get at the wives, yet there are thousands of husbands who are necessarily away at the time of the missionary's visit, who have not a word of rebuke, or exhortation, or invitation, or encouragement ever sounding in their ears at all, from the day of their birth to the day of their death; and they might, for all practical purposes, as well have been born in the center of Africa as in the city of London, for they are without God, without hope, aliens from the commonwealth of Israel, and far off, not by wicked works only, but also by dense ignorance of God.

These persons we may divide into two classes, upon neither of whom does the withering curse fall in this life. The first we look upon with hope. Although we see neither leaves nor fruit, we know that *it [is] not the season for figs.* They are God's *elect,* but they are *not called.* Their names are in the Lamb's Book of Life, and were there from before the foundations of the world; though they be dead in trespasses, they are the objects of divine love, and they must, in due time, be called by irresistible grace, and turned from darkness to light.

The Lord has *many people in this city,* and this should be the encouragement of every one of you, to try to do good, that God has among the vilest of the vile, the most reprobate, the most debauched and drunken, an elect people who *must* be saved. When you take the Word to them, you do so because God has ordained you to be the messenger of life to their souls, and they *must* receive it, for so the decree of predestination runs; they must be called in the fullness of time to be the brethren of Christ and children of the Most High. They are *redeemed,* beloved friends, but *not regenerated* – as much redeemed with precious blood as the saints before the eternal throne. They are Christ's property, and yet perhaps they are waiting around the alehouse at this very moment until the door shall open – bought with Jesus' precious blood, and yet spending their nights in a brothel, and their days in sin; but if Jesus Christ purchased them, he will have them. If he counted down the precious drops, God is not unfaithful to forget the price which his Son has paid. He will not permit his substitution to be in any case an ineffectual, dead thing.

Tens of thousands of redeemed ones are not regenerated yet, but regenerated they must be; and this is your comfort and mine, when we go out with the reviving Word of God. No, more than this, these ungodly ones are prayed for by Christ before the throne. *"I do not ask* on behalf of these alone," says the great Intercessor, "*but for those also who believe in Me through their word.*" They do not pray for themselves; poor, ignorant souls, they do not know anything about prayer, but Jesus prays for them. Their names are on his breast, and before long they must bow their stubborn knee, breathing the repentant sigh before the throne of grace. *It [is] not the season for figs.* The predestinated moment has not struck; but, when it comes, *they shall,* for God will have his own; *they must,* for the Spirit is not to be withstood when he comes forth with power – *they must* become the willing servants of the living God. *My Servant, will justify the many. As a result of the anguish of His soul, He will see it. I will allot Him a portion with the great, and He will divide the booty with the strong.*

No curse falls upon these; they deserve it, but eternal love prevents it. Their sins write it, but the finished sacrifice blots it out. They may well perish because they seek not mercy, but Christ intercedes for them, and live they shall.

Alas! However, among those who have neither leaves nor fruit, there is another class which *never* brings forth either the one or the other; they live in sin and die in ignorance, perishing without hope. As these leave the world, can they scold us for neglecting them? Are we clear of their blood? May not the blood of many of them cry from the ground against us? As they are condemned on account of sins, may they not accuse us because we did not take the gospel to them, but left them where they were? Dread thought! But let it not be shaken off; there are tens of thousands every day who pass into the world of spirits unsaved, and inherit the righteous wrath of God. Yet in this life, you see, no special curse falls upon them, and this miracle has no special bearing upon them; it bears upon a totally different class of people, of whom we will now speak.

We have before us a special case.

I have already said that in a fig tree, the fruit takes the precedence of the leaves, or the leaves and the fruit come at the same time; so that it is laid down as a general rule, that if there be leaves upon a fig tree, you may rightly expect to find fruit upon it.

To begin, then, with the explanation of this special case, *in a fig tree fruit comes before leaves.* So in a true Christian, fruit always takes the precedence of profession. Find a man anywhere who is a true servant of God, and before he united himself with the church, or attempted to engage in public prayer, or to identify himself with the people of God, he searched to see whether he had real repentance on account of sin. He desired to know whether he had a sincere and genuine faith in the Lord Jesus Christ, and he perhaps waited some little time to try himself to see whether there were the fruits of holiness in his daily life.

Indeed, I may say that there are some who wait too long; they are so afraid lest they should make a profession before they have grace in possession, that they will wait year after year – too long – and become unwise, and make what was a virtue become a vice. Still this is the rule with Christians: they first give themselves to the Lord, and afterwards to the Lord's people according to his will. You who are the servants of God – do you not scorn to vainly display yourselves beyond your line and measure? Would you not think it disgraceful on your part to profess anything which you have not felt? Do you not feel a holy jealousy when you are teaching others, lest you should teach more than God has taught you? And are you not afraid even in your prayers, lest you should use expressions which are beyond your own depth of meaning? I am sure the true Christian is always afraid of anything like having the leaves before he has the fruit.

Another remark follows from this – *where we see the leaves, we have a right to expect the fruit.* When I see a man a church member, when I hear him engage in prayer, I expect to see in him holiness – the character and the image of Christ. I have a right to expect it, because the man has solemnly declared that he is a partaker of divine grace. You cannot join a church without taking upon yourselves very solemn responsibilities. What do you declare when you come to see us and ask to be admitted into fellowship? You tell us that you have passed from death unto life, that you have been born again, that there has been a change in you, the like of which you never knew before, one which only God could have worked. You tell us you are in the habit of private prayer, that you have a desire for the conversion of others. If you did not so profess, we dare not receive you. Well now, having made these professions, it would be insincere on our part if we did not expect to see your character holy, and your conversation correct; we have a right to expect it from your own professions.

We have a right to expect it from the work of the Spirit which you claim to have received. Shall the Holy Spirit work in man's heart to produce a trifle? Do you think that the Spirit of God would have written us this Book, and that Jesus Christ would have shed his precious blood to produce a hypocrite? Is an inconsistent Christian the highest work of God? I suppose God's plan of salvation to be that which has more exercised his thoughts and wisdom than the making of all worlds and the sustenance of all providence; and shall this best, this highest, this darling work of God produce no more than that poor, mean, talking, inactive, and fruitless deceiver? You have no love for souls, no care for the spread of the Redeemer's kingdom, and yet you think that the Spirit has made you what you are! No zeal, no melting bowels of compassion, no cries of earnest pleading, no wrestling with God, no holiness, no self-denial, and yet you say that you are a vessel made by the Master and fitted for his use! How can this be?

No; if you profess to be a Christian, from the necessity of the Spirit's work, we have a right to expect fruit from you. Besides, in genuine professors we do get the fruit. We see a faithful attachment to the Redeemer's cause, and an endurance to the end, in poverty, in sickness, in shame, or in persecution. We see other professors holding fast to the truth. They are not led aside by temptation, neither do they disgrace the cause they have expressed support for; and, if you profess to be one of the same order, we have a right to look for the same blessed fruits of the Spirit in you, and if we see them not, you have misrepresented us.

> If you profess to be a Christian we have a right to expect fruit from you.

Observe further that *our Lord hungers for fruit*. A hungry person seeks for something which may satisfy him – for fruit, not leaves! Jesus hungers for your holiness. A strong expression, you will say, but I doubt not its accuracy. For what were we elected? We were predestinated to be conformed unto the image of God's Son; we were chosen to do good works, *which God prepared beforehand so that we would walk in them*. What is the end of our redemption? Why did Jesus Christ die? He *gave Himself for us to redeem us from every lawless deed, and to purify for*

Himself a people for His own possession, zealous for good deeds. Why have we been called but that we should be called to be saints? To what end are any of the great operations of the covenant of grace? Do they not all point to our holiness? If you will think of any privilege which the Lord confers upon his people through Christ, you will perceive that they all aim for the sanctification of the chosen people – the making of them to bring forth fruit that God the Father may be glorified in them.

O Christian, for this the tears of the Savior! For this the agony and bloody sweat! For this the five death-wounds! For this the burial and the resurrection, that he makes you holy, even perfectly holy like unto himself! And can it be, that when he hungers after fruit, you think nothing of fruit-bearing? O professor, how base are you, to call yourself a blood-bought child of God, and yet to live unto yourself! How dare you, O barren tree, professing to be watered by the bloody sweat, and dug by the griefs and woes of the wounded Savior – how dare you bring forth leaves and no fruit! Oh! Sacrilegious mockery of a hungry Savior! Oh! Blasphemous tantalizing of a hungry Lord! That you should profess to have cost him all this, and yet yield him nothing! When I think that Jesus hungers after fruit in me, it stirs me up to do more for him. Does it not have the same effect on you? He hungers for your good works; he hungers to see you useful. Jesus, the King of Kings, hungers after your prayers – hungers after your anxieties for the souls of others; and nothing ever will satisfy him for the labor of his soul but seeing you wholly devoted to his cause.

This brings us into the very midst and meaning of the miracle. *There are some, then, who make unusual profession, and yet disappoint the Savior in his just expectations.* The Jews did this. When Jesus Christ came it was not the time of figs. The time for great holiness was after the coming of Christ and the pouring out of the Spirit. All the other nations were without leaves. Greece, Rome – these showed no signs of progress; but there was the Jewish nation covered with leaves. They professed already to have obtained the blessings which he came to bring. There stood the Pharisee with his long prayers; there were the lawyers and the scribes with their deep knowledge of the things of the kingdom. They said they had the light. The time of figs was not come, but yet they had the leaves, though not a single fruit; and you know what a curse fell on Israel; how in the day of Jerusalem's destruction the tree was withered altogether from its root, because it had its leaves, but had no fruit.

The same will be true of any *church*. There are times when all the churches seem sunken alike in lethargy – such a time we had, say ten years ago – but one church, perhaps, seems to be all alive. The congregations are large. Much, apparently, is proposed for the growth of the Savior's kingdom. A deal of noise is made about it; there is much talk, and the people are all expectation. And, if there be no fruit, no real consecration to Christ, if there be no genuine liberality, no earnest vital godliness, no holy consistency, other churches may live on, but such a church as this, making so high a profession, and being so premature in the produce of leaves, shall have a curse from God. No man shall eat fruit of it forever, and it shall wither away.

In the case of *individuals,* the moral of our miracle runs thus. Some are looked upon as young believers who early on join the church. *It [is] not the season for figs;* it is not a very ordinary case to see children converted, but we do see some, and we are very grateful. We are jealous, however, lest we should see leaves but not fruit. These juveniles are extraordinary cases; and on that account we look for higher results. When we are disappointed, what shall come upon such but a curse upon their prematureness, which led them to the deception. Some of us were converted, or profess to have been, when young, and if we have lived up to this time, and all we have produced has been merely words, resolves, and professions, but not fruit unto God, we must expect the curse.

Again, *professors are distinguished in position.* There are necessarily but few ministers and few church officers; but when men so distinguish themselves by zeal, or by louder professions than others, so as to gain the ear of the Christian public and are placed in responsible positions – if they bring forth no fruit, they are the persons upon whom the curse will light. It may be with other Christians that *it [is] not the season for figs;* they have not made the advances which these profess to have made; but having been, upon their own profession, elected to an office which essentially requires fruit, since they yield it not, let them beware.

To those who make professions of much love for Christ, the same caution may be given. With most Christians, I am afraid, I must say that *it [is] not the season for figs,* for we are too much like the Laodicean church. But you meet with some men – how much they are in love with Christ! How sweetly they can *talk* about him, but what do they *do* for him? Nothing! Nothing! Their love lies just in the wind which comes out of their own mouths, and that is all. Now, when the Lord has a curse, he will deal it out on such. They went beyond all others in an untimely declaration of a very fervent love, and now they yield him no fruit. "Yes," said one, "I love God so much that I do not reckon that anything I have is my own. It is all the Lord's – all the Lord's, and I am his steward."

Well, this dear good man, of course, joined the church, and after a time, some mission work needed a little help. What was his reply? "When I pay my seat rent, I have done all I intend to do." A man of wealth and means! After a little time, this same man found it inconvenient even to pay for his seat, and goes now to a place not quite so full, where he can get a seat and do nothing to support the ministry! If there is a special thunderbolt anywhere, it is these fake hypocrites who whine about love for Christ and bow down at the shrine of wealth.

Or, take another case. You meet with others whose profession is not of so much love, but it is of *much experience.* Oh! what experience they have had! What deep experience! Ah! they know the humblings of heart and the plague of human nature! They know the depths of corruption, and the heights of divine fellowship, and so on. Yes, and if you go into the shop you find the corruption is carried on behind the counter, and the deceit in the journal; if they do not know the plague of their own hearts, at least they are a plague to their own household. Such people are abhorrent to all men, and much more to God.

> If you will watch these very critical people, the very faults they indicate in others they are indulging in themselves.

Others you meet with *who have a faultfinding tongue.* What good people they must be; they can see the faults of other people so plainly! This church is not right, and the other is not right, and yonder preacher – well, some people think him a very good man, but they do not. They can see the deficiencies in the various denominations, and they observe that very few really carry out Scripture as it should be carried out. They complain of lack of love and are the very people who create that lack.

Now, if you will watch these very critical people, the very faults they indicate in others they are indulging in themselves; and while they are seeking to find out the speck in their brother's eye, they have a beam in their own.

These are the people who are indicated by this fig tree, for they ought, according to their own showing, taking them on their own ground, to be better than other people. If what they say is true, they are bright particular stars, and they ought to give special light to the world. They are such that even Jesus Christ himself might expect to receive fruit from them, but they are nothing but deceivers, with these high soarings and proud boastings; they are nothing after all but pretenders. Like Jezebel with her painted eyes, which made her all the uglier, they would seem to be what they are not. As old Adam says, "They are candles with big wicks and no tallow, and when they go out they make a foul and nauseous smell." "They have summer sweating on their brow, and winter freezing in their hearts." You would think them the land of Goshen, but prove them the wilderness of sin. Let us search ourselves, lest such be the case with us.

And now to close, such a tree might well be withered. *Deception is despised by God.* There was the Jewish temple, there were the priests standing in solemn pomp, there were the abundant sacrifices on God's altar. But was God pleased with his temple? No, because in the temple you had all the leaves; you had all the externals of worship, but there was no true prayer, no belief in the great Lamb of God's Passover, no truth, no righteousness, no love for men, no care for the glory of God; and so the temple, which had been a house of prayer, had become a den of thieves. You do not marvel that the temple was destroyed. You and I may become just like that temple. We may go on with all the externals of religions, nobody may miss us out of our seat at the tabernacle, no, we may never miss our Christian engagements; we may be in all external matters more precise than we used to be, and yet for all that, we may have become in our hearts a den of thieves. The heart may be given to the world while external ceremonies are still kept up and maintained. Let us beware of this, for such a place cannot be long without a curse. It is abhorrent to God.

Again, *it is deceptive to man.* Look at that temple! What do men go there for? To see holiness and virtue. Why tread they its holy courts? To get nearer to God. And what do they find there? Instead of holiness, covetousness; instead of getting nearer to God, they get into the midst of a market where men are haggling about the price of doves, and bickering with one another about the changing of shekels. So men may watch to hear some seasonable word from our lips, and instead of that, they may get evil; and as that temple was cursed for deluding men, so may we be, because we deceive and disappoint the wants of mankind.

More than this, this barren fig tree *committed sacrilege upon Christ,* did it not? Might it not have exposed him to ridicule? Some might have said, "Why do you go to a tree, you prophet, upon which there is no fruit?" A false professor exposes Christ to ridicule. As the temple of old dishonored God, so does a Christian when his heart is not right; he does dishonor to God, and makes the holy cause to be trodden under foot of the adversary. Such men indeed have reason to beware.

Once more, this tree might well be cursed, because its bringing forth nothing but leaves was a plain evidence of its sterility. It had force and vitality, but it turned it to ill account, and would continue to do so. The curse of Christ was but a confirmation of what it already was. He did as good as say, "He that is unfruitful, let him be unfruitful still." And now, what if Christ should come into this tabernacle today, and should look on you and on me, and see in any of us great profession and great pomp of leaves, and yet no fruit? What if he should pronounce the curse on us; what would be the effect? We should wither away as others have done. What do we mean by this? Why, they have all of a sudden turned to the world. We could not understand why such fair saints should, all of a sudden, become such black devils; the fact was, Christ had pronounced the word, and they began to wither away. If he should pronounce the unmasking word on any mere professor here and say, *"No longer shall there ever be any fruit from you,"* you will go into gross outward sin and wither to your shame.

This will take place probably all of a sudden; and taking place, your case will be irretrievable, and you never afterwards will be restored. The blast which shall fall upon you will be eternal; you will live as a lasting monument of the terrible justice of Christ, as the great head of the church. You will be spared to let it be seen that a man outside the church may escape with impunity in this life, but a man inside the church shall have a present curse, and be made to stand as a tree blasted by the lightning of God forever.

Now, this is a heart-searching matter. It went through me yesterday when I thought, "Well, here am I. I have professed to be called of God to the ministry, I have forced myself into a leading place in God's church, and I have voluntarily put myself into a place where sevenfold damnation is my inevitable inheritance if I be not true and sincere." I could almost wish myself back out of the church, or at least in the obscurest place in her ranks, to escape the perils and responsibilities of my position; and so may you, if you have not the witness of the Spirit in you that you are born of God – you may wish that you never thought of Christ, and never dreamed of taking his name upon you. If you have by diligence worked yourself into a high position among God's people; if you have mere leaves without the fruit, the more sure is the curse, because the greater the disappointment of the Savior. The more you profess, the more is expected of you; and if you do not yield it, the more just the condemnation when you shall be left to stand forever withered by the curse of Christ.

> **The more you profess, the more is expected of you.**

O men and brethren, let us tremble before the heart-searching eye of God, but let us still remember that grace can make us fruitful yet. The way of mercy is open still. Let us appeal to the wounds of Christ today. If we have never begun, let us begin now. Now let us throw our arms about the Savior, and take him to be ours; and, having done this, let us seek divine grace, so that for the rest of our lives we may work for God. Oh! I do hope to do more for God, and I hope you will. O Holy Spirit, work in us mightily, for in you is our fruit found! Amen.

Chapter 4

The Moral of a Miracle

And Jesus answered saying to them, "Have faith in God."
(Mark 11:22)

This exhortation stands in connection with the miracle of the withering of the fig tree that was clad with leaves but was bearing no fruit. The peculiarity of the parable calls for a few words of explanation before we proceed to enforce the moral appended to it. To many readers it seems strange and inconsistent that, since it was not the time of figs, our Lord should have expected to find figs upon the tree at all. They wonder how it was that he should blame the fig tree for not having figs when the time of figs was not yet come. But it is because we do not live in the land of fig trees that we do not understand this; for according to the natural order of production, the fig fruit precedes the foliage. The fig tree first of all puts forth its figs, at the end of the shoots – the little knobs beginning to form in the early spring, and the figs becoming very fairly developed before any leaves appear – so that if a fig tree has leaves upon it, it ought to have figs in a considerable state of ripeness. This fig tree, at a time when no figs were expected, and far less any leaves, seemed to have outstripped all its fellow fig trees; to have gone far ahead of them; to have been in advance of its own responsibilities as a fig tree; to have exceeded all the demands of the season; to have reached a state of supernatural fruit-bearing which no other fig tree had dreamed of reaching. There were leaves. The Savior went up, and finding the leaves which ought to have denoted figs in a considerable state of ripeness he glanced around, but finding no single fig to justify the large pretense, he said, *"No longer shall there ever be any fruit from you."*

You know that occasionally trees do put on leaves at abnormal times. There is a famous oak tree in the New Forest which usually has well-developed leaves upon it around Christmas, when winter reigns on every side, and "dead the vegetable kingdom lies." There is a pretty superstition about it, as though the tree thrust forth its sudden honors at the birth of the great Lord. I have seen the tree, and it seems very strange that it should take to leaf-bearing when there is not a leaf throughout the forest anywhere else. This fig tree in like manner, for some reason or other, had got into leaf at a time when it ought not to have. If it did get into leaf, it ought to have figs, but it had leaves and no figs. As such it becomes a suitable and proper emblem of such a man as we sometimes meet with, who boasts of a righteousness he cannot verify; who seems more conspicuously devout in his character than he could reasonably have been expected to be; who makes a show of devotion that is altogether premature; who gives signs of maturity before the season; who professes much, though he yields nothing to corroborate it – a prodigy of self-conceit. He does not say he is absolutely perfect, but it needs very fine optics to distinguish the line. He outstrips all his fellows. His talk is something marvelous. His creed is more sound, his conscience more sensitive, his conduct more sanctimonious, and his standard in estimating others more critical than the rest of the community.

You wonder at it till you come near to him, and then you find it is all talk, tinsel, and trumpery. *Nothing but leaves,* and no real virtue, but a lush show thereof. Alas, I have known decent morality outraged by such monstrous duplicity. All the leafage and foliage of a godly life, and all the death and corruption of a graceless debauchery! Those round about him were ashamed to find themselves so inferior in their attainments, till presently the suddenness with which he withered astounded them more than the rapidity of his growth. There was nothing in it. The old proverb has it: "Great cry and little wool." Great cry, indeed, for holier voices are silenced by it, and there is no wool at all to repay the shearer – *nothing but leaves.* Now, if any man is withered, it is such a man as that.

One thing I have noticed in watching over a large church is that some brethren who have seemed too good to live, have turned out much too bad for us to want them to live very long. Such have been so pure, so white, so spotless, so stainless, so precise, so exact, so velvet-mouthed, so oily, so full of sugar, and so hyper-holy in their hypocrisy, that it seemed cruel to feel inward qualms when you were near them. Yet under a thin layer of this hollow pretension they have been so deficient in all spiritual life and reality and sincerity, that when we found them out, we could not help feeling a burning indignation in our own soul that men could go so far in lying unto the Holy Spirit. One does not wonder that Ananias and Sapphira fell dead, or that the fig tree was blasted that had so many leaves and no fruit. We have seen the same thing happen to men, and we have not wondered. We have only thought how righteously God has unmasked them and exposed their hideous vices to the curse even of the world, which though it lies in the wicked one, has yet some sense of scorn at a religious lie.

Now, our Savior performed this miracle by way of a parable, not that he cared for figs, or was angry because there were none, but because it furnished him with an opportunity of instructing his disciples. This was an object lesson. We never learn so well as from something we can actually see with our eyes. Jesus did this that they might see, and that their minds might be impressed with what they saw. The main impression upon the mind of Peter, and others, seems to have been the extraordinary power of Christ. One morning their Lord said, *"No longer shall there ever be any fruit from you,"* and the next day when they passed that way they found the fig tree withered, even from the roots – not simply all its shoots gone, but according to Mark, in the twentieth verse, they saw the fig tree dried up from the roots, or totally destroyed. It stood a wreck of a tree, the precise opposite of what it had seemed to be some four-and-twenty hours before. They were struck with the power of Christ's word: at the simple decree of his mouth the doom had fallen on the tree. He had not touched the tree that we know of. He simply spoke, and its bloom was past; its doom had come.

Now, our Lord did not go on to open up the parable to them, but perceiving the impression it made on their minds in one direction, he aimed at still further engraving on their souls the moral which had been conveyed to their senses. So he went on to speak about the great power of God that they were wondering at, and to tell them that they could have that power, that they could wield it, and that they might exert it as he did. And he practically told them how they could get that power, and go forth girded with it.

Our first observation, in order to bring out this vein of thought, shall be that it is good for us to observe the power of God.

These disciples saw the power of Christ, which is the power of God, in the withering of a fig tree. We do not see miracles now. We do not look for signs and wonders to supply the credentials and the seal of faith. The works of God in nature are, if rightly understood, testimonies to the eternal power and Godhead, at once simple and sublime. Perhaps, under some aspects, they convey higher lessons than miracles.

We ought, I think, to have our eyes open constantly to see the power of God in renewing the face of the earth. I like to observe it in the seasons. What a wonderful power was that which, all of a sudden, called up all sleeping bulbs and flowers from their graves, and caused that which had been black soil suddenly to blossom into a golden garden, or to bloom into beds adorned with many colors. Have you not seen lone places in the woods and nooks among the trees so glorious in color that it seemed as though the Lord had torn pieces of the robe of the sky and flung them down among the trees in the woods? We have seen the hyacinths all of a sudden in their deepest azure standing where all before had been black mold or dry leaf. We see it every year, but it is a marvelous thing, and we might stand and say, "How soon has the winter passed away! How speedily has earth put on her youth again!" See you no power of God in all this? These creations and resurrections of spring – are they nothing? And now at this season of the year when the leaves are falling all around us, though the trees are not withering away, how rapidly they are undergoing their wonderful process of disrobing. You passed by a tree the other day which was green, and you delighted to be beneath its foliage; and now in the setting sun of this afternoon it seemed as though it were blazing with golden fire: every leaf had turned yellow by the touch of autumn. How has God worked all this?

Silently and quietly, without sound of trumpet, from year to year these miracles of nature proceed, of which I am speaking very roughly now; but he that looks into them, and studies them, shall be filled with amazement at the extraordinary power of God. This world has been going around the sun making its revolutions. Who could hold it to its pathway but the Most High? Each day it revolves and gives us the delightful succession of day and night: it is the Lord that moves the world on its axis. We do not think at all adequately of the mighty power of God which is continually going forth. The creation of blood out of water by the plague of Egypt astonishes us a great deal more than does the revolution of the world, and yet this is by far the more amazing thing of the two.

It does us good, beloved friends, to stand sometimes at night and look up to the starry heavens and think what a God he is that calls all of them by name, leads them out in marching order so that not one of them fails, and sustains each one of those celestial orbs in its place throughout the ages. Marvelous are the works of God in nature. Can you read about Vesuvius beginning to pour forth its fires, or of earthquakes in diverse places shaking the mountains to their bases, and making the strongest works of men to rock and reel, without a sense of reverential awe? Can you be in a storm at sea, can you tremble while each timber starts as the waves beat upon the vessel, without feeling that this is a great God whom we serve? I invite you to think of the greatness, the majestic grandeur of God in nature, because the God of nature is the God of grace; and the God that rules on high, and thunders according to his pleasure, is the God whom we call Father, and who has taken us into his family that we may be his sons and daughters. Though we do not see fig trees withered away, yet often we ought to stand in holy wonder and say, "Great God, how wonderful are your works!"

> The God that rules on high, and thunders according to his pleasure, is the God whom we call Father.

Now, if you turn your eye from nature to Providence, which I invite you to do, you will observe stupendous examples of the great power of God. This withering of the fig tree has been repeated ten thousand times on a grand scale. I will only remind you of what has happened in our own day. A few years ago slavery seemed to have struck its roots into the soil of the Southern United States. Its branches ran over the wall: the Northern states were bound to return a fugitive slave. How quickly has that fig tree withered away! Slavery has gone, blessed be God, forever. And there treads not now on American soil a man of any color who is a slave. Across yonder channel frowned the great empire of Napoleon. It looked as if it was very mighty. It spread itself like a green bay tree. It was the main support of the papacy; but how quickly has that fig tree withered away! Over yonder, in Italy, there were a number of petty principalities with mean tyrants crushing down the people. God raised up an honest man who came forward as the champion of the oppressed, and how speedily did those little fig leaves fall. There stood the man of sin with his worldly power, and he was master of his own domains, and chiefly of the city of Rome, but how soon has that fig tree withered away.

One after another revolutions have occurred, and events have transpired in our own day which prove that the Lord is very great in power. All through history the ages bear their record that whenever an institution has sprung up that has brought forth no good fruit just at the very time when it was fullest of leaf, when everybody said, "Now we may expect fruit from it," and when it was supposed to be impossible that it should pass away, just then has the Lord spoken, and its hour of doom has come. One word from him, and how speedily has this fig tree withered away! All Providence is full of it. He that reads history looking for providences needs not turn two pages over without finding instances. He shall see the hand of God here and there, and there and there again, permitting for a while the growth of evil, but then speedily sweeping it away. So shall every system which defies his laws prove that its prosperity is the precursor of its utter destruction. It flowers and flourishes only to droop and die, to die just in its prime. While we stand trembling and astonished at its spread, so thick its leaves, so palpable its vitality, at that very moment we hear the powerful voice of Christ and see the inevitable result in the withering away of that which was in the prime of vigor.

Now, as we have opportunity to watch the power of God, let us always be ready to observe it; not, however, with vacant astonishment, nor with idle gossip to exclaim to one another, "How extraordinary!" Although the works of God are suitable subjects for adoring wonder, yet when we remember who he is and what he is, there is a sense in which we may well cease to wonder or be startled, as if our poor philosophy must forever reckon as strange phenomena the tokens of his presence, the proofs of his agency, and the imprint of his hand.

You know the story of the good woman who, on being told of some notable answers to prayer which had been received, was asked, "Is it not wonderful?" and she simply replied, "No, not at all; it is just like him. That is the way of him." And so when God puts away withered fig trees, and when he shows his power in other ways in his divine providence, it is wonderful for us to contemplate, and yet it is not wonderful for him to perform. *He breaks the bow and cuts the spear in two; He burns the chariots with fire,* and he bids us be still, and know that he is God. He will be exalted in the earth. It has been the way of him from the first, and it will be the way of him still.

We ought to watch these works of power so that we may feel that this power is altogether engaged upon our side. If we be indeed upon the side of God, if his grace has reconciled us to him, if we live now to promote his glory, if we are under his keeping and the guardian care of the Lord Jesus, then all the power that makes an earthquake will be put forth to shake heaven and earth sooner than we shall perish. All the power that shows itself in Providence shall be put forth to deliver us sooner than we shall famish. Our place of defense shall be the ammunitions of rocks: our bread shall be given us and our water shall be sure. The mighty God, Jehovah is his name, has pledged his omnipotence for the advance and the victory of his people, and stand they shall and win the day.

That is my first point: *it is good to observe the power of God.*

My second point is that God has called his people to works *which need all that power.* Our Lord Jesus Christ tells us this practically, when he says, *"Have faith in God. Truly I say to you, whoever says to this mountain, 'Be taken up and cast into the sea,' and does not doubt in his heart, but believes that what he says is going to happen, it will be granted him."* A Christian is a miracle. He is a mass of miracles. When he gets to heaven he will be a miracle of miracles. His story in the telling thereof will fill all heaven with enthusiasm, so marvelous is the work of God in the heirs of salvation. It is no small thing to be a soldier of the cross – a follower of the Lamb.

Now today, dear souls, if the Lord Jesus Christ by his Spirit should call any one of you to come to him, you would, perhaps, feel immediately the deepest anxiety in your heart. I think I hear you say, "If I come and trust him, how shall I be saved, for don't you see the difficulties that lie in my way? I see before me the vast mountain of my past sin. How can I come to Christ? Surely this alp of transgression must hide him from me." Have faith in God, dear friend, and God's power will be put forth to move this mountain; yes, Christ has moved it by his precious death. "Alas," says the poor heart, "but I feel such a mountain of despair, I cannot hope. I think I have sinned beyond grace." Have faith in God and you shall see this mountain of doubt and despair all swept away, and you shall find joy in him who blots out your sin like a cloud and your transgressions like a thick cloud. "Ah," says the soul, "but I seem so cold, so heavy, so dead. I do not feel as earnest and eager as I should. There is nothing in me that is good." Have faith in God's power to help you in this, and you shall find your lethargy and weariness giving place to energy and vigor, and your cold heart shall be thawed in the rivers of repentance.

"Oh," says one, "but I want everything. I am far off from God, as far as I can be. There are impassable barriers between me and God." Yes, but do you have faith in God? Do you but believe in his fatherly love and grace, his goodness, and faithfulness? Then do but trust Christ, and rely on the great Father's love in Jesus Christ, and you shall find that the mountains which appall you will melt away and no longer impede you.

I know what has happened to you. Your fig tree has been withered down to the roots. How full of leaves it used to be! You were a fine fellow once. If you did not bring forth any fruit to God, yet what fair promises you made – what grand resolutions! What a fine self-righteousness you had, but the power of God's will has already withered it down to the roots. Now, the selfsame power of his gospel by the Spirit will take up all the mountains that stand between you and God and cast them into the depths of the sea, and you shall rejoice in him.

God calls the coming sinner, then, to duties and obligations so far beyond his own natural capacity that it requires all the power of God to enable him to fulfill them. Even when bidden to repent and believe and come to Christ, he needs the Godhead to help him to do that;

the Godhead will enable him, and so he shall receive grace for obedience to the faith. Have faith in God, then, and faint not by reason of discouragements.

But after we have come to Christ we still find it no easy task to continue pressing on to God. You that have believed in him and are saved, do you not often cry out, "O weak and erring mortal that I am! How shall I ever reach perfection? How can I get rid of sin that haunts my imagination and irritates my heart? What heaven of bliss can I know unless my soul is purified from every stain?" Most true it is that there can be no such thing as perfect happiness till there is perfect holiness, and yet by faith the believer looks for both. "But," do I hear you say, "first, my ignorance is in the way"? Have faith in God, and you shall be taught of him, and that mountain of darkness shall disappear. "Oh, but then there is my old corruption in the way, and that comes in between me and every advance in grace." Have faith in God and you shall find that he will take away the stony heart out of your flesh and fill you with virtue and vitality through believing.

"Oh, but the trials and temptations of each day, how shall I stand against them?" You cannot stand against them alone. They are far too much for you, but have faith in God, and then fierce as those temptations may be, you shall be able to resist, for his power is able to hold you up. Though a legion of devils at once should tempt you, have faith in God, and they shall be put to defeat. You shall have sufficient grace to bear you through.

> Though a legion of devils should tempt you, have faith in God, and they shall be put to defeat.

"Alas," says another, "you do not know my trial." No, my dear friend, and you do not know mine, but both you and I may know this, that he who measured out the trial, for they are all measured and weighed to the last pennyweight, knows how to strengthen us so that we can bear them. We shall be able to say to the mountains of trial, "Depart," as truly as we bid the fruitless fig tree, "Be dried up." Rise, worm Jacob, and thresh the mountains and beat them small; yes, turn them into chaff and winnow them, and the wind shall carry them away. Only trust in the eternal power and Godhead, and there is nothing between here and heaven that need give you any fear. If we are without God we shall stumble at a straw, but if God be with us, who can be against us?

Even if our life should be extended to an advanced old age, our bones be full of pain, and our flesh infected with a thousand painful infirmities; even though we should spend years upon a weary bed, with poverty as well as pain to afflict us, he that has faith in God shall sing aloud upon his bed and praise the Lord because the power of God rests upon him. You are not called to be parade soldiers, to exhibit your regimentals and your fine feathers. You are called to fight. You must fight if you would reign. Do not mistake it; you are called to work miracles – moral miracles, spiritual miracles. You are called to do great wonders between here and heaven. You see your calling, brethren, and you will see, if you see correctly, that nothing but a divine power can help you to accomplish it.

Now, if this be true in respect to our own spiritual life, I am sure it is so in trying to win the souls of others to Christ. The man who brings a soul to Christ achieves a result which no genius or skill of the creature could bring about. The power which God puts upon a man to make him the means of turning a sinner from darkness to light has no parallel. If a man could tell me that he stopped Niagara at a word, I would not envy him his power if God would only allow me to stop a sinner in his mad career of sin. If a creature could put his finger on Vesuvius and quench its flame, I would not at all regret that I had no such power if I might but be the means of stopping a blasphemer, and teaching him to pray.

This spiritual power is the greatest power imaginable, and the most to be desired. If any of us aim to be useful, we cannot succeed unless we have this divine power, for without omnipotent spiritual help we can produce no spiritual result. You can read a sermon or preach a sermon, or hear your children read in your Sunday school class without any help from God, but then nothing will come of it. If there is to be living preaching and living teaching that really brings souls to Jesus Christ, the work must all be done in the power of the Holy Spirit from first to last. You see your calling then, brethren. You must have that power which speaks to fig trees and they wither – yes, a power sufficient to speak to a mountain and pluck it up by its roots, for nothing short of this will fit you for your work.

Take the larger scale for a minute and think of it. We are all called to try and extend the Redeemer's kingdom, and as Christians we are greatly concerned for the progress of the church and the truth of God. I am sure in these evil days there is not one of us that can look upon the signs of the times without considerable sorrow. I hope it is not because I am growing older that I take a gloomier view of things than I did some years ago; it is not my eyes, but I do actually see superstition much more rampant than it was. That particularly sweet fig tree of ritualism has spread its boughs amazingly. And then there is the very deceptive fig tree of skepticism that seems to overshadow a considerable portion of the professing church of Christ. Well now, what is to be done? Nothing is to be done except as the text tells us – *"Have faith in God."* And when we have faith in God we must speak with devotion and with authority too: we must show our faith by the testimony we bear; and the Word of God that comes out of faithful lips shall roll like thunder and flash like lightning, and strike with electric force. So the old effect it always had on these leafy, fruitless fig trees will be repeated: it shall make them wither away.

If you have ever read the history of skeptical thought in Germany – not that I recommend you to do so, for it is a sore labor and a weariness of spirit – but if you have ever waded through any of these histories of philosophy as I have myself, you will doubtless have observed a thought rising up like a cloud full of foreshadowings, and covering the fatherland with its fantastic shadows till the people are led to see everything in a new light, or under a fresh coloring. They give the poet, the essayist, and the critic of the new cloud region credit for inspiration, and all who abide under that shadow are written down as infallible. But how insecure the reign of human wisdom!

In about twenty-five years you could buy all the books of that day for the price of wastepaper, for a new philosophy has meanwhile sprung up, a fresh system which has rendered all that preceded it obsolete. The scholars are in ecstasy. They shout "Eureka!" and sneer contemptuously at all who refrain from echoing their cry. Wait a little while, and another meteor will attract their gaze, another short-lived glowworm will glimmer in the darkness. I have read of a plant *which came up overnight and perished overnight,* but the cedars of Lebanon grow slowly and endure longer. How soon this fig tree has withered away! Thus have I thought, and so have I said, as I have read one after another the various systems of nonsense that they call philosophy and metaphysics. How soon this fig tree has withered away! Now, in the lives of even some of the younger folks here you might have seen in England different systems of unbelief coming up in different quarters, under which the thinkers of the age (as they call themselves), or the triflers of the hour (as we might better call them), have sought shelter.

At one time we were all wrong because of some wonderful discovery of old bones. Geology had upset us. Then some other science was brought to the front. One has lived to see a number of little scares. The fig trees have come up with a vast show of foliage without any fruit. In looking back at them we can say, "How soon this fig tree has vanished away." And, as to the present claims, whatever they may be, we have only to wait a little while with confidence in God, and we shall see these fruitless fig trees also wither away. Yes, and if there be systems in the world which seem more enduring, as colossal as the Alps, with foundations as deep as hell, we have still but to exercise faith enough and cry to God loudly enough, and fling ourselves upon Omnipotence boldly enough, and then to speak, and in the speaking of the everlasting gospel we shall see these mountain systems plucked up by the roots and cast into the midst of the sea. There is the point: we must have divine strength to do it.

> Our faith must not be partly in God and partly in something else, but faith wholly in God.

My third point is this: our Savior shows us the connecting link between the divine power and our work.

How are we to acquire this power? We believe that God can do all things; we have seen something of the greatness of his power, so how can we be girded with it? Here is the answer: *"Have faith in God."* It is to be by faith, that is, trust, reliance, and belief. It must be in God. Our faith must not be partly in God and partly in something else, but faith wholly in God. And it is literally, *"Have the faith of God"* – the faith which is worked in us by God, and sustained by God, for that is the only faith that is worth having.

Have the faith of God. "Oh, but this is a very small thing," says one. It is. It is a child's instinct to trust his father, but it is the rarest grace in the world to trust our Father who is in heaven. *"When the Son of Man comes, will He find faith on the earth?"* If anybody could find it, he could. He knows where it is, for he is the author, the giver, and the nourisher of faith. Yet there is so little of it in culture that if he himself searched for it, he would not find many fields in which it grows, or many hearts in which it thrives. Why, some of us have faith in him whereby we are saved from this present evil world. How shocked at ourselves we have reason to be in respect to the little faith we have in him for the furtherance of his own work, and how our heart sinks under our own daily trials! He has given us justifying faith, but our faith still is a faith the weakness of which should make us humble ourselves before him. Doubt God! How monstrous it sounds, how foolish it appears, how impossible it seems. To an experienced Christian, at first sight, it really seems incredible that any disciple of Jesus should doubt God.

You, my dear brother, that have been fed and nourished all your life long by singular providences – you whose life is so remarkable, that if its incidents were all written down people would look on them as a romance; you who have seen his arm made bare on your behalf many times; you who have often been constrained to say, still has my life new wonders seen – do you doubt him? How can it be? Alas! Alas! is not this the fault, and the grievous, crying sin of many of the children of God? Therefore our Lord puts it thus. He not only speaks of the faith of God, but he also says, "Have it; have it. Have faith in God. Have it handy. Have it around you. Have it for daily use. Carry it with you." Some of you have got a good anchor somewhere, but you left it at home when the storm came. You have faith somewhere, but you do not seem to exercise it just at the time when faith is required. *"Have faith in God."* He does not tell you how much. There is no need to prescribe any limit. Have unlimited faith in God; have daily faith in God; have continual, perpetual, abounding faith in God. *"Have faith in God."* This is the connecting link between our weakness and the divine strength, by which we are made strong.

Have faith in God about every purpose and every peril that may arise. You saw how the fig tree withered away. Have faith about that. You have seen it. Now, have faith about mountains. Do not think that God's power is limited to withering fig trees. Have faith about things of magnitude and things minute, but more particularly about the things that at this moment distress you. When you feel that you could believe God about everything except one particular matter that just now frets your mind and breaks your peace, you evidently misjudge your own capacity for faith. You ought to measure its strength by the influence it exerts upon you under your present trial.

O my sister, have faith in God about that sickening little infant at home. Your heart is sad that the Lord's will in this must be done, but he will strengthen you to bear it. Have faith, too, about those simple family matters which are causing you so much irritation. You have been praying about them, now commit your cause to God, and have faith that he will grant your request. "Oh, but there is a matter of deep significance harassing my very soul, which I would not like to mention to anybody," say you. Have faith about it and mention it to your Lord. Do not go about and make mischief by talking of it, but have faith about it. "Alas, but I am out of employment," says a poor man over yonder, "and I am getting sternly oppressed." Dear brother, are you a true believer? Have faith about that now. I know you will say to me that I do not know your trial. No, I do not; but you do not know some troubles I have had! And if you were to tell me to have faith in God about them I would thank you for the exhortation, for that is the only way I have of getting over them. And, dear brother, it is the only way you will find of being extricated from your dilemmas.

What a mass of troubles are represented by this assembled multitude! If we could empty them out, what a heap they would be; and yet, if the living God is trusted, how the heap all vanishes! What does it matter? The burden is all gone when you have once left it to him. May the Lord the Holy Spirit help each one of us to have faith in God about the present difficulty, whether it is a fig tree or whether it is a mountain. I do not know what some of you do who have no God to trust in; some of you who are very poor and have to suffer a good deal in this life, and have no hope of the world to come. Ah, poor souls, the Lord have mercy upon you. Some of you seem to go through fire and water here, and yet you have no heaven in prospect, no hope in the world to come. Oh, see to it. May God grant you to have faith in Christ, so that there shall be no mountain between you and God, but you shall be with him where he is when your time comes to depart.

Now, I conclude with my fourth point, which is the connecting link between the divine power and ourselves.

To use a very simple figure, you remember how Franklin, when he knew there was an electric fluid in the cloud, sped his kite and brought down the lightning. Well now, there is the everlasting power of God up yonder, and I must learn to let my faith get up into the clouds to bring down the divine power to me. If I have faith enough I can have any quantity of power. *"It shall be done to you according to your faith."* If you are weak, it is because your faith is not a good conductor between you and the eternal strength. If you had better faith, is it possible to judge how strong you might be? There is no telling what a man might be able to accomplish if his faith were to increase with the occasion.

In Samson we see what physical strength came to in a man who had confidence in God, for that man Samson, though faulty in almost every point, had such confidence in God as hardly anybody ever had. There were a thousand Philistines, and they shouted against him, but what did that matter to that great big child Samson when the Spirit of the Lord came mightily on him? He said, *"With the jawbone of a donkey, heaps upon heaps, with the jawbone of a donkey I have killed a thousand men."* O glorious faith! And so ought we to feel. "I am nothing. I am nobody, yet God is with me, and on I go, dauntless and undismayed." If earth be all in arms abroad, it matters not if God be with us. When there is a minority of one, and that one is God, we are in the majority directly, for God is all, and all the people in the world are nothing before him.

The Lord gives us some hints as to how to use our faith. First, we must use it to expel every remaining doubt. *"Whoever says to this mountain, 'Be taken up and cast into the sea,' and does not doubt in his heart, but believes that what he says is going to happen, it will be granted him."* God will not bless the speaking of that man who is full of doubts. Get rid of the doubts. The gospel of this present half of the nineteenth century is, "Doubt." It does not say, "And you shall be saved," because it sees no immediate need of being saved. The gospel preached in numbers of our places of worship is, "Doubt, doubt; do not be as those nearly extinct Puritans that believe in the inspiration of the Bible, and hold to old-fashioned, exploded doctrines, but be a man and doubt." They will doubt themselves into a bad situation before long. Some of them are doubting till their chapels are empty; they are scaring their people away from them, as naturally they would, for doubt is a ghastly apparition.

But, dear brethren, you and I have to do the very opposite of this. We have to find out every lingering doubt, and draw it out and drive it away. A doubt! When a man is about to strike a blow in faith, it is a doubt which paralyzes him. A doubt! Why even a little doubt is like a small stone in a traveler's shoe: it lames him. It is a very little thing, but he had better spend a week in picking it out than go on with it there. Believer, you must get doubt right out of you, for until you believe, you will never travel well to heaven or be strong in the Lord. Only imagine Martin Luther agitated with doubts as he rode into Worms! Not quite sure about justification by faith when answering for his life! Agitated with doubts when he was carrying his life in his hand to confront the powers of the world in the name of God! Doubt would have ruined him. Let us chase the spirit of unbelief away. The Lord help us to do so, and to be filled with faith.

> If you desire the power of God to gird you, you must get rid of all malice from your heart.

The next hint the Savior gives us is to be much in prayer, because it is by prayer that faith exercises itself unto God. *"All things for which you pray and ask, believe that you have received them, and they will be granted to you."* Much prayer, but of a believing sort, should be offered by simple, trustful disciples, for the cry of faith which is true prayer touches the heart of the great Father, and he is prompt to grant his children their desires.

But one other hint. That is, we must see to it that we are purged of what would effectually prevent prayer from being heard. *If I regard wickedness in my heart, the Lord will not hear.* If you desire the power of God to gird you, you must get rid of all malice from your heart. You must forgive your brother. All selfishness and uncharitableness must be eradicated from your breast, for else the Lord cannot trust you with power. If you had tyrannical power linked with a pitiless disposition, you would not only curse a leafless fig tree, but you would also curse anything and everything that was contrary to your own likes. If you were endued with all manner of power, it would be no mercy to you, but an infinite misery, unless you were also partakers of the mind of Christ. Unless you have his heart of infinite purity and incomparable benevolence, power would be a most dangerous thing to trust you with. The Lord will only trust his children with power in proportion as they know his will and strive to do it. When they become completely like him, their very prayers which were sown in weakness shall be raised in power. But sin is awfully debilitating: it weakens, dampens, and utterly prostrates a man. For any kind of sin, whether it be tolerated in the will – that is, if there be a hankering and a lusting after self – if we think that power when acquired may be used for our own pleasure, profit, or honor, the power will not come, it cannot possibly be conferred on such terms. You shall move no mountain from its place till, first of all, the mountain of your selfishness is cast into the sea.

O Lord, purge your vessels and then fill them. Cleanse the instruments from rust, and then use them. Here we are now before you. Blessed be your name, you have saved us. Now make us fit to be serviceable in your cause and kingdom, poor unworthy things as we are, and you shall have honor of us and by us forever. Amen.

Chapter 5

And Why Not Me?

And a leper came to Him and bowed down before Him, and said, "Lord, if You are willing, You can make me clean." Jesus stretched out His hand and touched him, saying, "I am willing; be cleansed." And immediately his leprosy was cleansed. (Matthew 8:2-3)

Matthew has placed this miracle immediately after the Sermon on the Mount. In all probability, some little time intervened in which our Lord had preached at Capernaum, and had also healed the people in the street, as we read in the first chapter of Mark. It was not the object of Matthew to arrange his facts precisely in the order of time; he had another end in view. After the Sermon on the Mount, he gives us remarkable miracles, as if to teach us that *our Lord's words were confirmed by his works*. Our Lord was mighty in both word and deed. His kingdom comes not only with truth, but also with power. He worked miracles so that men might see with their eyes that the power of God was upon him, and might know that he spoke with divine authority.

At this day, beloved, it is even so. Power goes forth with the preaching of the gospel. The words of the Lord Jesus are spirit and life; they are in themselves full of authority, and we ought to accept them with ready faith. But since we are slow to believe, the Lord continues to work as well as speak; *the signs that followed* are still to be perceived – blind eyes are opened, deaf ears are unstopped, hearts of stone are turned to flesh, and the dead in sin are revived. Conversion by grace follows the proclamation of the doctrines of grace; for the word is with power. Beloved, we have beheld wonders of regenerating power in our own midst, and therefore we are bound to believe in Jesus more and more. Blessed be the divine power which confirms the word! Jesus is never known in the full authority of his word until the Holy Spirit makes us feel the glory of his work within our hearts. We have the word, and we pray for more of the work. The Lord speaks to us graciously in the gospel ministry. Oh, that he would now work with us also to his own glory!

When our Lord spoke, *his words were winged in such a way that they flew far afield.* He was heard not only by the nearer company of his disciples, and by a great multitude who gathered about him, but his words were also carried home by the people as they returned to their cottages among the hills, or to their dwellings by the sea. They flew abroad as doves whose wings were covered with silver, and they lighted in strange places. His words had so much pungency about them that they could not be forgotten; they had so much force in them that they worked mightily on the minds of men, and were repeated by those who heard them.

> Jesus is never known in the full authority of his word until the Holy Spirit makes us feel the glory of his work within our hearts.

Among the rest, the words of the Lord Jesus came to a poor leper, who dwelt alone outside a city wall. We know little about him; even his name is not mentioned, but to him also the glad tidings of a Savior came. He spent much of his time in solitude, or in begging, for he could not follow the pursuits of men, nor earn his bread like other men. The disease of despair was upon him, and none could help him in his trouble. He had heard of Jesus and, perhaps on the edge of the crowd, had heard him speak. He felt that there was something divine about the preacher who spoke as never man spoke. This aroused hope within him, and he came to Jesus and was healed. What was his name, or his descent, or his history, we do not know. He ranks among the notable anonymous of earth, whose names are written in heaven. No one among you knows where God's Word will fly this day: it may be blessed to some outcast in the bush, who will read it and find the mercy of the Lord.

Our congregation is a singular one, made up of persons of every condition of life, from almost every country under heaven; and in it there are specialties of character unknown to the preacher, but the Lord can bless all who hear it. God has brought them to this place, and since the word that shall be spoken is a repetition of Christ's own Word, and is the same gospel which Jesus preached, we expect that it will fly far and wide, and will call many a sin-sick soul to the Great Physician's feet. The Lord grant it!

As I have often preached upon this leper, you are well acquainted with the story, and must almost wonder why I should speak upon it again. I do so that I may dwell upon one single point of it, which I trust may encourage souls to come to Jesus. I have a burning thirst within me for the salvation of souls; where is the man or woman who will give me to drink, by coming to my Lord? Note the special object of observation – *A leper came to Him*. Upon this I have to say, in the first place, that *he came of himself,* that is, on his own account; secondly, that *he came by himself,* having no comrade to cheer him in the venture; and thirdly, that *he was in himself rewarded for coming.*

First, then – and this is the main point of this discourse – he came of himself. Read in Scripture concerning the miracles of Christ, and you will be struck with the way in which many were *led* to him. A friendly hand conducted the blind, or conducted the little children. Some were bodily *brought* to Christ. We read of a paralyzed man who was *carried by four men,* and they let him down by ropes through the ceiling to the place where Jesus stood. Others could not come or be brought, but the Lord went to them where they were, on their beds, or waiting at the pool. But here is a case of a man who came by himself, on his own account; and I want you to note this, because I am persuaded that we have around us those who have nobody to lead them to Christ, nobody to pray for them, nobody to persuade, exhort, or beg them, but these may come through the direct operations of the Spirit upon their souls. These are left outside the pale, dwelling on the other side of the line of Christian effort; but they are not beyond the grace of God. This leper did come of himself. Though none called him, he plucked up courage, and it is written as a wonder: *A leper came to Him and bowed down before Him.*

Note well that this man *knew in himself that his case was a terrible one.* I do not intend to describe the dreadful disease of leprosy; we have, on other occasions, viewed it as God's appointed picture of sin. It was a living death, a source of misery, a center of defilement – and such is sin. Medical men are not clear as to whether the leprosy was ordinarily infectious. It is now believed that it is contagious to a certain degree, but there was no pressing sanitary reason why lepers should have been shut out from all society. The Lord, who intended leprosy, under the old theocracy, to be the picture of sin, ordained that when once a man was a leper, he should be regarded as unclean in himself, and so polluting that every person and thing that he touched became unclean; therefore, the leper was dreaded in his every approach to his fellows. He was looked upon as dead while he lived, and his case was viewed as beyond human help.

Remember how the king of Israel cried out, *"Am I God, to kill and to make alive, that this man is sending word to me to cure a man of his leprosy?"* If a leper did recover, it was regarded as a making alive, a resurrection from death. This man knew, even better than anybody else, what a wretched and appalling state he was in. His disease was ever before him. Leprosy is awful to look upon; what must it be to feel? Leprosy is terrible in description; what must it be in actual endurance? He knew that now at length he had come to the last stage of his sickness, for Luke describes him as *covered with leprosy;* he had come to the final stage, and the disease was conspicuous upon him. His skin was foul, and his joints were rotting. Very likely his fingers, his teeth, and his hair were gone, and soon he would die. Such was the mass of moving death of which we read, *A leper came to Him.* He was not kept back by the fact that he was hopelessly and dreadfully diseased.

Let us learn the lesson well. I earnestly pray that some poor guilty one, conscious of sin, horrified at himself, may now venture to come to Jesus. Though he feels the foul disease within him, and fears that it has come to its worst, yet may he be emboldened to approach him who can at once make him clean. If you feel yourself to be a mass of dreadfulness and corruption, or, worse still, hardened and insensible in conscience, come to Jesus for healing. Even though you are truly described in our hymn as "self-despised," come to him who will not despise you. Come at once, saying, *"Lord, if You are willing, You can make me clean."* Let desperate cases come, let hopeless cases come. I am imploring the Lord to let it be so. O my brethren in the Lord, I beg you, plead with me!

Next, note with regard to this man, that *others gave him up as hopeless.* Persons hurried past him if he stood near the city gate. He was bound himself to warn them off by crying, "Unclean, unclean!" To him the sweetness of friendship and all the comforts of domestic life were unknown; he was a cast-off and a castaway. The rulers of his people had looked upon him and pronounced him unclean, and therefore he was banished from among men. Is there such a one before me? Do your relatives shun you? Do people in decent society avoid you? Oh, that you had grace and faith to come to Jesus just as you are, and fall at his feet and worship him; for, rest assured, he can make you clean, and give you a name and a place among his people. The hopeless are the very people whom Jesus loves to save.

> The hopeless are the very people whom Jesus loves to save.

No one could or would take him to Jesus. He was too foul to be touched, too far gone to be the subject of hope. Here and there we meet with persons who have so often disappointed their friends that it is small wonder that they now keep them at a distance. Even an affectionate mother has said, "We have tried him many times, sir, but it is of no use. We cannot help him anymore, for he has drained the family." The father almost prays to forget the prodigal, and the elder brother wishes never to see him again. It is a hard case when it comes to that, but such hard cases there are. The world has in it men of whom society is sick. The squanderer has been to this charitable person, and to the other benevolent individual, until everyone is weary of the ne'er-do-well, and no one feels that he could associate with him without becoming himself suspected of vice. By common consent he is judged to be unfit for a reformatory, but well worthy of a prison. No one reasons with him, pleads with him, or prays for him. He floats over the ocean of life as an abandoned wreck. He has turned infidel lately, and even his loving sister, who used to plead with him with tears in her eyes, now shudders when he comes near, because his language has grown so sarcastic and blasphemous that the dear girl cannot bear it. Now that no man cares for your soul, how earnestly do I wish that you would care for it yourself!

Oh, that you would form the singular and saving resolve that you will go to the Lord Jesus on your own account, and so frustrate all the evil prophecies which have been uttered concerning you! Why will you perish? Poor soul! Why will you die? If there be such a person now before me, I pray from the bottom of my soul that he or she may now, with fixed determination, come to Jesus. O you angels, may you now have cause to cry out again, *And a leper came to Him and bowed down before Him.* There is one hand which would willingly lead you to Jesus – I stretch it out to you today. There is yet one heart that would plead with you to seek salvation; and if there be not another in the world, yet come along with me, come just as you are, and show your misery to the Lord of mercy. Men have written out your death warrant, but the Lord Jesus has not signed it, and therefore it cannot be executed. They call you a castaway, but the Lord gathers together the outcasts of Israel. His longsuffering in sparing your life means your salvation.

> While the lamp holds out to burn,
> The vilest sinner may return.

Come, then, with all your sin around you, repent of your transgressions, and believe in Jesus, and you shall be clean.

In this man's case *there was no precedent to encourage him.* I do not find that our Lord had healed a leper up to that time. I do not think there was a case of the sort. Many diseases he had dealt with, but the Blessed One had not yet encountered *a man covered with leprosy.* When there are plenty of precedents, there is a kind of paved way for us to travel; but this man had to make his own track. We can reason – "My father and my brother came to Jesus, and were saved; why should not I?" This man could use no such argument. I wonder whether the poor creature had heard what Jesus said in the synagogue at Capernaum – it could not have been long before – *"There were many lepers in Israel in the time of Elisha the prophet; and none of them was cleansed, but only Naaman the Syrian."* I wonder whether he drew any kind of comfort from that utterance; perhaps not. In any case, he must boldly lead the way, and be the first leper that came to Jesus.

O my hearer, if never such a sinner as you are has been saved, make bold to lead the way. Dare to approach the living Lord who can make you clean, and do not despair, even though you may not have heard of another sinner of your sort that ever was forgiven.

As for most of you, my dear friends, you and the leper must part company on this point. He had no precedents, but you have very many. You know that Christ has saved sinners all around you. Some of you have at home a brother who was as bad as yourself, but he is now converted. You have heard your father tell how far he went astray, and yet the Lord brought him to himself. Many of us now present can assure you that *"this man receives sinners,"* for he received *us*. We can witness, assuredly, that he is abundantly able to save, for he has manifested that power in our cases. With these precedents, wherein the Lord Jesus has saved persons like yourself, come to him, I pray you, and prove that he is the same now as ever. Are you a drunkard? Many drunkards have been rescued from their degrading vice. Are you a thief? a liar? a Sabbath-breaker? Such were some of us, but we are washed and made clean. Yes, if you have been an adulterer, or a murderer – can I say worse? – *"any sin and blasphemy shall be forgiven people."* Men of the vilest sort have been saved; therefore, come to the Lord with confidence, even as this leper came, and put your trust in him.

Furthermore, *this man had no promise*. I do not find that Jesus ever said, "Come unto me, you lepers, and I will heal you." I do not know that any of his apostles had been sent forth to preach, saying, "Come to Jesus, all you lepers, and he will cleanse you." There was no promise to that effect, except that our Lord himself is a consolidated promise. The very fact of his being here below is a mountain range of promises to our fallen race. Without any verbal promise, this man came and said, *"Lord, if You are willing, You can."*

My dear friends, I cannot say to any of you that you may not come to Jesus because there is no promise for you. Far from it. If there were no promise, I would exhort you to seek mercy as the Ninevites did when they said, *"Who knows?"* But the promises are as plentiful as the stars. *Let the wicked forsake his way and the unrighteous man his thoughts; and let him return to the Lord, and He will have compassion on him, and to our God, for He will abundantly pardon* (Isaiah 55:7). *He who confesses and forsakes [his transgressions] will find compassion*

(Proverbs 28:13). *"He who has believed and has been baptized shall be saved"* (Mark 16:16). *"Believe in the Lord Jesus, and you will be saved"* (Acts 16:31). Will you not be drawn by these promises, and will you not come when such a word as this stands before you – *"The one who comes to Me I will certainly not cast out"*? The blessed doctrine of election does not hinder you, for all who come are elect. The sacred truth of the new birth does not bar you, for he that believes is born again. I pray you, come and show yourself to the great Healer, and he will not turn you away.

Again, *this man had no invitation.* Our Lord had not called him; he had never said, "Come, you lepers; come, and be healed." There was nobody to command or persuade him to come, nobody to cheer him in coming, much less any to compel him to come in. Of himself, constrained by a divine impulse unknown to anybody else, this leper resolved to come, and found himself welcome, though he had not been expressly bidden. To you, my dear friends, I cannot say that you have no invitation; for we are always crying to you, Come, you weary and heavy laden. Come, for Jesus calls. *The Spirit and the bride say, "Come." And let the one who is thirsty come; let the one who wishes take the water of life without cost.* The invitations of mercy are sent out on a broad scale, since we are bidden to *"preach the gospel to all creation."* Whoever will, let him come. Yes, those along the hedges and in the highways are to be compelled to come in. What shall I say? If you are lost, it will not be for lack of an invitation. If you turn your back on Christ, you shall not say in hell that you were not implored to come to him. I implore you to come to Jesus even as this leper came, and I pray the Holy Spirit to make my pleas effectual with you.

This leper was bold in coming to Jesus because, having nobody to encourage him, *he must have felt himself uncomfortable as a lone man in the midst of the multitude.* Well he might, for he had no right to be there. I wonder if anyone here today says, "Here am I, a stranger to everybody; nobody knows me, and if they did, they would not associate with me. I am out of place among the people of God." Are you laboring under an awful sense of sin? Are you bowed down under your own unworthiness? Do you feel as one lost in a crowd? The crowd being there was nothing very remarkable; but the leper's coming to Jesus was a very notable fact, a scene worth looking at. Therefore we see the word "behold". He is coming! Yes, he dares to come. The crowd makes way, and the leper falls at Jesus' feet and worships him, saying, *"Lord, if You are willing, You can make me clean."* Glory be to God, the leper is at the feet of Jesus, where infinite love and power are bending over him! O my friend, will not you make a dash for it at this moment? You need not rise up and make any obvious demonstration, but you can in spirit bow at the feet of our Lord.

Oh, that the Spirit of God would move you to come to Jesus now! Never mind the crowd. You are put apart by your own feelings; your broken heart has driven you into a solitary condition. Now come to Jesus before the crowd disperses. Though angels will see it, and devils will see it, yet come. Oh, that I could cry – Behold! Here is a sinner who, now, at once, and in this place, casts himself at Jesus' feet! Grant it, O God! O God the Holy Spirit, work it, and work it now, we pray you, and unto the name of Jesus shall be glory evermore!

This is our first topic: the leper came of himself, though no one aided or encouraged him.

Secondly, the leper came by himself. This is very unlike the case of the ten lepers, who came to Jesus in a company, concerning whom he asked the question, *"But the nine—where are they?"* It is easy to go where ten are going, but it is harder to go alone. There are many things which people readily do in company with others; but they would not venture upon them as separate individuals. My hearer, there is only one of you; and when that one feels himself to be repulsive and vile, it seems a daring thing for him to come to Jesus by himself. Yet I trust you will so come.

> There is always hope for a man when he begins to think about the Lord Jesus.

Here I would enlarge by observing, first, that no doubt *the leper thought out this matter by himself.* Being often alone, he meditated upon what he had heard concerning this great preacher, and he considered both his doctrine and his miracles, and drew his own conclusions. There is always hope for a man when he begins to think about the Lord Jesus; the worst of it is that so many hearers of the gospel put their thinking out, and do none of it at home. This man thought over the matter calmly, candidly, and hopefully; and he drew from it a solid, plain, and practical conclusion with reference to himself. He did not rest in a general theory about all the world, but he found out a truth which concerned himself.

Having done so, *he came to the conclusion that our Lord was omnipotent to heal.* Mark well that he came to this conclusion with regard to himself. Is it, "Lord, if You are willing, You can make *lepers* clean"? No, it was a far more personal conclusion. *"If You are willing, You can make me clean."* That was the crucial point. Jesus could save *him,* even him. Long ago I believed that Christ could save my brothers and sisters – I never had a doubt about that. I never doubted our Lord's power to save anybody until I thought of myself, and then there seemed to be just one case which his omnipotence did not cover. I did not see how Jesus was to save me. Singular as it may seem, when a man is under a sense of sin, he will not deny the omnipotent power of God's grace as to all the rest of mankind, but secretly he will shut himself out from the range of mercy. Strange cruelty to the self he loves so well. He thinks himself to be just over the border, just beyond the reach of grace. This man was not so foolish. He argued, "I am a leper. Yes; but God has healed lepers. I am a leper in the worst state, for I am full of leprosy; but with God all things are possible. This man is sent of God, and the power of God is with him; therefore I conclude that he can cleanse me if he will." It was well done by the leper.

It is a fine thing to have come to such a rational and just conclusion. I wish every person here would come to that conclusion about his own soul. Though you must condemn yourself, though the harshest expression I could use would not slander you in your own esteem, yet it comes to this, thinking it all over – "Christ can save you if he so wills." You are not shut out by any word of Scripture, or by any lack of love or power on the part of the Savior. If you are worse than others, the infinite grace of God will be seen all the more in your salvation. Jesus can save you – even you.

Still thinking the subject over, *he saw where the matter hinged.* Everything depended on our Lord's will. Some say that the leper doubted the willingness of Christ; I greatly doubt this interpretation of his words. He simply stated a great truth. If Jesus only willed it, the leper could be made clean without his saying or doing anything. The whole work depended on the Lord's will that it should be done. His will was the spring of the healing power. Does anybody doubt this? In the work of salvation, certain preachers are continually insisting upon the freedom of the human will; truly with these I raise no quarrel, but I would have them equally insist upon the freedom of the divine will. Christ has a right to save whom he pleases, and though he saves all who trust him, this also is not without his will. He said to this man, *"I am willing"*; and there is no instance in Scripture of one pleading for healing to whom he said, "I am *not* willing." Yet his saving grace lies under the control of his own sovereignty: he is no man's debtor, but he may do as he wills with his own. It is most certain that *it does not depend on the man who wills or the man who runs, but on God who has mercy. He has mercy on whom He desires.*

This man, in his lonely thoughts, had struck upon this golden nugget of truth. He saw that his hope lay in the will of Christ, and where could it lie better? I am afraid that in this matter he excelled some of you, for his own will was right enough; but I fear that, in the cases of some of you, your own will is not yet right with God. It goes without saying that the leper's will was in a right condition, and therefore he appeals to Jesus. Is Jesus willing? There was no fear as to that matter. I want all seekers to know that your salvation can now be worked by the will of Jesus. He has made you willing to receive, and he is assuredly willing to give. If you are saved, it will not be because you deserve it, but because he freely gives where he pleases, according to the royal bounty of his heart. This man had found out a grand truth when he saw that his healing depended upon the will of the Savior.

Then *he submitted himself to that will with joyful hope.* He could not know for certain that he would be healed, for Jesus had not as yet spoken of healing leprosy; but he was positive that he could do it if he willed to. It is a great thing to believe in the omnipotence of Jesus in the matter of salvation. We have a great advantage over the leper, for we know that he wills to save all sinners who come to him. The leper set himself before Christ and said, in effect, "Here am I. You see what a wretched creature I am; no worse can ever come to you, but yet, if you will, you can make me clean. I leave my case with you." He prayed intensely, but it was rather in dumb show than in words; but Jesus knew what he meant.

This was the man's practical conclusion from his lonely thinking, and *he expressed it before the Lord in words all his own.* In the few words he used he borrowed nothing from any book of prayers, or manual of devotion. He was, in fact, a man of his own order, standing apart from all others. The result of his private thoughts was a decided act, and a brave profession of his faith in the omnipotence of Jesus.

He did homage to Jesus, he knelt before him, and he worshiped him. I believe that he did this with the full persuasion of his deity; for I do not think he could have said, *"If You are willing, You can make me clean"* unless he had believed that Jesus was the Son of God. Our Savior did not say, "Rise up: you must not worship me, for I am only a man, and to worship me would be sheer idolatry." No. Our Lord did not repudiate divine honors when they were offered to him by his followers; but he accepted them as a matter of right, since he counted it not robbery to be equal with God. This man trusted him whom he worshiped, and worshiped him whom he trusted. With reverent, humble, and compelling prayer he set forth his case, and left it in the Savior's hands. Oh, that my hearer would imitate him! I groan in spirit till this be so.

The leper came alone. He came not through persuading friends. I am afraid that some people join the church because other people press them to do so; this is a mistake. Some will say that they believe in Jesus, because it will give pleasure to earnest friends; this is mischievous. The leper was under no excitement; he was not the fungus of a revival, but the fruit of grace. He did not go into an inquiry room, and see all the rest zealous about Jesus, and therefore become subject to an equal feeling. No; he came alone, and came deliberately, and bowed himself at Jesus' feet. I want any here who are quite unused to religious influences, who have no mother to put her arms around their neck and pray for them, no friends to explain the things of God to them, nevertheless to come to Jesus. You need a Savior; do you feel that you do? Though not accompanied by others, still come to Jesus. Come alone, and by yourself. Come at once to Christ, and cast yourself at his feet. The thoughtful

> The thoughtful individual believer is often one of the best converts, for he is most to be relied on.

individual believer is often one of the best converts, for he is most to be relied on. I like much those who are not imitators, but take their own course in coming to Jesus. Some are carried off their legs during a time of religious excitement, and think they are converted when they are not. Some profess faith because their brothers and sisters and friends are doing so, but it is not sufficiently an individual matter of heart with them. I set the leper before you as an example of the courage which comes to Jesus by itself, whether others will come or forego. I have kept to my one point up to this time, and I have all the while been praying the Lord to bring all my unconverted hearers to Jesus now.

I close by saying that this man himself was rewarded for coming.

Our Lord saw to it that he came not in vain. Poor soul! Suffering as he was, and in dread of a terrible death, he no sooner began to come to Christ than *our Lord rewarded him with his sympathy.* He looked at him with a different look from what the leper had ever received before. When others glanced at the leper they went by as quickly as they could; and if some came face to face with him they turned away their eyes from the ghastly spectacle. Nobody pitied lepers in those days, for they judged them to be struck by God. They were the objects of horror among men because they were viewed as objects of the wrath of the Most High. But when Jesus saw the afflicted man, we read in Mark 1 that he was *moved with compassion.* I do not think I could fully interpret the Greek word into English. I could hardly pronounce it, since there is such a complication of consonants in it. Did you ever see a man overcome with emotion? His heart seems to swell, his bosom heaves, and tears burst forth.

In our Lord's case his whole being was stirred. The depths of his spirit were agitated. He was moved – moved with a fellow-feeling. As soon as he saw the leper at his feet his very look said, "Alas, poor soul, what have you suffered! Into what a state of dreadfulness are you brought! You are to men as a living dunghill; but I do not despise you, I love you, I sympathize with you." Now, my hearer, if you will come to Christ, that is how he will meet you. If you sorrow, he sorrows for you. If you loathe sin, he loathes it more than you do; but he has pity for the sinner. He is moved with compassion over your miserable state.

As the man came, his lone coming was *rewarded by our Lord touching him.* Nobody else would have touched this man. Peter, James, and

John, and all the rest would have drawn back their garments lest they should come into contact with a leper. As for the crowd, he had no difficulty in making his way, for they gave way before him, and had a ready gangway for him. But now the Savior touched him. There was something wonderfully cheering in that touch.

I have heard of a lady who cared for poor crippled children. She found one which was so deformed, diseased, ill-tempered, and continually crying that no one felt able to love it. She was nursing the child, but the task was no pleasure to her because, do what she would, the poor child seemed always to cry, and always to act an unlovely part. The good woman pitied the child, but could not love it. As she had the poor creature in her lap, she dozed and dreamed that Jesus came and bowed over her, and told her that, as to her soul, she also was sick and repulsive in his sight; but yet he loved her and would manifest himself to her. When she came to herself, she looked at the poor, misshapen child and again felt an aversion to it because it was so wretchedly deformed, so disgustingly full of sores, and so passionate and fretful. Under the power of the vision she had beheld, however, all her feeling of disgust went from her; she felt great tenderness of soul, she pressed the little one to her bosom, and kissed its poor, blotchy face. The child opened its eyes with wonder, for it had never been kissed before; and by that kiss a new world was opened to it. The little one became grateful, happy, and patient, and was no longer a burden to those who cared for it. How much may come of a little!

Even thus our Lord's personal touch of us heals us. His touch, in effect, said to the leper, "I do not loathe you; I will not keep away from you. I will come very near to you. I will bring a heavenly poison to you, and, instead of your communicating disease, you shall receive of my health." Jesus Christ the Lord will come to you, poor seeker, and touch you, and prove himself to be your brother and your friend. Dear soul, if you will touch Jesus, he will touch you; if you believe in him, he will manifest himself to you; and today, you, who saw no image but your leprous selves when you came here, shall go home seeing no image but the incarnate God glorified in saving you.

The Lord rewarded his submission with the sovereign word, "I am willing." As I have already told you, Jesus never says to a seeking soul,

"I am not willing"; but if you cast yourself at his feet, and believe that he is able to save you, he will say, *"I am willing."* The "I am willing" of an emperor may have great power over his dominions, but the *"I am willing"* of Christ drives death and hell before him, conquers disease, removes despair, and floods the world with mercy. The Lord's *"I am willing"* can put away your leprosy of sin and make you perfectly whole. Let there be no mistake about it – I mean you, my hearer, even you upon whom I look at this moment. To you is the word of this salvation sent.

As a reward for the man's faith, our Lord gave a cure, and, to increase the wonder, an immediate cure. *Immediately his leprosy was cleansed.* How so great a change could be worked we cannot tell. To dissect a miracle is absurd. Every part of the body had been long out of order, certain secretions had been poisoned, and certain vessels destroyed; and yet that one command, *"Be cleansed,"* restored the leper's ruined frame, there and then. He that created can restore. Can God turn a sinner into a saint in a moment? He can. Niagara comes crashing down from the precipice of rock; could Omnipotence reverse those floods and make them leap upwards? God can do all things. In the moral world he is as mighty as in the outer universe. The heart is as hard as a stone, or as the lower millstone; can he make it soft? Yes, in a moment he can make it as tender as bleeding flesh. Do you believe this?

If so, submit yourself to the divine energy, and ask that this be done unto you. Only believe, without any sort of doubt, that Jesus is the incarnate God, and therefore has all power over human nature to pardon and to cleanse. Jesus can save you, though you stand between the open jaws of hell. Jesus can save you, though you be foulness itself, through lying soaked for so long in the filthy lye of lust and unbelief. He can with a word make you whiter than snow. Do you believe this? If you believe this, I say, test it by submitting yourself to Jesus, that he may be a Savior to you. He will say, *"I am willing; be cleansed."*

Now to close. I have set the gate of mercy wide open, will you not enter? Oh, that the secret power of the Holy Spirit may gently incline you! By God's help, I have thrown out a big net, and I hope some of you will be entangled in its meshes. I toil in birth for you this day till you are born unto Jesus.

One thing we may say about this poor leper's case – he could not be any worse if he came to Jesus and was refused, for already he was *covered with leprosy*. He could be no loser by his appeal to Jesus. And you, my hearer, if you will trust in Jesus, you can be no worse. You can but perish if you go to him. But, beloved, it is not possible for Jesus to repel a sinner who comes to him. He has said, *"The one who comes to Me I will certainly not cast out."* Though he be a leper, though he come without precedent, without promise, and without invitation, yet if he does but come, the Lord can in no way or manner cast him out. The gospel cry is, "Come and welcome."

Jesus loves to see men in good health. He takes no pleasure in disease and pain. It is a joy to him to cleanse and to make whole the souls of men. You will be a happy man if Christ saves you; but Christ will have the bigger share of the happiness, since this was the joy that was set before him, for which he endured the cross, despising the shame. Our Lord remembers well his wounds by which he procured our healing. He remembers the cruel tree by which he uplifts us from hell. He remembers his agony and bloody sweat, his cross and passion; and he has pity on the guilty for whom he died. Do you also remember the sufferings of your Lord, and trust him, trust him fully and alone? Look at once to him who lives, and was dead, and is alive forevermore; by that look you will live.

> **Jesus takes no pleasure in disease and pain.**

At this moment worship him. Bow at his feet. While yet in these seats prostrate your hearts before the Son of God, and leave yourselves with him, that he may give you eternal salvation. As surely as the Lord lives, if you, poor lonely one, do believe in the Lord Jesus Christ, you are saved. Go in peace, and rejoice yourself forever in the great salvation he has given you, and look to him yet more and more all the days of your life. I remember that on January the eighth, many years ago, I looked to Christ, and I am praying that this seventh day of September, I who looked may be the means of leading others to look to him and live. Why not? Dear men and women out of Christ, why not look to Jesus now? My heart breaks for your immediate salvation. Spirit of the living God, draw them to Christ, and to his name be glory forever and ever! Amen.

Chapter 6

The Lord and the Leper

And a leper came to Jesus, beseeching Him and falling on his knees before Him, and saying, "If You are willing, You can make me clean." Moved with compassion, Jesus stretched out His hand and touched him, and said to him, "I am willing; be cleansed." Immediately the leprosy left him and he was cleansed. (Mark 1:40-42)

Beloved, we saw in the reading that our Lord had been engaged in special prayer. He had gone alone on the mountainside to have communion with God. Simon and the rest search for him, and he comes away in the early morning with the burrs from the hillside upon his garments, the smell of the field upon him, even of a field that the Lord God had blessed. He comes forth among the people, charged with power which he had received in communion with the Father; and now we may expect to see wonders. And we do see them; for devils fear and fly when he speaks the word; and by and by there comes to him one, an extraordinary being, condemned to live apart from the rest of men lest he should spread defilement all around. A leper comes to him, and kneels before him, and expresses his confident faith in him, that he can make him whole. Now is the Son of Man glorious in his power to save.

The Lord Jesus Christ at this day has all power in heaven and in earth. He is charged with a divine energy to bless all who come to him for healing. Oh, that we may see today some great wonder of his power and grace! Oh, for one of the days of the Son of Man here and now! To that end it is absolutely needful that we should find a case for his spiritual power to work upon. Is there not one here in whom his grace may prove its omnipotence? Not you, you self-righteous one! You yield him no space to work in. You that are whole have no need of a physician; in you there is no opportunity for him to display his miraculous force. But yonder are the men we seek for. Forlorn and lost, full of evil and self-condemned, you are the characters we seek. You that feel as if you were possessed with evil spirits, and you that are leprous with sin, you are the persons in whom Jesus will find ample room and margin enough for the display of his holy skill. Of you I might say, as he once said of the man born blind, you are here that the works of God may be manifest in you. You, with your guilt and your depravity, you furnish the empty vessels into which his grace may be poured, the sick souls upon whom he may display his matchless power to bless and save.

Be hopeful, then, you sinful ones! Look up for the Lord's approach, and expect that even in you he will work great marvels. This leper shall be a picture – yes, I hope a mirror – in whom you will see yourselves. I do pray that as I go over the details of this miracle many here may put themselves in the leper's place, and do just as the leper did, and receive, just as the leper received, cleansing from the hand of Christ. O Spirit of the living God, the thousands of our Israel now beg you to work, that Jesus, the Son of God, may be glorified here and now!

I will begin my rehearsal of the gospel narrative by remarking, first, that this leper's faith made him eager to be healed. He was a leper. I will not stay just now to describe what horrors are compacted into that single word; but he believed that Jesus could cleanse him, and his belief stirred him to an anxious desire to be healed at once.

Alas! we have to deal with spiritual lepers eaten up with the foul disease of sin; but *some of them do not believe that they ever can be healed*, and the consequence is that despair makes them sin most greedily. "I may as well be hanged for a sheep as for a lamb," is the inward impression of many a sinner when he fears that there is no mercy and no help for *him*. Because there is no hope, therefore they plunge deeper and yet deeper into the swamp of iniquity. Oh, that you might be delivered from that false idea! Mercy still rules the hour. There is hope while Jesus sends his gospel to you and bids you repent. "I believe in the forgiveness of sins": this is a sweet sentence of a true creed. I believe also in the renewal of men's hearts, for the Lord can give new hearts and right spirits to the evil and the unthankful. I wish that you believed it, for if you did, I trust it would stimulate you into seeking that your sins might be forgiven and your minds might be renewed. Do you believe it? Then come to Jesus and receive the blessings of free grace.

We have a number of lepers who come in among us whose disease is white upon their brows, and visible to all beholders, and yet *they are indifferent;* they do not mourn their wickedness, nor wish to be cleansed from it. They sit among God's people, and they listen to the doctrine of a new birth, and the news of pardon, and they hear the teaching as though it had nothing to do with them. If now and then they half wish that salvation would come to them, it is too languid a wish to last. They have not yet so perceived their disease and their danger as to pray to be delivered from them. They sleep on upon the bed of sloth, and care neither for heaven nor hell. Indifference to spiritual things is the sin of the age. Men are empty of heart about eternal realities. An awful apathy is upon the multitude. The leper in our text was not so foolish as this. He eagerly desired to be delivered from his dreadful sickness; with heart and soul he longed to be cleansed from its terrible defilement. Oh, that it were so with you! May the Lord make you feel how depraved your heart is, and how diseased with sin are all the faculties of your soul!

Alas, dear friends, *there are some that even love their leprosy!* Is it not a sad thing to have to speak thus? Surely, madness is in men's hearts. Men do not wish to be saved from doing evil. They love the ways and wages of iniquity. They would like to go to heaven, but they must have their drunken frolics on the road; they would very well like to be saved from hell, but not from the sin which is the cause of it. Their notion of salvation is not to be saved from the love of evil, and to be made pure and clean; but that is God's meaning when he speaks of salvation. How can they hope to be the slaves of sin, and yet at the same time be free? Our first necessity is to be saved from sinning. The very name of Jesus tells us this: he is called *Jesus* because *"He will save His people from their sins."* These persons do not care for a salvation which would mean self-denial and the giving up of ungodly lusts.

O wretched lepers, that count their leprosy to be a beauty, and take pleasure in sin which in the sight of God is far more appalling than the worst disease of the body! Oh, that Christ Jesus would come and change their views of things until they were of the same mind as God towards sin; and you know he calls it *"this abominable thing which I hate."* Oh, if men could see their love for wrong things to be a disease more sickening than leprosy, they would willingly be saved, and saved at once! Holy Spirit, convince of sin, that sinners may be eager to be cleansed!

Lepers were obliged to consort together: lepers associated with lepers, and they must have made up a dreadful fraternal unity. How glad they would have been to escape from it! But I know spiritual lepers who *love the company of their fellow lepers.* Yes, and the more leprous a man becomes, the more do they admire him. A bold sinner is often the idol of his comrades. Though foul in his life, others cling to him for that very reason. Such persons like to learn some new bit of wickedness; they are eager to be initiated into a still darker form of impure pleasure. Oh, how they long to hear that last vulgar song, to read that last impure novel! It seems to be the desire of many to know as much evil as they can. They flock together, and take a dreadful pleasure in talk and action which is the horror of all pure minds.

Strange lepers, that heap up leprosy as a treasure! Even those who do not go into gross open sin, yet are pleased with infidel notions and skeptical opinions, which are a wretched form of mental leprosy. O horrible sickness, which makes men doubt the word of the living God!

Lepers were not allowed to associate with healthy persons except under severe restrictions. Thus were they separated from their nearest and dearest friends. What a sorrow! Alas! I know persons thus separated who *do not wish to associate with the godly;* to them holy company is dull and wearisome; they do not feel free and easy in such society, and therefore they avoid it as much as decency allows. How can they hope to live with saints forever when they shun them now as dull and moping acquaintances?

O my friends, I have come to this place in the hope that God would bless the word to some poor sinner who feels he is a sinner, and would willingly be cleansed; such is the leper I am seeking with my whole heart. I pray God to bless the word to those who wish to escape from evil company, who would no longer sit in the assembly of the mockers, nor run in the paths of the unholy. To those who have grown weary of their sinful companions, and would escape from them, lest they should be bound up in bundles with them to burn at the last great day – to such I speak at this time with a loving desire for their salvation. I hope my word will come with divine application to some poor heart here that is crying, "I wish I might be numbered with the people of God. I wish I were fit to be a doorkeeper in the house of the Lord.

Oh, that my dreadful sinfulness were conquered, so that I could have fellowship with the godly, and be myself one of them!" I hope my Lord has brought to this place just such lost ones, that he may find them. I am looking out for them with tearful eyes. But my feeble eyes cannot read inward character; and it is well that the loving Savior, who discerns the secrets of all hearts, and reads all inward desires, is looking from the watchtowers of heaven, that he may discover those who are coming to him, even though as yet they are a great way off. Oh, that sinners may now beg and pray to be rescued from their sins! May those who have become habituated to evil long to break off their evil habits! Happy will the preacher be if he finds himself surrounded with repentant persons who hate their sins, and guilty ones who cry to be forgiven, and to be so changed that they shall go and sin no more.

In the second place, let us remark that this leper's faith was strong enough to make him believe that he could be healed of his hideous disease. *Leprosy was an unutterably repulsive disease.* As it exists even now, it is described by those who have seen it in such a way that I will not afflict your feelings by repeating all the sickening details. The following quotation may be more than sufficient. Dr. Thomson, in his famous work, *The Land and the Book,* speaks of lepers in the East and says, "The hair falls from the head and eyebrows; the nails loosen, decay, and drop off; joint after joint of the fingers and toes shrink up and slowly fall away. The gums are absorbed, and the teeth disappear. The nose, the eyes, the tongue, and the palate are slowly consumed." This disease turns a man into a mass of dreadfulness, a walking pile of pests.

Leprosy is nothing better than a horrible and lingering death. The leper in the narrative before us had sad personal experience of this, and yet he believed that Jesus could cleanse him. Splendid faith! Oh, that you who are afflicted with moral and spiritual leprosy could believe in this fashion! Jesus Christ of Nazareth can heal even you. Over the horror of leprosy faith triumphed. Oh, that in your case it would overcome the terribleness of sin!

Leprosy was known to be incurable. There was no case of a man being cured of real leprosy by any medical or surgical treatment. This made the cure of Naaman in former ages so noteworthy. Observe, moreover, that our Savior himself, so far as I can see, had never healed a leper up to the moment when this poor wretch appeared upon the scene. He had cured fever, and had cast out devils, but the cure of leprosy was in the Savior's life as yet an unexampled thing. Yet this man, putting this and that together, and understanding something of the nature and character of the Lord Jesus Christ, believed that he could cure him of his incurable disease. He felt that even if the great Lord had not yet healed leprosy, he was assuredly capable of doing so great a deed, and he determined to make an appeal to him. Was not this grand faith? Oh, that such faith could be found among my hearers at this hour!

Hear me, O trembling sinner: if you be as full of sin as an egg is full of meat, Jesus can remove it all. If your propensities to sin be as untamable as the wild boar of the woods, still Jesus Christ, the Lord of all, can subdue your iniquities and make you the obedient servant of his love. Jesus can turn the lion into a lamb, and he can do it now. He can transform you where you are sitting, saving you in yonder pew while I am speaking the word. All things are possible to the Savior God; and all things are possible to him that believes. I wish you had such a faith as this leper had, although if it were even less it might serve your turn, since you have not all his difficulties to contend with, since Jesus has already saved many sinners like yourself, and changed many hearts as hard as yours. If he shall regenerate you, he will be doing for you no strange thing, but only one of the daily miracles of his grace. He has

> All things are possible to the Savior God; and all things are possible to him that believes.

now healed thousands of your fellow lepers; can you not believe that he can heal the leprosy in you?

This man had a marvelous faith thus to still believe while *he was personally the victim of that mortal disease.* It is one thing to trust a doctor when you are well, but quite another to confide in him when your body is rotting away. For a real, conscious sinner to trust the Savior is no average thing. When you hope that there is some good thing in you, it is easy to be confident; but to be conscious of total ruin and yet to believe in the divine remedy – this is real faith. To see in the sunshine is mere natural vision, but to see in the dark needs the eye of faith. To believe that Jesus has saved you when you see the signs of it, is the result of reason, but to trust him to cleanse you while you are still defiled with sin – this is the essence of saving faith.

The leprosy was firmly seated and fully developed in this man. Luke says that he was *covered with leprosy;* he had as much of the poison in him as one poor body could contain. It had come to its worst stage in him, and yet he believed that Jesus of Nazareth could make him clean. Glorious confidence! O my hearer, if you are full of sin, if your propensities and habits have become as bad as bad can be, I pray the Holy Spirit to give you faith enough to believe that the Son of God can forgive you and renew you, and can do it at once. With one word of his mouth Jesus can turn your death into life, your corruption into comeliness. Changes which we cannot work in others, much less in ourselves, Jesus, by his invincible Spirit, can work in the hearts of the ungodly. Of these stones he can raise up children unto Abraham. His moral and spiritual miracles are often worked upon cases which seem beyond all hope, cases which pity itself endeavors to forget because her efforts have been so long in vain.

I like best about this man's faith the fact that he did not merely believe that Jesus Christ could cleanse a leper, but that he could cleanse *him!* He said, *"Lord, if You are willing, You can make **me** clean"* (emphasis added). It is very easy to believe for other people. There is really no faith in such impersonal, substitute confidence. The true faith believes for itself first, and then for others. Oh, I know some of you are saying, "I believe that Jesus can save my brother. I believe that he can save the vilest of the vile. If I heard that he had saved the biggest drunkard in Southwark I would not wonder."

Can you believe all this and yet fear that he cannot save you? This is strange inconsistency. If he heals another man's leprosy, can he not heal your leprosy? If one drunkard is saved, why not another? If in one man a passionate temper is subdued, why not in another? If lust, and covetousness, and lying, and pride have been cured in many men, why not in you? Even if you are a blasphemer, blasphemy has been cured; why should it not be so in your case? He can heal you of that particular form of sin which possesses you, however high a degree its power may have reached, for nothing is too hard for the Lord. Jesus can change and cleanse you now. In a moment he can impart a new life and commence a new character. Can you believe this? This is the faith which glorified Jesus and brought healing to this leper, and it is the faith which will save you at once if you now exercise it. O Spirit of the living God, work this faith in the minds of my dear hearers, that they may thus win their appeal with the Lord Jesus, and go their way healed of the plague of sin!

Now notice, thirdly, that this man's faith was fixed on Jesus Christ alone. Let me read the man's words again. He said unto Jesus, *"If You are willing, You can make me clean."* Throw the emphasis upon the pronouns. See him kneeling before the Lord Jesus, and hear him say, *"If **You** are willing, **You** can make me clean"* (emphasis added). He has no idea of looking to the disciples; no, not to one of them or to all of them. He had no notion of trusting in a measure to the medicine which physicians would prescribe for him. All that is gone. No dream of other hope remains; but with his eye fully fixed on the blessed Miracle-worker of Nazareth, he cries, *"If **You** are willing, **You** can make me clean"* (emphasis added). In himself he had no shade of confidence; every delusion of that kind had been banished by a fierce experience of his disease. He knew that none on earth could deliver him, and that by no innate power of constitution could he throw out the poison; but he confidently believed that the Son of God could by himself effect the cure. This was God-given faith – the faith of God's elect, and Jesus was its sole object.

How did this man come to have such faith? I cannot tell you the outward means, but I think we may guess without presumption. Had he not *heard our Lord preach*? Matthew puts this story immediately after the Sermon on the Mount, and says, *When Jesus came down from the mountain, large crowds followed Him. And a leper came to Him and bowed down before Him, and said, "Lord, if You are willing, You can make me clean."* Had this man managed to stand at the edge of the crowd and hear Jesus speak, and did those wondrous words convince him that the great Teacher was something more than man? As he noted the style, and manner, and matter of that marvelous sermon, did he say within himself, "Never a man spoke like this man. Truly he is the Son of God. I believe in him. I trust him. He can cleanse me"? May God bless the preaching of Christ crucified to you who hear me this day! Is not this used of the Lord, and made to be the power of God unto salvation to everyone that believes?

Perhaps this man had *seen our Lord's miracles.* I feel sure he had. He had seen the devils cast out, and had heard of Peter's mother-in-law, who had lain sick of a fever, and had been instantaneously recovered. The leper might very properly argue: To do this requires omnipotence; and once granted that omnipotence is at work, then omnipotence can as well deal with leprosy as with fever. Did he not reason well if he argued thus: What the Lord has done, he can do again. If in one case he has displayed almighty power, he can display that same power in another case. Thus would the acts of the Lord corroborate his words and furnish a sure foundation for the leper's hope. My hearer, have you not seen Jesus save others? Have you not at least read of his miracles of grace? Believe him, then, for his works' sake, and say to him, *"Lord, if You are willing, You can make me clean."*

Besides, I think this man may have *heard something of the story of Christ,* and may have been familiar with the Old Testament prophecies concerning the Messiah. We cannot tell but some disciple may have informed him of John's witness concerning the Christ, and of the signs and tokens which supported John's testimony. He may thus have discerned in the Son of Man the Messiah of God, the Incarnate Deity. At any rate, as knowledge must come before faith, he had received knowledge enough to feel that he could trust this glorious personage, and to believe that, if he willed it, Jesus could make him clean.

O my dear friends, can you not trust the Lord Jesus Christ in this way? Do you not believe – I hope you do – that he is the Son of God;

and if so, why not trust him? He that was born of Mary at Bethlehem was God over all, blessed forever! Do you not believe this? Why, then, do you not rely upon God in our nature? You believe in his consecrated life, his suffering death, his resurrection, his ascension, and his sitting in power at the right hand of the Father; why do you not trust him? God has highly exalted him, and caused all fullness to dwell in him. He is able to save unto the uttermost; why do you not come to him? Believe that he is able, and then with all your sins before you, red like scarlet – and with all your sinful habits and your evil propensities before you, ingrained like the leopard's spots – believe that the Savior of men can at once make you whiter than snow as to past guilt, and free you from the present and future tyranny of evil.

A divine Savior must be able to cleanse you from all sin. Only Jesus can do it, but he can do it – do it himself alone, do it now, do it in you, do it with a word. If Jesus wills to do it, it is all that is needed; for his will is the will of the almighty Lord. Say, *"Lord, if You are willing, You can make me clean."* Faith must be fixed alone on Jesus. No other name is given among men whereby we must be saved. I do pray the Lord to give that faith to all my dear friends who as yet have not received cleansing at the Lord's hands. Jesus is God's ultimatum of salvation: the unique hope of guilty men both as to pardon and renewal. Accept him even now.

Now let me go a step further. This man's faith had respect to a real matter-of-fact cure. He did not think of the Lord Jesus Christ as a priest who would perform certain ceremonies over him and formally say, "You are clean," for that would not have been true. He wanted really to be delivered from the leprosy; to have those dry scales, into which his skin kept turning, taken all away, that his flesh might become as the flesh of a little child; he wanted the rottenness which was eating up his body to be stopped, and his health be actually restored. Friends, it is easy enough to believe in a mere priestly pardon if you have enough naiveness; but we need more than this. It is very easy to believe in baptismal regeneration, but what is the good of it? What practical result does it produce? A child remains the same after it has been baptismally regenerated as it was before, and it grows up to prove it. It is easy to believe in sacramentalism if you are foolish enough, but there is nothing in it when you believe in it. No sanctifying power comes with outward ceremonials in and of themselves. To believe that the Lord Jesus Christ can make us love the good things which once we despised, and shun those evil things in which we once took pleasure – this is to believe in him indeed and certainly. Jesus can totally change the nature, and make a sinner into a saint. This is faith of a practical kind; this is a faith worth having.

None of us would imagine that this leper meant that the Lord Jesus could make him feel comfortable in remaining a leper. Some seem to imagine that Jesus came to let us go on in our sins with a quiet conscience; but he did nothing of the kind. His salvation is cleansing from sin, and if we love sin we are not saved from it. We cannot have justification without sanctification. There is no use in quibbling about it; there must be a change, a radical change, a change of heart, or else we are not saved. I put it now to you, Do you desire a moral and a spiritual change, a change of life, thought, and motive? This is what Jesus gives. Just as this leper needed a thorough physical change, so do you need an entire renewal of your spiritual nature so as to become a new creature in Jesus Christ. Oh, that many here would desire this, for it would be a cheering sign.

The man who desires to be pure is beginning to be pure; the man who sincerely longs to conquer sin has struck the first blow already. The power of sin is shaken in that man who looks to Jesus for deliverance from it. The man who frets under the yoke of sin will not long be a slave to it; if he can believe that Jesus Christ is able to set him free, he shall soon leave his bondage. Some sins which have hardened down into habits disappear in a moment when Jesus Christ looks upon a man in love.

I have known many instances of persons who, for many years, had never spoken without an oath, or a filthy expression, who, being converted, have never been known to use such language again, and have scarcely ever been tempted in that direction. This is one of the sins which seems to die at the first shot, and it is a very wonderful thing that it should be so. Others I have known so altered at once that the very propensity which was strongest in them has been the last to annoy them afterwards. They have had such a reversal of the mind's action that while other sins have worried them for years, and they have had to set a strict watch against them, yet their favorite and dominant sin has never again had the slightest influence over them except to excite an outburst of horror and deep repentance. Oh, that you had faith in Jesus that he could thus cast down and cast out your reigning sins! Believe in the conquering arm of the Lord Jesus, and he will do it. Conversion is the standing miracle of the church. Where it is genuine, it is as clear a proof of divine power going with the gospel as was the casting out of devils, or even the raising of the dead in our Lord's day. We see these conversions still, and have proof that Jesus is able to work great moral marvels still.

O my hearer, where are you? Can you not believe that Jesus is able to make a new man of you? O brethren who have been saved, I beg you to breathe a prayer at this time for those who are not yet cleansed from the foul disease of sin. Pray that they may have grace to believe in the Lord Jesus for purification of heart, pardon of sin, and the implantation of eternal life. Then when faith is given, the Lord Jesus will work their sanctification, and none shall effectually hinder it. In silence let us pray for a moment. (Here there was a pause, and silent prayer went up to heaven.)

And now we will go another step. This man's faith was accompanied by what appears to be a hesitancy. But after thinking it over a good deal, I am hardly inclined to think it such a hesitancy as many have judged it to be. He said, *"If You are willing, You can make me clean."* There was an *if* in this speech, and that *if* has aroused the suspicions of many preachers. Some think it supposes that he doubted our Lord's willingness. I hardly think that the language justly bears so harsh a construction. What he meant may have been this – "Lord, I do not know yet that you are sent to heal lepers; I have not seen that you have ever done so; but still, if it be within the scope of your commission, I believe you will do it, and assuredly you can if you will. You can heal not only some lepers, but also me in particular; you can make me clean." Now, I think this was a legitimate thing for him to say, as he had not seen a leper healed – "If it be within the scope of your commission, I believe you can make me whole."

Moreover, I admire in this text *the deference which the leper pays to the sovereignty of Christ's will as to the bestowal of his gifts.* "If You are willing, You can make me clean" – as much as to say, "I know you have a right to distribute these great favors exactly as you please. I have no claim upon you; I cannot say that you are bound to make me clean; I appeal to your pity and free favor. The matter remains with your will." The man had never read the text which says, *So then it does not depend on the man who wills or the man who runs, but on God who has mercy*, for it was not yet written; but he had in his mind the humble spirit suggested by that grand truth. He owned that grace must come as a free gift of God's good pleasure when he said, *"Lord, if You are willing."*

Beloved, we need never raise a question as to the Lord's willingness to give grace when we have the willingness to receive it; but still, I would have every sinner feel that he has no claim upon God for anything. O sinner, if the Lord should give you up, as he did the heathen described in the first chapter of the epistle to the Romans, you deserve it. If he should never look upon you with an eye of love, what could you say against his righteous sentence? You have willfully sinned, and you deserve to be left in your sin. Confessing all this, we still cling to our firm belief in the power of grace, and cry, *"Lord, if You are willing, You can."* We appeal to our Savior's pitying love, relying upon his boundless power.

See also how the leper, to my mind, *really speaks without any hesitancy,* if you understand him. He does not say, "Lord, if you put out your hand, you can make me clean," nor, "Lord, if you speak, you can make me clean," but only, *"Lord, **if You are willing**, You can make me clean"* (emphasis added). Your mere will can do it." Oh, splendid faith! If you are inclined to see a little unsureness in it, I would have you admire it for running so well with a lame foot. If there was a weakness anywhere in his faith, still it was so strong that the weakness only manifests its strength. Sinner, it is so; and I pray God that your heart may grasp it – if the Lord is willing, he can make you clean. Do you believe this? If so, carry out practically what your faith will suggest to you, namely, that you come to Jesus and plead with him, and get from him the cleansing which you need. To that end I am hoping to lead you, as the Holy Spirit shall enable me.

In the sixth place, notice that this man's faith had earnest action flowing out of it. Believing that, if Jesus was willing, he could make him clean, what did the leper do? At once he came to Jesus. I know not from what distance, but he came as near to Jesus as he could. Then we read that he implored him; that is to say, he pleaded, and pleaded, and pleaded again. He cried, "Lord, cleanse me! Lord, heal my leprosy!" Nor was this all; he fell on his knees and worshiped, for we read that he *bowed down before Him.* He not only knelt, but also knelt before Jesus. He had no difficulty as to paying him divine honor. He worshiped the Lord Christ, paying him reverent homage. He then went on to honor him by an open acknowledgment of his power, his marvelous power, his infinite power, by saying, *"Lord, if You are willing, You can make me clean."* I should not wonder if some who stood by began to smile at what they thought of the poor man's fanatical naiveness. They murmured, "What a poor fool this leper is, to think that Jesus of Nazareth can cure him of his leprosy!" Such a confession of faith had seldom been heard. But whatever critics and skeptics might think, this brave man boldly declared, "Lord, this is my confession of faith: I believe that if you are willing, you can make me clean."

Now, poor soul, you that are full of guilt, and hardened in sin, and yet anxious to be healed, look straight away to the Lord Jesus Christ. He is here now. In the preaching of the gospel he is with us always. With the eyes of your mind behold him, for he beholds you. You know that he lives, even though you see him not. Believe in this living Jesus; believe for perfect cleansing. Cry to him, worship him, adore him, trust him. He is very God of very God. Bow before him, and cast yourself upon his mercy. Go home, and on your knees say, "Lord, I believe that you can make me clean." He will hear your cry and will save you. There will be no interval between your prayer and the gracious reward of faith, of which I am now to speak.

> There will be no interval between your prayer and the gracious reward of faith.

Lastly, his faith had its reward. Have patience with me just a minute. The reward of this man's faith was, first, that *his very words were treasured up.* Matthew, Mark, and Luke, all three of them record the precise words which this man used: *"Lord, if You are willing, You can make me clean."* They evidently did not see so much to find fault within them as some have done; on the contrary, they thought them gems to be placed in the setting of their gospels. Three times over are they recorded, because they are such a splendid confession of faith for a poor diseased leper to have made. I believe that God is as much glorified by that one sentence of the leper as by the song of cherubim and seraphim when they continually cry, *"Holy, holy, holy is the Lord God, the Almighty."* A sinner's lips declaring his confident faith in God's own Son can breathe sonnets unto God more sweet than those of the angelic choirs. This man's first faith words are folded up in the fair linen of three of the Gospels, and laid up in the treasury of the house of the Lord. God values the language of humble confidence.

His next reward was that *Jesus echoed his words.* He said, *"Lord, if You are willing, You can make me clean,"* and Jesus said, *"I am willing; be cleansed."* As an echo answers to the voice, so did Jesus to his petitioner. The Lord Jesus was so pleased with this man's words that he caught them as they leaped out of his mouth, and used them himself, saying, *"I am willing; be cleansed."* If you can only get, then, as far as this leper's confession, I believe that our Lord Jesus from his throne above will answer your prayer.

So potent were the words of this leper that *they moved our Lord very wonderfully.* Read the forty-first verse: *Moved with compassion.* The Greek word here used, if I were to pronounce it in your hearing, would half suggest its own meaning. It expresses a stirring of the entire manhood, a commotion in all the inward parts. The heart and all the vitals of the man are in active movement. The Savior was greatly moved. You have seen a man moved, have you not? When a strong man is unable any longer to restrain himself, and is forced to give way to his feelings, you have seen him tremble all over, and at last burst out into an evident breakdown. It was just so with the Savior: his pity moved him, his delight in the leper's faith mastered him. When he heard the man speak with such confidence in him, the Savior was moved with a sacred passion which, as it was in sympathy with the leper, is called *compassion.* Oh, to think that a poor leper should have such power over the divine Son of God! Yet, my hearer, in all your sin and misery, if you can believe in Jesus, you can move the heart of your blessed Savior. Yes, even now his bowels yearn towards you.

No sooner was our Lord Jesus thus moved than *out went his hand,*

and he touched the man and healed him immediately. It did not require a long time for the working of the cure, but the leper's blood was cooled and cleansed in a single second. Our Lord could work this miracle, and make all things new in the man; for *all things came into being through Him, and apart from Him nothing came into being that has come into being.* He restored the poor, decaying, putrefying body of this man, and he was cleansed at once. To make him quite sure that he was cleansed, the Lord Jesus bid him to go to the priest and seek a certificate of health. He was so clean that he might be examined by the appointed sanitary authority and come off without suspicion. The cure which he had received was a real and radical one, and therefore he might go away at once and get the certificate of it.

If our converts will not bear practical tests, they are worth nothing; let even our enemies judge whether they are not better men and women when Jesus has renewed them. If Jesus saves a sinner, he does not mind all men testing the change. Jesus does not seek display, but he seeks examination from those able to judge. Our converts will bear the test. Come to this place, angels! Come to this place, pure intelligences, able to observe men in secret! Here is a wretch of a sinner. He seemed first cousin to the devil, but the Lord Jesus Christ has converted him and changed him. Now look at him, you angels; look at him at home in his chamber! Watch him in private life. We can read your verdict. *"There is joy in the presence of the angels of God over one sinner who repents,"* and this proves what you think. It is such a wonderful change, and angels are so sure of it that they give their certificates at once. How do they give their certificates? Why, each one manifests his joy as he sees the sinner turning from his sinful ways. Oh, that the angels might have work of this kind to do today!

Dear hearer, may you be one over whom they rejoice! If you believe on Jesus Christ, and if you will trust him as the sent One of God fully and entirely with your soul, he will make you clean. Behold him on the cross, and see sin put away. Behold him risen from the dead, and see new life bestowed. Behold him enthroned in power, and see evil conquered. I am ready to be bound for my Lord, to be his surety, that if you, my hearer, will come to him, he will make you clean. Believe your Savior, and your cure is worked. God help you, for Jesus Christ's sake! Amen.

Chapter 7

First Healing and Then Service

When Jesus came into Peter's home, He saw his mother-in-law lying sick in bed with a fever. He touched her hand, and the fever left her; and she got up and waited on Him.
(Matthew 8:14-15)

This event took place at Capernaum, but Peter's residence was at Bethsaida; for we read, *Now Philip was from Bethsaida, of the city of Andrew and Peter.* How did Peter come to have a house at Capernaum? Poor fishermen do not often have two houses. May not the conjecture be highly probable that, finding the Lord Jesus Christ was frequently at Capernaum, Peter thought it best to have a dwelling there, that he might always be present when the Master was preaching, and that he might do his best to entertain him sometimes? I like to think that the servant changed his place of abode for his Master's sake.

Would it not be well if many Christian people had some little consideration when they are choosing a house, as to whether it will be convenient for the hearing of the Word? Do you not think that a great many professors look chiefly for every other kind of advantage, and, when they have virtually made their choice, they afterwards inquire into the very secondary item of their nearness to a place where they may worship God, enjoy Christian fellowship, and be useful? There are some in this congregation who have moved to this part of town to become members of an earnest, prayerful church. Such believers feel that the first consideration in life must be the health of their souls, the benefiting of their children, and their usefulness in promoting the cause of Christ. When they have made the selection of a house in that way and for that reason, they have found a blessing resting upon them, according to the promise, *"But seek first His kingdom and His righteousness, and all these things will be added to you."*

Some who have forgotten this rule, and, like Lot, have chosen the well-watered plains of Sodom, have lived to regret their choice. Although the house may be commodious, and the position convenient, these advantages will not make up for losing the means of grace and missing opportunities of holy service. When Mephibosheth lived at Lodebar, the place of no pasture, David fetched him up to Jerusalem, where he himself delighted to dwell. It would be well for many a limping brother if he made a similar change. Thus, before we actually cross the threshold of Peter's house we learn a lesson.

Our Lord Jesus Christ had been having a heavy day: he had been to the synagogue, and he had preached and had worked miracles; he had moved in the midst of a great throng, and now that the Sabbath was drawing to a close he needed refreshment, and it was most convenient that Peter had a house into which the Lord could go. I do not suppose it was a stately mansion; probably it was little better than a hut, for Peter was only a fisherman; but the Lord Jesus made it honorable enough by entering it. Where the king is there the palace is.

Though our Lord went to Peter's house to rest, he did not find it free from trouble. It was a hospital before he made it a palace. Peter's mother-in-law was on her bed prostrate with a fever. Typhus of the worst kind was burning out her life. However good a man may be, he will not escape trial in the flesh. You may have a house full of sanctity and full of sickness at the same time. We find it true while we are here, that *the body is dead because of sin, yet the spirit is alive because of righteousness.* The regenerated spirit has risen to life, but the body lingers under the power of death and its accompanying pain and weakness. Certain persons attribute all sickness to the devil, and impute special sin to those who are grievously afflicted. This teaching is as false as it is cruel. *"For those whom the Lord loves He disciplines."* I can bear witness that some of the saintliest persons I have ever known have been bedridden for years together; and others in whom the very image of Christ was conspicuous, from whose lips all the country around gathered up the choicest sentences of holy experience, have been invalids for twenty or thirty years at a stretch.

Our sicknesses are of the Lord's appointing, however painful they may be, and we may without doubt say, as David did, *The Lord has disciplined me severely.* "Lord, behold, he whom You love is sick" is still a truth. Even Peter's house, though it be the abode of a chosen saint and a leading apostle, whose very shadow would one day heal the sick, had a terrible fever in it which threatened death. Yet Jesus came where the fever polluted the air. If the disease had come, the Great Physician had come also. We are not alarmed at the cross if Christ comes with it.

> Jesus came where the fever polluted the air.

Notice, with regard to our Lord's entering the house of Peter, that he came there with his three most favored disciples. If you read the statement given by Mark in his first chapter, you may be somewhat surprised to discover Peter, James, and John there. We read, *And immediately after they came out of the synagogue, they came into the house of Simon and Andrew, with James and John.* Whether Andrew was there or not I cannot tell; he was joint proprietor of the house, but he is not mentioned as being there. Whenever you see Peter, James, and John present together with the Lord, you may look for special wonders. These were the men who beheld the Lord's exceeding glory on the Mount. These were nearest to the agony of Gethsemane. These were admitted to the room to behold the raising from the dead of the young girl when the Lord put out all the gathered company. To this most select threesome did Jesus display himself as he did not to the rest of the apostles, and much less to the world.

Did not the Savior thus give us notice that the healing of Peter's mother-in-law was a choice manifestation of his power and grace, and was intended to convey a lesson to the choicer spirits among his followers? I think so, and therefore I shall so use the incident. To you who love Jesus much, and live in special nearness to him, there is a voice from the bed of her who rose from the fever to minister to her Lord. You also are called from your weakness that you may pay personal service to him who heals all your diseases.

Yet though Jesus and Peter and James and John were there, nothing is before you but a family group, a scene in a house. True religion displays its greatest marvels around the domestic hearth. A fisherman's mother-in-law becomes an historic personage through the Lord's touching her. What glory Jesus casts upon common things! With what grandeur he adorns a room in a poor man's house! A fisherman's hut becomes the headquarters of the Captain of our salvation. He heals a woman within its doors, and before long *the whole city had gathered at the door.* O that we may see the like: our own dear ones saved, and then the whole city roused to seek divine healing!

We will arrange our discourse under the headings of four observations.

First, let us observe that it may be we have some in our house who need the ministry of the Lord Jesus. One in Peter's house could not as yet minister to Christ, for she needed Christ to minister to her. She was sick with a fever, and quite prostrated by it, so as to be altogether unable to rise. Let us think whether we have not some around us who are spiritually sick in a way which may be likened to a fever.

What would the fever represent? Those who have a fever represent spiritually those who are *on fire with sin.* The original word for *fever* bears a close relation to the word *fire.* The world's great poet speaks of "the fiery fever." A burning heat inflames the body, accelerates the pulse to an unnatural pace, parches the mouth and tongue, and dries up the entire system. Those who have a fever in their souls are hot after sin, dried up with ill desires, and inflamed with evil lusts. What unhealthy energy many even show in the indulgence of their passions, or in the pursuit of their ambitions; they are so inflamed with their desires that their life is consumed.

Have we not seen some whom we dearly loved afflicted with this fierce distemper? Touch upon certain points, and we discover that they are diseased in reference to them; they are in an inflamed state of mind; they cannot be made to think coolly or judge calmly, but they grow excited and angry. Their touch is that of a fevered hand; their whole nature is burning with the fire of sin. Such persons are not always alike inflamed; they are frequently gentle and docile, so much so that we are filled with hope concerning them. Often fever is intermittent; the patient is hot at one time, and cold at another; and in many sinners the fever of sin is intermittent in its symptoms. They are not always drinking; sometimes they are sober for a long period, and express themselves as deeply repentant for former falls. What pleasant company, what fine pleasant spirits they are at such times! The fever returns, and nothing can restrain them; they drink even to delirium. Alas, the misery which is thus caused! Others are gentle, and loving for a season; and then they suddenly give way to anger, and there is no knowing what they will say or do. When once the fever is on them, they become as inflamed as ever. We know persons from whom the heat of the fever is so long gone that we think surely they are healed; but alas, their cool times are only a pause between the attacks, and the evil returns with increased energy. Their goodness is as the morning cloud and as the early dew; it comes hopefully, but it disappears utterly.

We have mistaken the period between the fever fits for the calm of a cure, but it has not turned out to be so. They have, perhaps, been even worse after their hopeful times than ever they were before; like him from whom the evil spirit went out of his own accord, only to return again, and bring with him seven other spirits more wicked than himself to enter in and dwell there. Have you not such cases under your own roofs, or among your next of kin – poor souls inflamed with the terrible heat of sin?

These fevered people are *frequently very restless*. It is one effect of the fever that the man cannot lie long together either on this side or on the other, but turns to and fro. Even his sleep is broken; neither by day nor by night can he find rest. He is dried up, and he feels as weak as if he were brought into the dust of death and utterly dissolved. His experience is not so much pain as something worse than pain, an utter absence of rest. Have you not friends who in this sense are feverish? I had almost said I hope they are so, if they are, indeed, under the power of sin. There are signs of life where unrest abounds. We know young men with happy homes who cannot be content; they seem resolved to break their mothers' hearts, and their fathers know not what to do with them. Nothing pleases them, they are always unsettled. They have been put to half a dozen businesses already, and have left each one of them;

they are now longing for a foreign country, or for enlistment in the army, or for anything other than their present calling. We have known them to go to the colonies and come back again, finding nothing there; a sea voyage was to cure them, but alas, a sinner on land is a sinner at sea. The sickness is inward, and it needs a change of self rather than a change of place.

Under the influence of the fever of sin men wish, and do not know what they wish; they are like a rolling thing before the whirlwind, or as waves of the sea driven with the wind and tossed. No part of them seems to be at rest, and a sort of madness possesses them. Above all, there is a restlessness about them in reference to sin. They sin, but they are not pleased; and after they have sinned they are eaten up by remorse, a remorse, however, which is not practically operative, for they go back to sin again, flying like the moth to the candle wherein they have already burned their wings. Such persons often become irritable towards their friends when checked in their wrongdoing, and even become at last, like Pashhur in the book of Jeremiah, a terror to themselves and to their friends.

I may be treading upon tender ground in all this. I believe my words are true to the letter. I shall ask Christian people who do not have this heavy trouble to be very thankful, and to pray to God for those who have it. With those dear friends who have to endure the sore affliction of having such in their family I desire to sympathize, and to encourage them to bring these feverish spirits to the Lord Jesus by prayer and faith, that in them the parable of the prodigal may be literally fulfilled.

One symptom of a fever is that a man *loses his appetite for that which would be good for him*. Some of our unconverted friends have no taste for the gospel; we cannot easily induce them to come to hear it. If you could get them under the sound of the Word, you would sit and pray and even agonize for them, all while the truth was being preached, but alas! they will not come near. They have no taste, no liking, and no care for heavenly things; the thing they most require is that for which they have the least desire. Yet, fear not; Jesus can give them appetite, and everything else which is necessary to a perfect cure.

On the other hand, a fevered patient often *feels a great thirst,* which he cannot by any means relieve. He longs to drink and drink again, and with all his drinking the heat is not abated. Sometimes the sick man has *an appetite for what he must not taste;* he craves the most injurious and even unnatural things; foods which would be most harmful he prefers. So is it with unconverted ones when under the full power of sin; they are eager enough to hear a godless lecture, or to listen to opinions which are the opposite of truth; they would go through any hardship to indulge their passions, and sacrifice any amount to be allowed their desires.

As the leech cries, *"Give," "Give,"* so is sin insatiable. Sin can never yield satisfaction to the soul of man; as well might the thirsty hope to relieve their anguish by drafts of salt water. As it is with cups of wine, so it is with sin; one makes room for another. He that has sinned will sin. It is an awful part of the punishment of sin that it grows into a habit and increases in intensity as it is indulged. I may rightly say of the black well of sin, "He that drinks of this water shall thirst again and thirst more." Sin is a thing of rapid propagation, and it never abides alone. You cannot retain one sin in the house by itself, for it will before long produce numerous offspring, a generation of vipers, as many as the hairs of your head. What a dreadful thing it is for a man to have a fever upon him which makes him thirst for that which increases his thirst.

> Sin can never yield satisfaction to the soul of man.

But the worst point in the case of the sinner is this, that this fever of his *will prove fatal.* This son, daughter, husband, or wife of yours will perish through the fever of sin, if it be not cured. A great fever is a great danger, and so is sin. In our Lord's days men did not know how to deal with fever so well as now; therefore, those who were taken with it were doomed. This poor woman would have died if Jesus had not interceded; thus is it with the sinful ones whose cases we deplore.

I have thus described the disease; what shall we do with it? Let us see what the disciples did.

Mark says *they spoke to Jesus about her.* I would earnestly persuade you to do the same. Take the case of the person who is laid upon your heart and spread it before the Lord. Go over the matter in detail; not for his information, but to excite your own prayerfulness. Look the matter in the face, making no excuses for the sinner, and in all truthfulness tell the Lord what ails the sinful one. Pour out your heart before the Lord, and sorrow over the lost one, even as Samuel mourned over Saul, only with better hope. Tell the case to Jesus just as you would mention a physical case to a doctor. He is ready to hear it all, and to consider it. Make a *confidant* of Jesus. Do not go and complain all over the neighborhood, "My boy does this," or "My husband does that," for you may increase the evil in that way by incensing the person against yourself and your religion. You may tell Jesus all about it, without restraint. No harm can come of such a relation. It will be a relief to your own mind, and it will be the most proper way of engaging your Lord to help you.

Luke tells us *they asked Him to help her.* After you have stated the case to your Lord, then plead with him, plead his promises, and plead his nature, plead the need of the case, and the glory which a cure will bring. Let it be no cold prayer, but a warm, hearty, intense plea. Do not wrangle with sinners about religion, but wrestle with Christ about them. Beg the sinners for Christ, but never fail to beg Christ for the sinners. When little can be done with men, you can still do much with Jesus. It will be of very little use to be always worrying them with saying, "You should not do this," and "You should not do that"; but it will be of infinite service to go and say, "Lord, have mercy upon these poor souls who know you not." Never give up praying for your prodigals as long as there is breath in their bodies; no, not even if they curse you for doing so.

We find also that when they had thus told Jesus of her, and had implored him, then they brought him into the chamber, so that we read in our text, *When Jesus came into Peter's home, He saw his mother-in-law lying sick in bed with a fever.* They seemed to say, "Lord, this is all we can do. We would have you look upon the dying woman and consider her. There she is." Can you not by faith so realize the presence of the Lord Jesus Christ that you see him viewing the lost estate of those for whom you are concerned? Your friend is fevered with sin, but Jesus sees it. Your boy is restless, but Jesus watches him. Your daughter is likely to perish, but Christ looks upon her. Every day let your compelling prayers keep them under Christ's eye. Bring unto Jesus all your sinful ones; lay them at his feet, leave them in his presence. When you have done all this – when you have told him of her, and begged him about her, and brought him to the house to look upon her – then you may expect his healing touch and saving word.

That is our first remark.

Secondly, the ministry of Jesus must precede the ministry of the saved ones. We anxiously desire that these friends of ours who are now sick of the fever of sin should yet become the servants of Christ, and should minister to him. I can imagine the joy of that anxious mother over yonder if she should ever be privileged to hear her boy preach the gospel – that boy who has even been known to swear. What delight would fill the wife's bosom if she could hear her infidel husband engage publicly in prayer. Some of you are thinking now of certain gifted persons who are using all their abilities against the cause of Christ, and "Oh," say you, "if they might be converted, my heart would dance with delight." This is a right desire, but do not indulge it unwisely. Do not ask them to do anything for Jesus while they are unregenerate. Healing must come before serving. When a person is *lying sick . . . with a fever,* do not ask her to rise and wait upon the Lord Jesus Christ. No; *his* ministry to Peter's mother-in-law preceded *her* ministry to him. She was *lying,* that is, prostrated by the terrible sickness. As a body greatly weakened seems to cling to the bed and almost sink into it, so was she. She was like a crushed thing, or a sheep cast upon its back in a trench, and so she was powerless to do anything.

Thus is it with the sinner. What can he do for Christ? *For while we were still helpless, at the right time Christ died for the ungodly.* There is no strength in an ungodly man by which to serve God. He has no faith, and without faith it is impossible to please God. He has no love, and even if a deed were done rightly, if there was no love as the motive, it could not be acceptable with God. The sinner, in fact, has no spiritual life, and if he should try to do good works they would be dead works, and could not please the living God. Out of a foul spring no clean waters can come, and out of a corrupt heart no acceptable works can proceed. Christ must give us strength, and cause us both to will and to do of his own good pleasure, for without him we can do nothing.

Moreover, this sick woman was *utterly unfit* to do anything for Jesus and his disciples with a great fever upon her. Everywhere she went she would spread the poison of her sickness. Everything she touched would be infected; any food she prepared would be nauseous even to think upon. Let her stay in her bed, by all means, and let none go near her unless they are compelled to do so, for fever soon seizes upon fresh victims. So you that are ungodly cannot serve Christ, for everything you do is defiled: you cannot lay your hand even upon holy things without polluting them. Your thoughts are feverish, your words are feverish, your acts are feverish; therefore, we cannot invite your cooperation in the work of the Lord. You would do more hurt than good, if as sinful men you pretended to render service to a holy God. Such is your natural depravity that you would spread infection all around, even if you attempted to minister to the Lord Jesus.

What is more, a person with a fever, if in her feverishness she were to arise and wait upon guests, would get no good, but would *run terrible risks.* Persons with a fever must not be exposed to drafts, or be driven to exert themselves. Every doctor would judge it to be most injurious to a person in a high state of fever to attempt to work. I solemnly believe that unconverted people get hurt when they attempt religious duties. To preach with an unrenewed heart must be to pronounce one's own death warrant. If unrenewed men come to the sacramental table, they eat and drink condemnation to themselves; and if they in any way make a profession of faith, they are enacting a falsehood in the sight of high heaven, seeing they have no such faith. *But to the wicked God says, "What right have you to tell of My statutes?"* No, you must stand back, you that have never been washed in the blood of the Lamb. You cannot minister to Christ while the red fever is on your brow. He who has seraphim for his servants does not want feverish services from souls diseased with iniquity. King Jesus wants no slaves to swell his train; you must be freed first from the yoke of sin, and then you shall become the servants of the Lord.

Listen to me, any fevered ones who are here, while I briefly describe how the Lord Jesus Christ ministered to this woman.

He ministered to her by *his presence.* His being in the room with her meant that salvation had come to her house. Beloved, believe that Jesus Christ is here. To his ministers he has said, *"Lo, I am with you always, even to the end of the age."* I want you to know that he is not shut up within the heavenly gates, but he is here, and his power to save is present in the midst of this assembly, and will be present in your room when you go home and fall upon your knees.

The next thing that blessed this woman was *his look*. "Jesus saw her." There is more here than appears upon the surface. You know what a physician means when he says, "I will come and see your sick child." He does not mean that he will barely look at it; he intends to search into the matter, study it, and see what can be done. Will you try to think that the Lord Jesus Christ sees you, that he reads your heart, knows your secret thoughts, hears your secret groanings, and notes your inward desires? He perceives the power which sin has over you, the difficulty you find in coming to him; he sees it all, and knows how to deal with it. Not only is Jesus near at hand, but he is present with his eyes open, observing all that ails you. He sees it with a mind which is deeply sympathetic, and a heart quick to relieve.

The next thing the Lord Jesus Christ used was *his touch*. This is the healing point. He *raised her up, taking her by the hand*. There was a contact established. Oh, that glorious doctrine of the incarnation of Christ, there is healing in it! I do not mean in the doctrine but in the fact itself, that the Lord Jesus Christ took our flesh, and became man, bone of our bone, and flesh of our flesh. Thus he touches us and heals us. Had he not been man he could not have died, and had he not died we would have died forever. God in Christ Jesus is very near to you, poor soul; he is so near to you that if you do by faith touch the hem of his garment, you are saved. If you believe in the Lord Jesus, he is in contact with you. His cool hand is grasping your fevered hand; and as your fever dissolves into him – for *He Himself took our infirmities* – his health flows into you so that you may arise and minister unto him. Contact by faith with Jesus Christ our Lord is the ordained means of salvation.

> Contact by faith with Jesus Christ our Lord is the ordained means of salvation.

And there was, besides this contact, another form of power: our Lord spoke to the fever. *His word* is a word of might. If the touch of our Lord represents incarnation, his word represents resurrection; for by hearing the voice of the Son of God shall all the dead arise from their graves. His word is stimulating, and where it falls it proves itself to be a living and incorruptible seed. By the word of the Lord, even by the gospel of Jesus, the fever of sin is driven out of men and women. Oh, that the Lord Jesus may now speak to you by these lips of mine – speak with almighty power to your hearts! Oh, that you, poor sin-sick sinner, may hear the word of the Lord with your inner ears, for such hearing is eternal life! God help you so to hear.

There is healing for you, and I warn you again that you must have this healing before you can work for Jesus. Your Lord must begin with you before you can begin with him. Do not go blundering out of the tabernacle and say, "I will take a class in the Sunday school"; "I will try to preach"; "I will give my money to the Lord's cause." No; stand back till you are healed; weep and pray and agonize till you are healed. You must receive from Jesus all he has to give before you can give anything to him.

This may sound harsh to you who mean well, but God forbid that I should bolster you up in a zeal for God which is not according to knowledge. Aliens cannot stand in the Lord's courts; you must be made Israelites before you can be priests unto God. First salvation, then service.

Thirdly, it is plainly taught in the text that strength to minister comes with healing. *And she immediately got up and waited on them.* Fever causes extreme weakness, and when it leaves the patient, he is for a considerable time greatly debilitated. The cures of nature are slow, but when Jesus cures, he does it at once. Though he uses only a touch and a word, yet he cures so perfectly that no weakness remains. The woman did not lie in bed a week or two, and feed upon a nourishing diet, and so recover her strength; but there and then she arose from her bed, put on her garments, and went about the duties of the household. Is it not wonderful to see her hasten to the kitchen to prepare the evening meal for the Lord Jesus Christ and his friends? With gratitude beaming from her face, she placed each dish upon the table, and brought forth water with which her guests might wash their feet. The moment the Lord Jesus Christ saves a soul, he gives that soul strength for its appointed service.

I want to call your attention to this, that her service was *immediate* service, rendered on the spot, without delay. Some of you have been converted during our late special services; let me instruct you to serve the Lord at once, even as the Lord has served you. "What, get to work directly?" Yes, immediately; for there is something very beautiful about that which is done by new converts. Oh, the beauty of that first look of love! Oh, the sweetness of those first notes of praise! Oh, the power of those first sentences of testimony! I do not find any fault with our dear old saints; there is a richness and maturity about them, but still my soul desires the first ripe fruits. There is a pungency of flavor about the first berries of grace, and even a kind of tartness about them which makes their taste all the more perceptible to those who are dull and careless. Give me fruit with the dew of the morning upon it. New blood in the veins of the church is a great promoter of its health and vigor. The first fruits are in some respects the best fruits. I would not have a converted person wait a week before trying to do something for Jesus. Run as soon as you find your feet.

But notice that what this good woman did was very *appropriate*. Peter's mother-in-law did not get out of bed and go down the street and deliver an address to an assembled multitude. Women are best when they are quiet. I share the apostle Paul's feelings when he bid women to be silent in the assembly. Yet there is work for holy women, and we read of Peter's mother-in-law that she arose and ministered to Christ. She did what she could and what she should. She arose and ministered to him. Some people can do nothing that they are allowed to do, but waste their energies in lamenting that they are not called on to do other people's work.

Blessed are they who do what they should do. It is better to be a good housewife, or nurse, or domestic servant, than to be a powerless preacher or a graceless talker. She did not arise and prepare a lecture, nor preach a sermon, but she arose and prepared a supper, and that was what she was fitted to do. Was she not a housewife? As a housewife let her serve the Lord. I do not say that if you were converted a week ago you are at once to preach. No; but you are to minister to the Lord in the way for which you are best qualified, and that may happen to be by a living testimony to his grace in your daily calling. We greatly err when we dream that only a preacher can minister to the Lord, for Jesus has work of all sorts for all sorts of followers. Paul speaks of women who helped him much, and, assuredly, as there is no idle angel there ought to be no idle Christian. We are not saved for our own sakes, but that we may be of service to the Lord and to his people; let us not miss our calling.

When healed of her fever, Peter's mother-in-law had strength to perform a *suitable* ministry, such as the peculiar occasion required. She did for Jesus and the three companions that which was needful there and then. Jesus had had a hard day's preaching, and that is hungry work; he had spent a heavy day in healing, and that is exhausting work; and now he more or less wanted to eat, and therefore he came into Peter's house. The principal worker there was laid aside, and so our Lord did not ask for refreshment. He always thought of others before himself; and when he was faint and hungry he put back his own needs till he restored health to the fevered woman. This being done, the next necessary thing was that the wearied preacher and physician should be refreshed, and this the grateful woman attended to. When our Lord sat on the well and talked with the woman of Samaria, he was faint and weary, and asked for drink; but the claims of nature he put aside till he had preached the gospel to her. Then came the disciples with the meat which they had bought.

On this occasion at Peter's house the refreshment was ministered by her who had just left her bed. *She immediately got up and waited on them.* Now, dear friends, you who are converted may minister to Christ in a way which is as necessary as the service of his ablest preachers and pastors. There is something for you to do which will be a refreshment to him and to his servants. He condescendingly permits it, and will graciously accept it. You can personally minister to a personal Christ. You cannot do everything, but you can do something that will be acceptable to him. You may, you can, and you ought. Ministry to Jesus is feasible, permissible, acceptable, and obligatory. You owe your very life to him. Come, spend that life in his service. Immediately, this very day, minister to Jesus. If you have only been saved this day, yet there is a somewhat incumbent duty for the day; and in its place it is as necessary to the glory of God as the ministry of cherubim and seraphim. Now then, do it. I will not urge you, because I can see in my last head something that will move you to it.

The desire to minister always arises out of healing. Here was a woman, a poor woman, an old woman, a widow woman, one who had just been sick, and she desires at once to minister to Christ, and she can do it, and she does do it. How do you think she was moved to this? Was it not that *strength naturally suggests* activity as soon as you ever get it? When you are very prostrate you do not want to do anything. You feel as if you must lie still; there is no power in you, and there is no industry in you; but persons who have recovered want something to do. Sometimes they try to do more than they can, such is the suggestion of revived strength. Now, if the Lord has given you spiritual life, that life will want to work; if he has given you light, that light will shine. "Now candle, do not shine." Will the candle take any notice of you? No, it cannot help shining if it has been lighted. If Christ has given you his grace, and it is in you as a well of living water, it must flow out that others may drink. It is no use saying, "Water, do not flow; fountain, cease." The fountain cannot help it, it must send forth its streams; and it must be so with you. The strength God has given you in Christ suggests activity.

> If the Lord has given you spiritual life, that life will want to work; if he has given you light, that light will shine.

And then the *gratitude for this strength impels you to activity*. How can a man be still when Christ has spoken for him and delivered him? We read in the paper some time ago that the king of Italy, to his great honor, appeared in a court of law on behalf of a man brought up under the charge of causing a death. The king had seen the accident, and he came forward as a common witness in the court to say that the horse had mastered the driver, and the man was not to be blamed. I do not know the name of the man, but I feel pretty sure that Jacobi or Antonio, whoever he may be, if ever King Humbert wants somebody to speak up for him, will find a friend in him. He will say, "My king came into the court and spoke for me, and I will as long as ever I live speak up for him." Now, the Lord Jesus Christ is an advocate for you; therefore, be an advocate for him. Can you ever be silent for Christ now that the Lord Christ has redeemed you from the curse of the law and the penalty of sin? I tell you, if you can be quiet and do nothing for Christ, I am afraid you have never tasted of his love and grace.

Once more, I think I may say that those who are healed by Christ are sure to do something for him of the right sort, because *their former predispositions will assist them.* I do not mean by this that sinful activity can ever help us into holy activity, but I do mean this: that we can turn our old habits to account for Jesus.

I believe that Peter's mother-in-law was a particularly nice old lady. There is rather a prejudice against a mother-in-law, and if Peter found it the proper thing to have her living in the house, I am sure she was an especially good woman. I have a picture of her in my mind's eye – a dear old soul, always busy and happy. When there was nothing else to do she would mend the stockings, or do any commonplace work. She was always busy. You never had to ask her to work, she did it of her own accord. At cooking the meals and preparing everything for the house she was perfectly at home, never grumbling, never complaining, never setting the husband against the wife, but always looking out to do everything that possibly could be done to make the household go along in all its concerns with oiled wheels. When she had the fever she did not like to be laid aside, and so the moment she is restored, there she is at it again. The ruling passion is strong now that death has been removed. She begins to serve Jesus, for she had always been serving somebody. When Jesus came into the house with Peter, and James, and John, she could not bear to think that there was nothing for supper; but the moment she felt well, away she went to the kitchen, with all the utensils of her cookery craft, to prepare the best meal in her power. You people who, when you were not converted, were always active, ought to be doubly active now. In the family do all for the Lord Jesus Christ.

Those commonplace things – sweeten and flavor them with love for him. Reverence him and glorify him in all that you do. Is not there something you can do for your neighbor, something you can do for your children, some part of the Lord's work you can undertake?

As for you, young men who have been so restless, so vigorous, so spirited in sin, it seems to me that this habitual energy ought to be placed under consecration to Christ. A horse that has no spirit in it is easily managed; still, a horse with a little spirit, though he may kick, and plunge, and do a great deal of mischief, is all the better horse when he is broken in. If he be under proper management, if he answers to the bit, you like the spirit. So it is with a man when he is converted. If he had spirit in him that led him to kick and plunge when he served the devil, if he did so much mischief and damage against the kingdom of Christ, he is the very man to pull well in Jesus Christ's chariot. I pray the Master, therefore, that he will come and heal that young man of his feverishness and make his blood cool within him this day, and restore him by his grace. Oh, that the Lord would touch all sick folk and make them healthy! Then when all are healed, let us rise to serve him who has served us, and unto him be glory forever and ever. Amen and amen.

Chapter 8

The Best House-Visitation

And immediately after they came out of the synagogue, they came into the house of Simon and Andrew, with James and John. Now Simon's mother-in-law was lying sick with a fever; and immediately they spoke to Jesus about her. And He came to her and raised her up, taking her by the hand, and the fever left her, and she waited on them. When evening came, after the sun had set, they began bringing to Him all who were ill and those who were demon-possessed. And the whole city had gathered at the door. (Mark 1:29-33)

We see before us small beginnings and grand endings. One man is called by the voice of Jesus, and then another; the house wherein they dwell is consecrated by the Lord's presence, and by and by the whole city is stirred from end to end with the name and fame of the Great Teacher. We are often wishing that God would do some great thing in the world, and we look abroad for instruments which we think would be peculiarly fit, and think of places where the work might suitably begin. It might be quite as well if we asked the Lord to make use *of us,* and if we were believingly to hope that even our feeble instrumentality might produce great results by his power, and that *our home* might become the central point from which streams of blessing should flow forth to refresh the neighborhood.

Peter's house was by no means the most notable building in the town of Capernaum. It was probably not the poorest dwelling in the place, for Peter had a boat of his own, or perhaps a half share in a boat with his brother Andrew, or possibly he and Andrew and James and John were proprietors of some two or three fishing boats, for they were partners, and they appear to have employed hired servants (Mark 1:20.) Still, Peter was not rich nor famous, he was neither a ruler of the synagogue nor an eminent scribe, and his house was not at all remarkable among the habitations which made up the little fishing suburb down by the seashore. Yet to this house did Jesus go. He had foreknown and chosen it of old, and had resolved to make it renowned by his presence and miraculous power. There hung the fisherman's nets outside the door – the sole escutcheon and hatchment of one who was ordained to sit upon a throne and judge with his fellow apostles the twelve tribes of Israel. Beneath that lowly roof Immanuel stooped to unveil himself; "God-with-us" showed himself God to Simon. Little did Peter know how divine a blessing entered his house when Jesus crossed the threshold, nor how vast a river of mercy would stream forth from his door down the streets of Capernaum.

Now, dear friend, it may be that your dwelling, though very dear to you, is not very much thought of by anybody else; no poet or historian has ever written its history, nor artist engraved its image. Perhaps it is not the very poorest small house in the place in which you live; still it is obscure enough, and no one as he rides along asks, "Who dwells there?" or "What remarkable house is that?" Yet is there no reason why the Lord should not visit you and make your house like that of Obed-edom, in which the ark abided, or like that of Zaccheus to whom salvation came. Our Lord can make your dwelling the center of mercy for the whole region, a little sun scattering light in all directions, a spiritual dispensary distributing health to the multitudes around. There is no reason except in yourself why the Lord should not make your residence in a city a greater blessing to it than the cathedral and all its clergy.

> Our Lord can make your dwelling the center of mercy for the whole region.

Jesus cares not for fine buildings and carved stones; he will not scorn coming beneath your cottage roof, and coming there he will bring a treasury of blessings with him which shall enrich your house, and shall ensure the richest of benefits to your neighbors. Why should it not be? Have you faith to pray this moment that it may be so? How much do I wish you would! More good by far will be done by a silent prayer now offered by yourself to that effect than by anything which can be spoken by me. If every Christian here will now put up the plea, "Lord, dwell where I dwell, and in so doing make my house a blessing to the neighborhood," marvelous results must follow.

I am going to speak of three things. The first is, *how grace came to Peter's house;* secondly, *what grace did when it got there;* and thirdly, *how grace flowed forth from Peter's house.*

How grace came to Peter's house. The first link in the chain of causes was that *a relative was converted.* Andrew had heard John the Baptist preach and had been impressed. The text which was blessed to him was probably *"Behold, the Lamb of God who takes away the sin of the world!"* Andrew followed Jesus, and having become a disciple, he desired to lead others to be disciples too. He began, as we all ought to begin, with those nearest to him by ties of relationship; *he found first his own brother Simon.*

Beloved friend, if you are saved, you should look around you and inquire, "To what house may I become a messenger of salvation?" Perhaps you have no family of your own; I do not know whether Andrew had family, for he seems at the time of this narrative to have lived in a part of the same house as Peter. Perhaps they had each of them a house at Bethsaida, which was their own city, but they lived together when they went on business to Capernaum. Perhaps Andrew had no wife and no children; I cannot tell. If it were so, I feel sure that he said to himself, "I must seek the good of my brother and his family." I believe, if we are really lively and thoughtful Christians, our conversion is an omen for good to all our relatives. We shall not idly say, "I ought to have looked after my own children and household, if I had owned any, and having none I am excused"; but we shall consider ourselves to be debtors to those who are kindred householders. I hope that some Andrew is here who, being himself enlisted for Jesus, will be the means of conquering for Jesus a brother and a brother's household. If there be no Andrew, I hope some of the Marys and Marthas will be fired up with zeal to make up for the deficiency of the men, and will bring brother Lazarus to the Lord.

Uncles and aunts should feel an interest in the spiritual condition of nephews and nieces; cousins should be concerned for cousins, and all ties of blood should be consecrated by being used for purposes of grace. Moses, when he led the people out of Egypt, would not leave a hoof behind, nor ought we to be content to leave one kinsman a slave to sin. Abraham, in his old age, took up sword and buckler for his nephew Lot, and aged believers should look around them and seek the good of the most distant members of their families; if it were always so, the power of the gospel would be felt far and wide. The household of which Peter was master might never have known the gospel if a relative had not been converted.

This first link of grace drew on another of much greater importance, namely, that *the head of the family became a convert.* Andrew sought out his brother and spoke to him of having found the Messiah; then he brought him to Jesus, and our Lord at once accepted the new recruit and gave him a new name. Peter believed and became a follower of Christ, and so the head of the house was on the right side. Heads of families, what responsibilities rest upon us! We cannot shake them off, let us do what we may! God has given us little kingdoms in which our authority and influence will speak for the better or the worse to all eternity. There is not a child or a servant in our house but what will be impressed for good or evil by what we do. True, we may have no wish to influence them, and we may endeavor to ignore our responsibility, but it cannot be done; parental influence is a throne which no man can abdicate. The members of our family come under our shadow, and we either drip poison upon them like a deadly upas tree, or else beneath our shade they breathe an atmosphere perfumed with our devotion. The little boats are fastened to our larger vessel and are drawn along in our wake.

O fathers and mothers, the ruin of your children or their salvation will, under God, very much depend upon you. The gracious Spirit may use you for their conversion, or Satan may employ you as the instruments of their destruction. Which is it likely to be? I charge you, consider this. It is a notable event in family history when the grace of God takes up its headquarters in the heart of the husband and the father: that household's story will henceforth be written by another pen. Let those of us who are the Lord's gratefully acknowledge his mercy to us personally, and then let us return to bless our household. If the clouds be full of rain, they empty themselves upon the earth; let us pray to be as clouds of grace to our families. Whether we have only an Isaac and an Ishmael like Abraham, or twelve children like Jacob, let us pray for each and all that they may live before the Lord, and that we and all that belong to us may be bound up in the bundle of life.

Note, further, that the third step in the coming of grace to Peter's house was that after the conversion of the brother and Peter, *there were certain others converted who were partners and companions with the two brothers.* It is a great help to a man to find godly workfellows. If he needs to go a-fishing like Peter, it is a grand thing to have a James and a John as one's partners in the business. How helpful it is to devotion when Christian men associate from day to day with their fellow Christians, and speak often one to another concerning the best things. Firebrands placed closely together will burn all the more freely, coals laid in a heap will glow and blaze, and so hearts touching hearts in divine things cause an inward burning and a sacred fervor seldom reached by those who walk alone.

> Firebrands placed closely together will burn all the more freely.

Many Christians are called to struggle hard for spiritual existence through having to work with unbelievers; they are not only sneered at and persecuted, but also all sorts of doubts and blasphemies are suggested, and these materially hinder their growth in the heavenly life. When they are brought into this trial in the course of Providence, they have need of great grace to remain firm under it. Beloved brother, if in your daily business you meet with none to help you but many to hinder you, you must live all the nearer to God, for you require a double measure of grace; but if in the providence of God you happen to be placed where there are helpful Christian companions, do not readily change that position, even though your income would be doubled thereby. I would sooner work with James and John for twenty shillings a week than with swearers and drunkards for sixty. You who reside with really consistent Christians are much favored, and ought to become eminent

Christians. You are like flowers in a conservatory, and you ought to bloom to perfection. You live in a lavender garden, and you ought to smell sweetly. Prove that you appreciate and rightly use your privileged position by endeavoring to bring grace to your house, that it may be altogether the Lord's.

A fourth and more evident step was taken when *Peter and his friends were drawn closer to their Lord.* The good man of the house was already saved, and his brother and companions too, but by the grace of God they rose to be something more than merely saved, for they received a call to a higher occupation and a nobler service; from fishers they were to rise into fishers of men, and from rowing in their own boats they rose to become pilots of the small boats of the church. Peter was already a disciple, but he was in the background; he must come to the front. He had been more a fisherman than a disciple, but now he must be more a disciple than a fisherman. He must now follow Jesus by a more open declaration, a more constant service, a nearer communion, a more attentive discipleship, a fuller fellowship in suffering; and for this he must receive an inward preparation by the divine Spirit. He was, in fact, by the call of his Lord and Master, lifted to a higher platform altogether, upon which he would abide and learn by the Spirit what flesh and blood could never reveal.

Beloved, what a difference there may be between one Christian and another. I have sometimes seen it with astonishment; and though I would not go so far as to say that I have seen as much difference between one Christian and another as between a Christian and a worldling, for there must ever be between the lowest grade of life and the fairest form of death a wider distinction than between the lowest and highest grades of life, yet still it is a very solemn difference. We know some who are saved – at least we hope they are – but oh, how few are the fruits of the Spirit, how feeble is the light they give, how slender is their consecration, and how small is their likeness to him whom they call Master and Lord.

Thank God, we have seen others who live in quite another atmosphere and exhibit a far different life. It is not a higher life, I hardly like that term, for the life of God is one and the same in all believers; but it is a higher condition of the life, more developed, more vigorous, more influential; a condition of life which has a clearer eye, and a nimbler hand, a quicker ear, and a more musical speech; a life of health, whereas too many only know life as laboring under disease, and ready to give up the ghost. There are Mephibosheths among the king's favorites, but give me the life of Naphtali, *satisfied with favor, and full of the blessing of the Lord;* or of Asher, of whom it is written, *may he dip his foot in oil.* An owl is alive though it loves the darkness, and a mole is alive though it is always digging its own grave; but give me the life of those who mount up as on the wings of eagles, who live upon the fat things, full of marrow, and drink the wines on the dregs well refined. These are the mighty ones of Israel, whose joyous energy far surpasses that of the weary and faint, whose faith is feeble and whose love is cold.

Now, Peter and his friends at this time had been called from their fishing tackle and their boats to abide with Jesus in his humiliation, and learn of him the secrets of the kingdom, which afterwards they were to teach to others. They had heard the Master say, *"Follow me,"* and they had left all at his bidding. They were in the path of fellowship, boldly pressing on at their Lord's command, so that now they had taken a grand stride in their Christian career; and that is the time, beloved, when men bring blessings on their houses. Oh, I could sigh to think of the capacities which lie dormant in some Christians! It is sad to think how their children might grow up, and with God's blessing become pillars in the House of the Lord, and perhaps ministers of the gospel, under the influence of an earnest, consecrated father and mother; but instead of that, the dullness, the lukewarmness, the worldliness, and the inconsistencies of parents are hindering the children from coming to Christ, hampering them as to any great advances in the divine life, dwarfing their stature in grace, and doing them lifelong injury.

Brethren, you do not know the possibilities which are in you when God's Spirit rests upon you; but this much is certain: if you yourselves be called into a higher form of divine life, you shall then become a means of blessing to your relatives. Your husband, your wife, your child, your friend, and the whole of your family shall be the better for your advance in spiritual things.

Now, observe further, that at this time when the Lord was about to bless the household of Peter, *he had been further instructing Peter and Andrew and James and John,* for he took them to the synagogue and they heard him preach. A delightful sermon it was – a sermon very full of energy and very unlike the discourses of ordinary preachers, for it had authority and power about it; and it was when they came home from the synagogue, after hearing such a sermon, that the blessing descended upon the house. The best of us need instruction. It is unwise for Christian people to be so busy about Christ's work that they cannot listen to Christ's words. We must be fed, or we cannot feed others. The synagogue must not be deserted, if it be a synagogue where Christ is present. And oh, sometimes, when the Master is present, what a power there is in the word. It is not the preacher's eloquence, it is neither the flow of language, nor the novelty of thought; there is a secret, quiet influence which enters into the soul and subdues it to the majesty of divine love. You feel the vital energy of the divine word, and it is not man's word to you, but the stimulating voice of God sounding through the chambers of your spirit, and making your whole being to live in his sight. At such times the sermon is as manna from the skies, or as the bread and wine with which Melchizedek met Abraham; you are cheered and strengthened by it, and go away refreshed.

My dear brother, my dear sister, then is the time to go home and take your Lord home with you. Peter and his friends had so enjoyed the great Teacher's company at the synagogue that they begged him to abide with them, and so they went straightaway with him from the synagogue into the house. Can you do that? If my Lord shall come and smile upon you and warm your hearts, do not lose him as you go down the aisles, do not let him go when you reach the streets and are walking home. Do not grieve him by chitchat about worthless matters, but take Jesus home with you. Tell him it is noonday, and beg him to wait with you during the heat of the day; or if it be evening, tell him the day is far spent, and implore him to abide with you. You can always find some good reason for detaining your Lord. Do as did the spouse of old, when she said, *"I found him whom my soul loves; I held on to him and would not let him go until I had brought him to my mother's house, and into the room of her who conceived me."* Is there not a sick one at home? Take Jesus home to her. Is there no sorrow at home? Implore your Lord to come home to help you in your distress. Is there no sin at home? I am sure there is. Take Jesus home to purge it away.

But remember, you cannot take him home with you unless you first have him with you personally. Labor after this then; be not satisfied without it. Resolve to be his servant – that I trust you are; to be his servant walking in the light as he is in the light, and having fellowship with him – that I hope you are; and then, having gone so far, resolve that you will take him to your friends and to your relatives, that so your whole house may be blessed.

I desire, before I pass to the second point, to lay great stress upon this. We have an old proverb that benevolence must begin at home, but let me shape it into this – devotion must begin with yourself. Before you ask salvation for your family, lay hold upon it for yourself. This is not selfishness; indeed, the purest benevolence makes a man desire to be qualified to benefit others, and you cannot be prepared to bless others unless God has first blessed you. Is it selfishness which makes a man stand at the fountain to fill his own cup, when he intends to hand that cup around for others to drink? Is it any selfishness for us to pray that in us there may be a well of water springing up unto everlasting life, when our second thought is that out of us may flow rivers of living water whereby others may be replenished? It is no selfishness to wish that the power of the Lord may be upon you, if you long to exercise that power upon the hearts of others for their good. Look well, brethren, to yourselves; you cannot bless your children, you cannot bless your households till first of all upon yourselves the anointing of the Lord rests. O Spirit of the living God, breathe upon us, that we may live yet more abundantly, and then shall we be chosen vessels to bear the name of Jesus to others.

Now we take the second step, and show what grace did in Peter's house when it came there.

The first effect that grace produced was that *it led the family to prayer*. The four friends have come in, and no sooner are they in than they begin to speak with the Master, for the text tells us, *immediately they spoke to Jesus about her* – of Peter's mother-in-law who lay sick. I like that expression – I do not know whether you have noticed it – *immediately they spoke to Jesus about her*. Luke tells us *they asked Him*.

I have no doubt Luke is right, but Mark is right too. *They spoke to Jesus about her.* It looks to me as if it taught me this – that sometimes all I may do with my sore affliction is just to tell my own dear Lord about it, and leave it to his loving judgment to act as he sees fit. Have you any trouble or sickness in the house? Tell Jesus of it. Sometimes that is almost as much as you may do. You may beg him to heal that dear one, but you will have to say, *"Not as I will, but as You will,"* and so will feel that all you may do is to tell Jesus the case and leave it with him. He is so gentle and loving that he is sure to do the kindest thing and the thing which is most right to do; therefore, we may be content to *speak to Jesus about her.*

With regard to spiritual things, we may press and be very urgent, but with regard to secular things, we must draw a line and be satisfied when we have told Jesus and left the matter to his discretion. Some parents may, when their children are ill, plead with God in a way which shows more of nature than of grace, more clearly the affection of the mother than the submissiveness of the Christian; but such should not be the case. If we have committed our way unto the Lord in prayer, and meekly told him of our grief, it will be our wisdom to be still and watch till God the Lord shall speak. He cannot be either unjust or unkind; therefore should we say, *"Let Him do what seems good to Him."*

Very likely this good woman, Peter's mother-in-law, was herself a believer in Christ; but I venture to take her case as typical of spiritual sickness, not at all wishing, however, to insinuate that she was spiritually sick, for she may have been one of the most devoted of Christians. But now, suppose you take Jesus Christ home with you, dear friend, if you have an unconverted one in the house, then you will immediately begin to *speak to Jesus about her. They spoke to Jesus about her.* That is a very simple type of prayer, is it not? Yes, in some respects it is, and therefore I urge you to use it. Do not say you cannot pray for your child; you can tell Jesus about her. Do not say you cannot plead for your brother or your sister; you can go, and in a childlike manner tell Jesus about the case, and that is prayer. To describe your needs is often the best way of asking for help. I have known a person say to a man of whom he needed aid, "Now, I am not going to ask you for anything; I only want you to hear my story, and then you shall do as you like," and if he wisely tells his story, the other begins to smile, and says, "You do not call that asking, I suppose?" Tell Jesus Christ all about it; his view of the matter will be to your advantage.

This elementary form of prayer is very powerful. The police do not allow people to beg in the streets, but I do not know that there is any law to prevent their sitting down in attitudes of misery and exhibiting holes at the knees of their trousers and bare feet staring through soleless shoes. I saw that exhibition today. The man was not begging, but it was wonderfully like it, and answered the purpose better than words. To tell Jesus Christ about your unconverted relative or friend may have in it a great deal of power. It may be, in fact, one of the most earnest things you could do, because the absence of spoken pleas and arguments may arise from your being so burdened with anxiety that you cannot find words to say, "Lord relieve me," but you stand there and sigh under the burden, and those groanings which cannot be uttered act as urgent pleas with the pitiful heart of Christ, and cry aloud in his ear, *"Lord, help me!"*

Telling Jesus is a simple mode of praying, but I think it is a very believing mode. It is as if they felt, "We only need to tell the case, and our blessed Lord will attend to it. If immediately we tell him about her, there shall be no need to clasp his knees and cry with bitter tears for pity upon the fevered one; for as soon as he hears, so loving is his heart, that he will stretch out his hand of power." Go to Jesus, then, dear friends, in that spirit, about your unconverted friend or child, and *speak to Jesus about her.*

There is something very instructive about this particular case, because we are apt to think we must not tell the Lord of the more common troubles which occur in our family; but this is a great error. Too common? How can the commonness of an evil put it out of the list of proper subjects for begging? The seacoast of Capernaum in which Peter dwelt is said by travelers to be a peculiarly damp, marshy, fever-causing place. There was no end to the number of people who had the fever just around the house, but Peter and Andrew did not argue that they must not tell the Lord because it was a common disease. Do not let Satan get an advantage over you by persuading you to keep back commonplace troubles or sins from your loving Lord.

Beloved, if he counts the hairs of your head, if not a sparrow falls to the ground without his knowledge, depend upon it that your most common trouble will be sympathized in by him. *In **all** their affliction He was afflicted* (emphasis added). It is a great mistake to think you may not carry to your Redeemer the ordinary trials of the day; tell him, yes, tell him all. If your child is only a common sinner, if there is no unusual depravity in him, if your son has never grieved you by perverseness, if your daughter has always been amiable and gentle, do not think there is no need to pray. If it is only a common case of the fever of sin, it will still be deadly in the end unless a balm be found; therefore, tell Jesus about it at once. Do not wait till your son becomes a prodigal, pray at once! Do not delay till your child is at death's door, pray now!

But sometimes a difficulty arises from the other side of the matter. Peter's mother-in-law was attacked by no ordinary fever. We are told it was *a high fever*. The expression used implies that she was burning with fever; and she was intensely debilitated, for she was lying down or prostrate. Now the devil will sometimes insinuate, "It is of no use for you to take such a case to Jesus; your son has acted so shamefully, your daughter is so willful that such a case will never yield to divine grace in answer to prayer." Do not be held back by this wicked suggestion. Our Lord Jesus Christ can rebuke great fevers, and he can lift up those who are broken down and rendered powerless by raging sin. Wonders of grace to God belong. Go and tell Jesus about the case – common or uncommon, ordinary or extraordinary – even as they told Jesus about her.

Now, notice one or two reasons why we think they were driven to tell Jesus about her. I know the great reason, but I will mention the little ones first. I imagine they told Jesus about her, at first, because it was a contagious fever, and it is hardly right to bring a person into a house that has a great fever in it, without letting them know. If there is a great sin in your house, you may perhaps feel in your heart, "How can Jesus Christ come to my house while my drunken husband acts as he does?" Perhaps, more sorrowful still, the wife drinks in secret, and the husband, who sees it with deep regret, says, "How can I expect the Lord to bless us?" Or perhaps some great, sad sin has defiled your child, and you may well say, "How can I expect the Lord to smile on this house? I might as well expect a man to come into a house which is infected with typhus fever." Never mind. Tell Jesus all about it, and he will come, fever or no fever, sin or no sin.

I think perhaps they told him about her because it would be some excuse for the scantiness of the entertainment they were likely to give. What could Peter and Andrew do in preparing a meal? The principal person in the house was ill and could not serve. We poor men are miserable hands at spreading a table; we need a Mary or a Martha to help us, or a Peter's wife, or a Peter's mother-in-law. And so they say with long faces, "Good Master, we would gladly entertain you well, but she who would delight to serve you is sick." How often a family is hindered from entertaining Christ through some sick soul that is in the house. "O Lord, we would have family prayer, but we cannot: the husband will not permit it." "Lord, we would make this household ring with your praises, but we would make one tenant in it so angry that we are obliged to be quiet." "We cannot give you a feast, good Lord; we have to set before you a little as best we can, or the house would grow too hot to hold us." Never mind. Tell Jesus about it, and Jesus will come and dine with you, and turn the impediment into an assistance.

Moreover, the faces of the friends looked so sad. I dare say while in the synagogue Peter had almost forgotten about his mother-in-law because he had been so pleased with the preaching. But when he reached home, the first question when he came through the door was, "How is she now?" The servants replied, "Alas, master, the fever rages terribly." Down went Peter's spirits, a cloud came over his countenance, and he turned to Jesus and cried, "Good Master, I cannot help being sad, even though you are here, for my mother-in-law, whom I love much, is sick with a fever." That sadness may have helped Peter to *speak to Jesus about her*.

But I think the grand reason was this: that our blessed Lord had such a sympathetic heart that he always drew everybody's grief out of them. Men could not keep anything to themselves where he was. He looked like one who was so much like yourself, so much in all points tested like as you are, that you could not help telling him. I exhort you who love my Lord to allow his sweet sympathy to extract from you the grief which wrings your heart, and let it constrain you to tell him of your unconverted relative. He endured the contradiction of sinners against himself, he loved the souls of men, and died for them; therefore, he can tenderly enter into the anxieties which you feel for souls rebellious and hardened in sin. Therefore, *speak to Jesus about her.*

I think, however, that they told him about her because they expected that he would heal her. Tell Jesus about your child, or your friend, who is unconverted, and expect that he will look upon them with an eye of love. He can save. It is like him to do it. He delights to do it. It will honor him to do it. Expect him to do it, and tell him the case of your unregenerate friend this very day.

May I put the question all around? You have each of you, probably, someone left in your family unsaved, and you have said, "I was in hopes that this one would be converted." Have you ever told Jesus about her or about him? Oh, I hope you can answer, "Yes, I have many times"; but it is just possible you have not made an intentional business of it. Begin now, and go upstairs and take time every day to tell the Lord every bit about Jane, or Mary, or Thomas, or John. Wrestle with God, if need be, all night long, and say, *"I will not let you go unless you bless me."* I do not think that many of you will be very long with that trouble to carry when you have in that manner told it to your Lord. This is what they did when Jesus came. *Immediately* they told him of her, for the word *anon* is really in the Greek "immediately." *Immediately* when Christ went in they told him about her, and *immediately* Christ went to heal her.

So the first work that grace brought about in the house was to lead them to pray; and secondly, *this led the Savior to heal their sick.* He went into the chamber, spoke a word, gave a touch, lifted up the sick woman, and she was restored; and the wonderful thing was that she was able to rise from the bed immediately and wait upon them. This never occurs in the cure of a fever, for when a fever goes it leaves the patient very weak, and he needs days and weeks, and sometimes months, to recover his usual strength. But the cures of Christ are perfect; and so at once the patient rose and ministered unto them.

Thus we see that when grace came into that house and worked its cure, *it quite transformed the family.* Look at the difference. There is the poor woman: the patient, shivering, and then again burning, for the fever is on her; she can scarcely lift hand or foot. Now look at her: she is busily serving, with a smiling face, no one more happy or healthy than she. So when God's grace comes, the one who has been the object of the most anxiety becomes the happiest of all; the sinner, saved by sovereign grace, becomes a servant of the Lord; the patient becomes the hostess.

Note the change in the rest of them. They had all been heavy of heart, but now they are rejoicing. There is no anxiety on Peter's face now, Andrew is no more troubled, the skeleton in the closet has disappeared, the sickness has been chased out, and they can all sing a gladsome hymn. The house is changed from a hospital to a church, from an infirmary to a banqueting hall. The Lord himself seems changed too, if change can come over him, for, from a physician, going carefully into a sick room, he comes forth a King who has subdued an enemy, and they all look upon him with wonder and reverence as the mighty Lord, victorious over invisible spirits. Now, I pray God that our household may be transformed and transfigured in this way: our Luz become a Bethel, our valley of Achor a door of hope, our sons of perverseness a seed to serve the Lord. If you yourself get a fullness of grace, the next step is for your families to receive the boundless fullness till not one shall be soul-sick at home, but all shall be happy in the Lord, and all, all shall serve him.

When mercy had once entered, let us see how grace flowed forth from the house. They could not keep the fact hidden indoors that Peter's mother-in-law was cured. I do not know who told about it. Had it been in our day I would have thought it was one of the servants over the fence pickets in the backyard, where they are so fond of talking; or perhaps some friend who came in and was told the news. Perhaps the doctor came around to see the good woman, and, to his utter astonishment, found her up and about the house. He goes to his next patient, and says, "My business will soon come to an end; my patient who had a fever yesterday has been made perfectly whole by one Jesus, a prophet of Nazareth." Somehow or other it oozed out. You cannot keep the grace of God a secret; it will reveal itself. You need not advertise your religion; live it, and other people will talk about it. It is good to speak for Christ whenever you have a fair opportunity, but your life will be the best sermon.

The story went through the town, and a poor man upon crutches said to himself, "I will hobble out to Peter's house!" Another who used to creep through the streets on all fours quietly whispered, "I will go to Peter's house and see." Others, moved by the same impulse, started for the same place. Many who had sick ones said, "We will carry our friends to Peter's house"; so the house grew popular, and lo, around the door there was such a sight as Peter had never seen before. It was a great hospital, all down the street patients were clamoring to see the great prophet. "Almost the whole city came round about the door." And now, what say you to Peter's house? We began with calling it a humble lodging, where a fisherman dwelt; why, it has become a royal hospital, a palace of mercy. Here they come with every kind of complaint, lepers, and lame, and withered, and there is the loving Master, moving here and there till he has healed every one of them. The streets of Capernaum rang that night with songs of joy. There was dancing in the street of a new kind, for the lame man was leaping; and the music that accompanied the dancing was of a new kind too, for then did the tongue of the dumb sing, "Glory be to God." It was out of Peter's house that all this mercy came.

Ah, brethren, I wish to God he would look first on Peter, and then on Peter's mother-in-law, or Peter's child or relative, and then on the whole house, and then from the house cause an influence to stream forth and to be felt by all the neighborhood. "It cannot be so with my home," says one. Why not, dear brother? If you are hampered at all, you are not hampered in God; you are hampered in yourself. "But I live in a place," says one, "where the ministry is lifeless." All the more reason why you should be a blessing to the town. "Oh, but I live where many active Christians are doing a great deal of good." All the more reason why you should be encouraged to do good too. "Oh, but ours is an aristocratic neighborhood." They need the gospel most of all. How few of the great and mighty are ever saved! "Oh, but ours is such a low neighborhood." That is just the place where the gospel is likely to meet with a glad reception, for the poor have the gospel preached to them, and they will hear it.

You cannot invent an excuse which will hold water for a moment: God can make your house to be the center of blessing to all who dwell around it, if you are willing to have it so. But the way to have it so, I have described. First, you yourself must be saved, yourself called to the highest form of life, yourself warmed in heart by the presence of your Master; then your family must be blessed, and after that the widening circle around your habitation. Oh, that it might be so. I know some brethren who, wherever they are, are burning and shining lights; but I know some others who are lamps, and it would be difficult to say whether they are lit or not. I think I see a flicker, but I am not sure. Brethren, aspire to be abundantly useful. Do you wish to live inferior lives? Do you wish to be bound to the disgusting carcass of a dead Christianity? I abhor lukewarmness from my soul, let us be done with it! We have a very short time in which to bear our testimony, for we shall soon be at rest; let us work while we can. The shadows are lengthening, the day is drawing to a close. Up! Brethren, up! If you are to bring jewels to Jesus, if you are to crown his head with many crowns, up, I pray you, and labor for him while you can.

There are some here who are unconverted. I have not spoken to them, but I have tried to set you all speaking to them. Will you do it, or shall I keep you to hear the second half of my sermon? No, I will trust you to deliver it, and may God bless you for Jesus' sake. Amen.

Chapter 9

Fever, and Its Cure

Then He got up and left the synagogue, and entered Simon's home. Now Simon's mother-in-law was suffering from a high fever, and they asked Him to help her. And standing over her, He rebuked the fever, and it left her; and she immediately got up and waited on them. (Luke 4:38-39)

Peter was from Bethsaida, but yet he had a house at Capernaum. Is it not highly probable that he had moved there to be near our Lord's headquarters, to hear everything that he said, to see all his miracles, and to yield him constant attendance and service? I think it was so. This is what we should expect from the Lord's truehearted followers, and I am sad when I remember how many professed disciples of Jesus nowadays act on another principle. When they are removing themselves they do not consider whether they shall be near the house of prayer or the place of usefulness. Though their souls have been fed, and they have declared intense love for the church and the pastor, they nevertheless go away with a light heart to places where there are no means of grace. Should these things be so? In choosing our residence, we should have great respect to its relation to our soul's work and welfare. We should ask, "Shall we be where we can honor our Lord?"

In his house, Simon willingly entertained his mother-in-law, which is presumptive evidence that he was a good man, willing out of love to run the risk of discomfort. We have evidence that his mother-in-law was a good woman, for the moment that she was healed, she arose and ministered unto them, whereas, in too many cases, an invalid and aged person would demand to be waited upon. She was a blessing to any house, for she evidently lent all the strength she had to the work of the family. I know just such women, whose very lives are to minister to others. Happy Peter to have such a mother-in-law! Happy mother-in-law to have such a son-in-law!

Good as the tenants were, sickness came to the house. Capernaum was situated, like several other towns, in that low, marshy district which surrounds the northern part of the Sea of Galilee, near the spot where the Jordan runs into it. There was always a great deal of fever there; and that fever, putting on its very worst form, had come to Peter's house as *a high fever,* and had laid low his excellent mother-in-law, much to the grief of all. However dear you may be to the heart of God, and however near you live to him, you will be liable to sorrow. *"For affliction does not come from the dust, nor does trouble sprout from the ground, for man is born for trouble, as sparks fly upward"* (Job 5:6-7). None of us can hope for entire exemption from affliction; I am not sure that we should wish for it.

But then, it so happened – and it so happens always – that just when the trial came, Jesus came too. It is very beautiful to see the Lord of life close on the track of the fever, ready to deliver his chosen one. When a great affliction comes to a house, a great blessing is coming too. As our tribulations abound, so do our consolations. I have often noticed that when we are exceedingly glad, some ill news will hurry up to calm our excitement. It has happened so to me this very week: returning from a happy meeting, a telegram met me to announce a sorrowful bereavement. On the other hand, when we are exceedingly sorrowful, the Lord, by his Holy Spirit, causes a sense of peace and rest to steal over us and sustain us. How often have I found the divine presence more consciously revealed and more sweetly sustaining in the hour of trouble than at any other season! I would not invite the fever to my house, but if Jesus would come with it, I would not be alarmed at its approach. If we do see our Lord riding on the pale horse, we will welcome the horse for the sake of its rider. Come, Lord Jesus, come how you will, but permit not the trial to come alone!

When Jesus came, they told him of her. Make a practice of telling the Lord about all your family concerns. Bring sicknesses and other troubles to your best friend. Do it at family prayer, but do it also at your bedside alone. If Jesus has come to stay with you, he will not hold himself aloof from your anxieties. He comes with his great sympathetic heart to be afflicted in your afflictions. Keep no secret from him, since he keeps none from you; for *the secret of the Lord is for those who fear Him.* So Peter and the rest told Jesus of the good woman who was bedridden with fever, and at once the Lord Jesus went into the room, and brought his divine power to bear upon the disease, that she might be at once restored. He stood over her; he rebuked the fever; he took her by the hand and lifted her up, and in a moment the fever was gone, and she was not only well, but also strong.

> **Make a practice of telling the Lord about all your family concerns.**

You have heard this incident preached from before, but not in the way in which I shall use it. It is a very singular thing that, as far as I know, in the whole range of homiletics there is not one in which this cure of the fever is treated as the other healing miracles have been. The other miraculous cures have been legitimately regarded by preachers of the Word as types of the removal of certain forms of sin. When we preach about the leper, we talk to you concerning great sin and grievous defilement. When we consider the story of Lazarus, who had been dead, we perceive that every point of his resurrection bristles with spiritual teaching. If it is so in other miracles, why not in this one? Why is one miracle to be looked upon as instructive as to spiritual and moral truth, and another be left unused? I shall use this miracle of the healing of the fevered one for ourselves, since it may be that some of us are mentally or spiritually sick with a fever. There is a fever of soul, which comes even upon gracious people, which only Christ can heal. Oh, that he may heal us now!

Here will be the run of my discourse. First, *spiritual fevers are common;* secondly, *they arise from several causes;* thirdly, *these are mischievous in their action;* and fourthly, *there is One who can cure these fevers.* Oh, that I may be helped so to speak of this spiritual disease at this time, that while you hear my voice, you may also feel my Master's touch, and go your way restored from your fever!

Let me first remind you that spiritual fevers are very common. *A fever begins with a kind of restlessness.* The patient cannot be quiet, nor be at ease in any position. He is not pleased with anything for more than a moment. He cannot help it; he is tossed to and fro, and is like the troubled sea. He suspects everybody, and has confidence in nothing. Are there not many who are in that condition with regard to spiritual things? Their religion is a question, rather than a doctrine; an experiment, and not an experience. Their own interest in Christ is a grave anxiety, rather than an assured delight. They believe the promise, but cannot grasp it for themselves, so as to feel sure and happy. A sermon full of good cheer does not afford them a cup of comfort. They are so feverish that they settle to nothing. No promise, no truth, no heavenly gift can yield them rest: they are tossed up and down like the locust.

This restlessness affects them with regard to worldly things too: they are always anxious, doubtful, and fearful. There is that excellent woman Martha. She is here today, but she has had a task to tear herself away from the washing and mending; and while she has been sitting here, she has been wondering all the while whether she put the guard before the fire when she came out. She has felt three or four times in her pocket for her keys. She is half afraid that an accident will happen to the baby before she gets back. She is anxious about everything she can think of, and anxious about some things she has not thought of. Will her husband be home before she gets back? How will he be? Will he like his supper? Will the children all be well tomorrow? Evidently she has the domestic fever upon her, and rest is out of the question. She must worry and fidget; there is no consoling her. I know what it is as a minister to feel very feverish about the characters and proceedings of the members of the church. I have been told that farmers are very liable to the weather fever. It is either too wet or too dry. There may be good times for the root crops; but then, it is bad for the corn. Merchants have the speculative fever, and workmen the strike fever. Some of you tradesfolk are wonderfully feverish in reference to your shop and your stocktaking. Will you, after all, have a good season, and make a fair profit? When a man falls into that state, although we do not call in a doctor, there is great need to call in the heavenly physician.

A Christian in good, sound spiritual health, is calm, quiet, peaceful, happy, and full of rest, for he is obedient to that sweet verse of the psalm: *Rest in the Lord, and wait patiently for Him.* This restlessness is a sign of the times, but it is a great pity that it should afflict the people of God.

Some folks with this fever are troubled with the *burning heat of irritability.* They take offense where none is intended. You cannot put your words in the right order to satisfy them. Members of churches who get into this irritable state are always imagining that they have enemies all around them. Everybody has not been quite respectful to their royal highnesses; they treasure up little slights, and feel highly indignant. I know more people with this fever than I should like to mention. It is a happy thing to live with a brother who is spiritually and mentally sound, for then you may speak freely, and you need not be afraid of being misunderstood; but feverish folk make you an offender for a word or a look. They are grieved because you did not see them, or did see them: either way you are wrong. One feels that he is like a man walking among eggs: he has to be careful, even to a painful degree. Let us be gentle with the irritable brother. He cannot help it, poor man! It is not the man so much as it is the fever that is on him.

The influence of fever is seen in other ways. It is *intermittent,* and it makes the patient *change from hot to cold.* Feverish persons love a religion of excitement. They are eager and impatient, omit repentance, and leap into a false security. Their zeal is not according to knowledge, and so it is as fierce as the blaze of thorns under a pot, and it dies out as soon. What haste they make! Everything must be done immediately; the patient waiting of faith is too slow for them. They are determined to drive the church before them and drag the world after them; but to plod on in scriptural ways they cannot endure. We like to see the healthy heat of earnestness, but theirs is the burning heat of passion. This fever heat soon turns to a chill, and they shiver with dislike of the very thing they cried about so loudly. They are as cold as they were hot; and again they turn to be as hot as they were cold. A strange fever is upon them, and you know not where to find them. The steady warmth of vital principle, intelligent faith, true love for Christ, and zeal for the conversion of souls has little in common with the fever of fanaticism. May God grant that we may always have the warmth of healthy life, but may we be saved from being delirious one day and lethargic the next! Religious inflammation is the dangerous counterfeit of holy zeal. Be as hot as you will, but do not turn cold directly, or else we shall tremble for you.

A worse kind of fever, perhaps, is that which shows itself in *thirst* of different kinds. Some suffer from the yellow fever of greed: they thirst for gold water, and the more they drink, the more the thirst consumes them. They rise up early, they sit up late, they eat the bread of carefulness, and all they long for is to gain and hoard; but the love of Jesus is not near their hearts. They are all hack and hurry, toil and turmoil, woe and worry. The deadly yellow fever is upon them – they must lay up many goods for many years, and add field to field till they are left alone in the earth. God save his people from even a touch of this fever!

Some are struck with the scarlet fever of ambition. They must be everybody. Some would be great, greater, greatest, and then greater still, always sighing for the preeminence, like Diotrephes. Ambition, kept in due check, may be right enough, but when it rises to fever heat, it is a great sin. The man does not enjoy what he has because he is lusting for more; and meanwhile, he treads down his brethren and becomes high-minded and unkind. While anyone is still a little higher than him, he is envious and malicious. May the Lord cure us of these fevers, if we have even the smallest trace of them!

Alas! I have to mention one other fever, which is a kind of gastric fever, *a fever of the stomach*. It comes to men who have degraded themselves below the brutes by intoxication. When they seek to abstain from and quit the cup, a drink-fever hinders them. Some imagine that it is an easy thing to escape from drunkenness, but it is not so. Those who are now true children of God have given us an awful description of the hankering which came upon them months after they had given up the drink. Often it seemed to them nothing but a miracle that they kept clear of the temptation: they felt as if they must drink or die. O dear friends, have great pity on the drunkard in his struggle to escape. Help him all you can by words of encouragement, and especially by the grand encouragement of your own example, for, believe me, it is a horrible fever, and happy is he who has never felt it. If any of you have it upon you, look to almighty grace for deliverance; for if you look to anything short of this, I fear you will go back to your sin.

Yet one more fever I would mention. There is one which I may well call *brain fever* – a very common disease nowadays. Persons cannot be satisfied with the old doctrines of the gospel; they must have something new. They do not know that in theology nothing new is true, and nothing true is new. God has given us a faith which he once for all delivered unto the saints, with no intent that it should ever be changed. Do you think that revelation is imperfect, and that we are to improve upon it? After all, then, it is not God's revelation that we are to believe, but our own deductions therefrom, and our own improvements thereupon. God forbid that we should fall under such a delusion!

Very many young men – and I dare say young women too, though I do not so often meet with them – have begun to feel that they must *think* which, also, we should be glad for them to do. But they dream that they must think their own thoughts, and they will not submit their thoughts to the instruction of the Spirit of God. This is a vain thought. They claim that they may think as they please; and so it comes to pass that their thoughts are not God's thoughts. They diverge more and more from the eternal truth of God, till they wander among the dark mountains of error, and perish in utter infidelity. God keep us from this. If this fever is upon any one of you, may the cooling hand of the Holy Spirit, and the sobering influence of a divine experience, bring you back to spiritual and mental health again. These fevers are as common as they are fatal. If you, dear hearer, have not suffered from them, many others have done so, and we are anxious for their cure; therefore, we would desire to bring them to Jesus, who can rebuke the fever and heal the sick ones.

> God has given us a faith which he once for all delivered unto the saints, with no intent that it should ever be changed.

Secondly, these fevers arise from many causes. Peter's mother-in-law may have been struck with fever through the undrained and boggy spots around the Sea of Galilee, especially where the Jordan makes a marsh. *She dwelt in a low spot,* where the air was full of malaria, and the fever pounced upon her. Ah, Christian people! If you live below your privileges, if you live in the marshland of worldliness, if prayer is neglected, if the Bible is not read, if the great truths of the gospel do not fill your meditations, if you sojourn much among ungodly folk, and make them your companions, then you are living in a low situation, where you will get one or another of these fevers before long. If you climb the mountains of confidence in God, and dwell near to God, and rest your souls upon him, the fever will soon vanish; but if you continue in the hollows of unbelief, and the damp places of worldliness, you will grow more and more anxious and restless, and will thirst for evil things. You who dwell in the misty lowlands doubt your own love for Jesus. If you climbed the hills of joy, and dwelt on the heights of fellowship, you would know your love for God, and find it daily growing. The sunlight of his countenance is a sure cure for the fever of anxiety. Abide with him, and the heat of anxiety will depart, and your irritability will disappear, and you will be calm and joyful.

A second great cause of spiritual fever is *allowing things to stagnate*. The moment the sanitary authorities cut drains, and let the waters run out of the land, and carry away the filth, the fever begins to abate. Stagnant water breeds miasma, and fever is sure to come. When the waters are no longer putrid, but have free course, then the source of fever is taken away. How many people get into a feverish state through having everything stagnant! You do not teach in the Sunday school: your teaching power is stagnant. You never go out to the village station to preach: your talking power is stagnant. You have nobody to pray for: your intercessory power is stagnant. Everything about you is still and stale. You have nothing to live for, nothing to do; and therefore your whole being is shut up within itself, and this breeds mischief. The Lord help you to cut a good wide drain, and let your life run out to some useful purpose, instead of hoarding it up by selfishness. Spiritual fever soon disappears before holy, unselfish activity.

Fevers, again, come on through excessive heat. In countries where the temperature rises high, fever is more common and fatal than with us. The white man dies, and even the black man finds it hard to live in parts of Africa. I fear that life in London is growing very much like the tropical regions. Our forefathers took things rather more coolly than we do. In Cromwell's time, a writer tells us that he walked all down Cheapside in the early morning, and found all the blinds down, because at every house they were having family prayer. Where will you go to find such a state of things in this burning age? You are up in the morning, and at it; and all day long you are at it, and at it, and at it. Little rest is given to our minds, and yet we want holy rest. We need to sit at Jesus' feet with Mary, and because we do not do so, the burden and heat of the day are forceful upon our spiritual constitutions, and we are not strong as we need to be.

But, worst of all, *fever is often born of filth.* I suppose that even excessive heat would not produce it if it were not for decaying matter which, in rotting, gives out evil vapors and deadly gases. There is nothing more putrid in the natural world than sin is in the moral world. Flee from sin as you would from a reeking dunghill of rottenness. I charge you, children of God, be clean in yourselves and your surroundings. *Purify yourselves, you who carry the vessels of the Lord* (Isaiah 52:11). It is hard to avoid contact with evil in these days, but yet we must aim at it. Our public walls disgust us with indecencies of the most blaring kind: they make us blush for the times.

We can, however, keep ourselves from the resorts of the frivolous, the vicious, and the drunken; and I implore you, as you love the Lord, and as you desire to be healthy in his sight, stand not in the way of sinners, nor sit in the seat of the scorners. Run not with the multitude to do evil. Come out from among them; be separate; touch not the unclean thing, for then God will be a Father unto you, and you shall be his sons and daughters. The corruption which reeks around us has the dread tendency to breed fevers in our minds of the most perilous kind; we must, therefore, use our utmost endeavors to keep ourselves disinfected by the grace of God.

> **Flee from sin as you would from a reeking dunghill of rottenness.**

Fever also comes from overcrowding. Where people are closely packed together in their sleeping places, breathing exhausted air, there disease lurks as in its chosen lair. I am afraid that most of us get too crowded by fellowship with men: conversing with them from morning to night, working with them, dealing with them in business, and thus learning their ways and catching their spirit. Oh, to get into the purer atmosphere of heaven, and to be alone with God! In the spiritual realm we find space and air enough for a soul to breathe freely. Where God manifests himself to us, we are refreshed with breezes from the eternal hills. Why are we wearied with man's talk, or with women's chat, when conversing with God would revive our spirits? Oh, to be left by men, and quiet with God! Amid this crowd we find our souls suffocating; but when we are on the mount of God we breathe freely and feel revived.

Not to leave out any one thing which may instruct us, I would remind you that *fevers are often caused by poor diet.* Persons have not enough to eat, and the fever germs bear fruit in their weakness. With many Christians the rule seems to be one spiritual meal a week. Sunday morning is the occasion for baiting the religious horse. Your very respectable Christian person goes out to worship on Sunday morning, but at no other time. What does he do on Sunday afternoon? This witness says nothing. What does he do on Sunday evening? He is at home taking his ease. At a prayer meeting, some time ago, one brother prayed that the Lord would bless those who were at home "on beds of sickness *and on sofas of wellness.*" The last words were unexpected, but very needful. Certain of our friends practice the art of waiting at home; but I fear they do not divide the spoil.

As to prayer meetings and weeknight lectures, these are regarded rather as tasks than privileges by many professors. They live on one meal a week. Would any of you who are doing this oblige me with a trial of this regimen in reference to your bodies? Will you only eat on a Sunday morning? You shall take what you please at that one meal, and consume as much as you can of it; but you must have only that one meal till next week. Do you decline the experiment? I think you are wise. I should not expect to see you here often to report your experience. I feel sure you would break through the regulation before it had reached its full result. Therefore, I pray you, do not carry out the experiment of spiritual starvation, lest you die in the operation.

This neglect of heavenly food brings many Christians into so low a state that spiritual fever readily fastens upon them. Alas! many have a poor spiritual diet. Spiritual meals nowadays, when they are taken, do not amount to much. In many a place where Christ was preached by the good old man, who is now in heaven, you will find that anything else is held forth except the Lord Jesus. Your cultured gentleman sickens at the idea of preaching about the precious blood. He calls the cardinal doctrine of the atonement "the theology of the shambles." Shame on his profane tongue! He is ashamed to speak of original sin, or the new birth, or to tell men that if they are not saved, they will be cast into hell. He is too refined to speak plain truth. You may eat a thousand meals of his sort of meat before you will know that you have had a mouthful; for it is all light as air, and unsubstantial as froth. Such wind can never satisfy a hungering soul; but it can starve it down so low that disease preys upon it.

Some become fevered not so much by what they do themselves, but by being in *contact with others who are full of the disease,* for it is exceedingly contagious. I can bear witness to that. It has been my lot to deal with the fevers of doubt, depression, anxiety, and despair, and it is hard to deal with these without catching them. I remember that one day I saw several mournful cases of depression. I will not say that the patients ought to have been in an asylum; but I am sure that many in those places are as reasonable as those I conversed with. They were sadly doubting, fearing, trembling, and dreading; and it was no light work to treat their unhappy cases. I tried to comfort them, and I hope that I succeeded in a measure; but by the time that I had borne the burdens of a half dozen of them, I needed comfort myself. It is not easy to lift others up without finding yourself exhausted. I went over all the gospel arguments for salvation by faith, and I heard their objections, and pressed the truth upon them, and when they went away smiling, I stayed behind to pray God to make the work effectual, and also to lift up the light of his countenance upon *me,* for I needed to be filled again after pouring out my soul for others.

The fever of depression may be caught while we are acting as surgeons to other fevered ones. If you live with a friend who is always playing on the minor key, you will find your own music growing mournful. If you have companions in life who are nervous, fretful, fearful, melancholy – or, what is worse, full of doubts about God – you will be likely to be warped as they are, and you will soon feel that the sunlight has gone out of your life. What must you do? Run away from these sorrowful ones? By no means. But you must seek more grace, so that, instead of being dragged down by them, you may draw them upward to God and to brighter things. Be filled with spiritual life, and then you will survive your contact with the feeble and the diseased. I could not help mentioning this, for to me it is a frequent cause of fever, and I wish that I could rise far above it.

Thirdly, and as briefly as I can, this fever, in any of its forms, is mischievous. What does it do? Well, fever *puts you altogether out of order*. You cannot precisely say where a fever begins or ends, or in what organ it operates most powerfully, for it puts the whole system out of gear. Nothing is right. You feel as if you cannot sit, or lie, or be quiet in any position. You cannot do anything, and yet you must be doing something. Now, when a soul gets into the fever of unbelief, and fear, and anxiety, it is in general disorder. The prayer is fevered; the song languishes; the patience fails; the service drags. The mind is like a harp whose strings are out of tune. It is a mischievous thing, this fever – mischievous to every faculty.

And then *it brings pain and misery*. In the commencement of a fever, pain is usually felt in the joints and other parts of the body. If I am fearful and anxious, I am in mental pain. If I am doubting and dreading, I am in pain. If I am fretty, irritable, short-tempered, and grumbling, I must have pain; and therefore it is an evil thing to be overtaken by a spiritual fever.

Mental fever *takes away his beauty* from the Christian. A man who has a fever has his features pinched and drawn. A practiced doctor can tell when a patient has the fever by the very look on his face. Looking at his eyes, and other features, he says, "This man has a typhoid upon him. I am sure of it." Are there not some Christians who do not look as they used to look? For they are ill-tempered, or timid, or fretful, or hasty, and all through the inward fever. Their voice has lost the joyful note it used to have, and their whole demeanor is dreary. The hallelujahs have gone; the hosannas have died out. The Lord would have his people beautiful and gladsome. He made them that they might show forth his praise. It is no small evil when the heat of spiritual fever dries up the moisture of our graces, and turns our comeliness into corruption.

This mental heat brings with it *weariness and weakness*. The man is a Christian, but he is not much of a Christian. He lives, but he does not grow, nor exhibit strength. What a difference there is between the able-bodied worker and the invalid! Here is a railway cutting to be made through a hill, and we need a number of working men to do it. They tell me that we can get a hundred men at once if we appeal to the Hospital for Consumptives. But we do not see the wisdom of the advice. Poor fellows, what a misery it would be to see them doing their little best with pain and labor! I had rather not be the leader of such a band. Give me a company of stout English laborers, with bone and muscle. Why, the mountain flies before their spades like the waters before the blast of the north wind. The road is cut through the mountain, and the men are gone to perform similar wonders elsewhere. We want, in these days, Christian men with stamina in them. What work healthy souls will do! But when they catch fever in their souls, what painful and futile efforts they make!

Dear friends, it is to be feared that *those who give way to fever may drift into delirium* by and by, for fevers often lead to that. My good friend who begins complaining just a little, does not know that he will grow to be one of the most obstinate grumblers in the world. My good sister yonder, who is only a little nervous and fretty, does not know into what an abyss of unbelief she will yet plunge. If you say one word against God, there is no reason why you should not say two; and if you say two, the devil will soon teach you to say twenty, till at last you rave at the Lord God. Oh, that we could be silent before him, in holy calm and peace! We should then escape that delirium of rebellious dread into which so many are hurried.

If by God's grace we are delivered from this fever, *it may leave behind it sad remains.* Any doctor will tell you that fevers are to be dreaded not only for what they are, but also for what they leave behind them. When a man is cured of a fever, he may still be injured for the rest of his life; and if you and I do not keep quiet before God, and calm and happy, but begin to get anxious, and willful, and covetous, and ambitious, we may hurt ourselves seriously for all time; and, it may be, even on our deathbed we shall look back with sorrow to that day of unbelief when we grieved the Lord and lost his presence. The Lord keep us from these fevers in every degree!

I must also remind you of one thing more, beloved: *this disease,* as I have said, *is catching.* I brought this fact forward under our second head, but I must mention it yet again. If some of you could fret, and trouble, and worry yourselves, and did not at the same time injure others, it might not so much matter; but the sad fact is, there are some Christians who drag others down into their own wretchedness. You spoil the joys of the saints. They are willing to comfort you, but you ought not to be so ready to cause them anxiety. Some of you are enough to give the fever of despondency to a whole parish. God's ministers are willing to comfort you, but they ought not to be called upon to spend so much time in entering into your case. It is a dreadful waste of time and thought – this looking after the fevered ones.

When an army has to carry half its number in ambulances, it takes nearly the other half to carry them, and no fighting can be done. The cruelties of war are great; but I am told that the aim is now to be, not to kill the opposite party, but to wound them. If you kill a man, he counts one as a loss to the other side; but if you wound a man, and another man is called out to look after him, that counts as a loss of two from the fight. This is the sort of craft whereby Satan injures the host of God. He does not kill off some of you by leading you into gross sin, but he wounds you, so that you need more than one to look after you; and thus the strength of the army of salvation is greatly diminished. I ought to be spending my strength in winning souls; instead of which I have to look after you who have the fever. I am content to be a nurse, but I had rather be winning souls.

Lastly, there is one who can cure the fever. I am afraid that I have given rather a sad description, and I am sorry that some of you have been obliged to say, "However sad, it is true of us." But observe, dear friends, the cure, which is not brought about by medicine, or surgery, or any profound system of the doctors. The cure lies here. The poor patient lies flat in her bed. We read that she was *lying sick in bed with a fever.* She could not therefore sit up, much less rise from the bed. When she opened her eyes and looked up, she saw the Lord Jesus Christ *standing over her.* O fevered soul! Open your eyes today, and see Jesus standing over you. With tender love and infinite compassion he looks down upon you; he shields you, thinks of you, and watches over you for good. He will help you; therefore, fear not. Over you today he broods, as does an eagle over its young. Jehovah-Jesus bows over you with fullness of love and power. In your present trouble, fear, and depression of spirit, Jesus stands over you, and his eye and his heart are upon you.

Then, next, to her great surprise, *the Lord touched her.* Dear Master, touch the fevered ones today. Oh, to feel that he is a real man like yourself, your brother, very near to you! This is the touch which will drive out the fever. I love the old verse:

> A man there was, a real man,
> > Who once on Calvary died;
> That same dear man exalted sits
> > High at his Father's side.

The Lord Jesus is a real man, and so he touches you in your feeble and suffering nature, and he seems to say, "In all your afflictions I am afflicted." When saints are in the furnace, one like unto the Son of God is there with them. They are sufferers, but he is *a man of sorrows and acquainted with grief.* The Lord give you to feel the touch of the true humanity of Christ!

We read that, when our Lord had touched her, *He rebuked the fever.* Your feverishness deserves his rebuke. Oh, that he would command it to be gone! Oh, that he would say today, "Be gone, unbelief! Be gone, anxiety! Be gone, fretfulness! Be gone, doubt and fear!" The winds and the waves heard his rebuke, and from their noise and clamor they hushed themselves to a great calm. Oh, that Jesus would come now, and speak to your feverishness, and you shall be as happy as the birds of paradise. I had a great trouble last night. I will not tell you what it was – a great trouble to my heart; but this morning I had a great joy, which I will tell to you.

It is this note: "Dear Sir, I feel so happy to tell you that the Lord has pardoned a poor outcast of society. I got into your place in a crowd, hoping nobody would see me. I had been out all night, and was miserable. While you were preaching about the leper, my whole life of sin rose up before me. I saw myself worse than the leper, cast away by everybody. There is not a sin I was not guilty of. *As you went on I looked straight away to Jesus.* A gracious answer came: 'Your sins, which are many, are forgiven.' I never heard any more of your sermon. I felt such joy to think that Jesus died even for a poor harlot. Long before you get this letter I trust to be on the way to my dear home I ran away from. Do please pray for me, that I may be kept by God's almighty power. I can never thank you enough for bringing me to Jesus" – and so on. If it had not been for that bit about going home, I might have had some doubt about it; but when a fallen girl goes home to her father and mother, it is a safe case. This gives me joy; do you wonder? To see souls saved is heaven to me. I find that my Lord has a gracious way of laying on a plaster where he makes a sore. If the heart be heavy with grief, he can balance it with consolation.

The next thing Jesus did was to raise her up. You must have felt, when lying very ill, as if you were buried in the bed. So the Savior gave his hand to her, and he *raised her up*. She did not think that she could rise, but with his aid she sat up. Then he gave her an instant cure, and at the same time renewed her strength. No trace of fever remained. She was perfectly well. Her instinct, as a matronly woman and head of the household, was to rise at once to prepare a meal for her Benefactor and his disciples.

Oh, that you doubting ones, you fevered ones, might at once be cured and lifted up, so that you would immediately set about serving the Lord and ministering to those around you! Come, let us be as happy as ever we can be, and as useful as it lies in our power to be, and may the fever never visit any one of us again! On the contrary, as you go home, trip over the pavements with a sense of spiritual health; and when you get home, say at once, "I must minister unto Jesus. He has driven out my cares and fears, and soothed my mind, and therefore out of love I will spend and be spent to his praise." God bless you, for the Savior's sake! Amen.

Chapter 10

The Ministry of Gratitude

And she immediately got up and waited on them.
(Luke 4:39)

Peter's mother-in-law had been sick with a great fever, and had been restored by the touch of the Savior's hands, and by the power of the Savior's word. The grace of God does not secure us from trial. The house of Peter and of Andrew (for it was shared by them both) was a highly favored one; the grace of God had passed by many other houses, but had selected this for its dwelling place; and yet in that abode there was great sickness – the mother-in-law lay sick of a fever, and was near death. This was no small grief to the household, but that grief was for their lasting benefit. God loves his chosen too well to let them always live without the rod. If he loved us less he might allow us undiluted pleasure, but the love of our wise Father is too great to deprive us of the sacred benefits of affliction. Sickness came to that house not as an enemy, but as a friend; for it was the means whereby Christ's great power was made manifest to that family, and through his power, his love.

The mother-in-law could never have been so distinguished a subject of the Redeemer's power if she had not been prostrated with fever. The malaria from the marshes around the city occasioned her being made a trophy of our Lord's divine energy; the worst of ills are often the black horses upon which the very best of blessings ride to us. It was no small honor to Peter that his house became the headquarters of the Savior. The sick thronged the door; as the sun went down, and the Sabbath was over, the multitude brought persons afflicted with all manner of diseases and panted to reach that favored dwelling to lay them before the Lord. The healing power which had displayed itself within, poured forth from the house like a mighty flood, and all who drank of it were restored; that house contained the springhead, and was beyond measure honored thereby. Surely for many a year that house would be one of the most notable in the city – surely it would be called the House of the Great Physician. It would not be like that ancient house in Antwerp that was detestable because it was the den of the Inquisition, but this one would be dear to many of the healed ones and their sons, as the Hospital of Mercy, the Palace of Blessing.

Peter among the apostles is singularly honored, for everything about him was in some way or another connected with a miracle. In regard to his person – it was by a miracle that he had walked the waters; it was by a miracle that he had been saved from drowning when the Savior stretched out his hand and bid him to stand fast upon the liquid wave. There was a miracle in connection with his boat, for it was from that boat that the miraculous haul of fish had been taken, and it was filled so full that it began to sink, and Peter knelt down and adored the Savior.

There was a miracle in connection with Peter's rusty sword; he cut off with it the ear of the high priest's servant, but the Master healed the wound that his rash defender made. And here, in this case, there was a miracle performed upon his relative – his mother-in-law was restored from a great fever by the almighty power of the Lord Jesus Christ. Every Christian man should be ambitious to have the hand of God connected with everything that he has, so that when he looks upon his house he may see God's providence in giving it to him; when he looks upon the garments that he wears he may see them to be the garb of love, and may view the food upon his table as the daily gift of divine charity. In looking back upon his whole biography, the believer may see bright spots where the presence of God flames forth and makes the humblest circumstances to be illustrious; but, above all,

> **Every Christian man should be ambitious to have the hand of God connected with everything that he has.**

it ought to be his prayer that God's hand should be very conspicuous in connection with his relatives, that of every one of them it might be said, "The Lord restored her," or "The Lord gave him spiritual life in answer to my prayer." May husband, wife, children, servants, all receive healing from the beloved physician; may our whole household be *holy to the Lord,* and may all sing for joy, because the Lord has done great things for them by which we are glad.

The occurrence about which we are to speak happened on a Sabbath day. Sabbaths were generally Christ's great chosen field days to break down the superstitiously rigid observance of the Sabbath among the Pharisees, and because it seemed as a holy day to be peculiarly adapted for the display of the greatest works of the holy Savior. It was a Sabbath day, and the poor patient was probably lying there complaining in her soul that she could not go to the synagogue, or mingle with the people where prayer was accustomed to being made. Perhaps her fever had reduced her to such a state that she was quite unable to remember Christ the healer, and unable to breathe a prayer to him. But Peter and Andrew went to him, and told the case, and implored him to come and heal her.

It is a blessing for you, my friend, even though you be sick in soul, to have saints for your relatives – to have some in the household who will remember you in prayer, and speak into the ear of Christ on your behalf. If through despair or depression of spirit you cannot pray for yourself, happy are you that there are compassionate friends who will speak unto the King on your behalf. One Christian in a family may bring a great blessing to it, but here were two, for Simon and his brother Andrew were both here; and if two of you are agreed as touching any one thing concerning the Master's kingdom, it shall be done unto you. The two prevailed with the Savior, and, on that Sabbath day, when the patient little dreamed it, the Savior came to her lowly room, and, standing over her in infinite pity, he first spoke a royal word of rebuke to the disease, and then, lifting her up gently in his own kind and familiar manner she found herself perfectly restored to health. What love she must have felt for her gracious benefactor! Little wonder is it that thankfulness glowed in her heart, and being healed, she rose at once and began to serve her healer. Her ministering commenced from the very hour of her recovery. Of that ministering we are about to speak. *She immediately got up and waited on them.*

Now, the fact that this restored woman began at once to minister to Christ and to his disciples proves, first, the certainty of her cure; and there are no better ways of proving the thoroughness of our conversion than by conduct similar to hers. Suppose now, in order to prove that this woman was really restored, we were critically to examine the *modus operandi* of Christ, the way in which he usually worked, and show that on this occasion he operated in the regular orthodox fashion. Suppose the Master had been accustomed, as he was not, to using one set of ceremonies over everybody whom he healed, and we were to say, "Well, he has done this, that, and the other, as he is accustomed to doing; therefore, the woman is healed." It would not be at all conclusive reasoning; yet this is the reasoning of a great many.

This child was baptized, this young person was confirmed, and afterwards took the sacrament, and consequently this individual is regenerated in baptism, and established in grace, and so on. The ceremonials are correct, and therefore the work is done. Some may believe such reasoning; I marvel that they should. But to us it seems that there is a far better way of testing whether persons have grace or not; and, moreover, if these aforesaid baptismally regenerated people and sacramentally confirmed people live in sin like other people, it appears to us that they have none of the grace of God in them, however much they may pretend to have received it. If the woman had still been hot with fever and had all the symptoms of her disease continued in her, it would have profited nothing to have said, "This has been done and the other"; the woman would not have been healed. And if men live like unregenerate sinners, depend upon it that the work of the Holy Spirit is not in them.

Suppose the patient had lain there and had begun to talk about how she felt, how much better she was, what a strange sensation passed through her when the Savior rebuked the disease, and how strangely well she felt; yet if she had not risen up, but had lain there still, there would have been no evidence of her restoration, or at any rate none that you or I could judge of. So when persons tell us that they have felt great changes of heart, that they know they are renewed because they enjoy this, and love that, and hate the other, we are very hopeful, and desire to believe what they say. But, after all, trees are known by their fruits, and converted people, while they will themselves know their inward experience, cannot convince us by it; we must see their outward ministerings for Christ. If their actions be holy, if their lives be purified, then shall we know – but not till then – that their nature is renewed.

Suppose this good woman, still lying upon her bed, had begun to say, "Well, I hope I am healed," and had begun to express some feeble expectation that one day she would be able to exercise the functions of health – we could not have known that she was restored. Something more was needed than mere hopes and expectations. Or suppose she had leaped out of her bed in wild excitement, rushed down the street, and performed strange antics. It would have been no proof that she was recovered, but it would have made us feel sure that she was in a delirium, and that the fever was still strong upon her. So when we see persons inactive as to holiness, we cannot believe that they are saved; or when we see them full of empty excitement about religion, but not serving God in the common acts of life, we think them to be in the delirium of a sinful presumption, but cannot regard them as healed by the cooling, calming hand of the Great Physician, who, when he puts out the fever, restores the soul to quiet and peace. The woman gave a much better proof than any of these could be. This leads us to remark that the only irresistible proof with onlookers of a person being spiritually healed by Christ must be found in the change in his conduct, and especially in his living from this point on to serve Christ and to be obedient to him. This is the test and nothing short of it.

When we see holy living in the man who was once a gross offender, we are quite sure that Christ has healed him, because the man begins to do what he could not have done before. Perhaps this poor fevered woman might have made some shift to have done something for the Savior, but the unconverted man is dead in trespasses and sin. He may go through forms of religion, but real holiness is far above and out of his sight; he cannot obey the law of God; his nature is set against it; he is unable to walk in the way of God's commandments; and therefore, when we see him doing so, we exclaim, "This is the finger of God. God has healed that man, or else he would not be able to live as he is now living." Besides, the unconverted man before conversion hates holiness. He is disinclined to it, so that in his case, when his life becomes pure and upright, when he spends and is spent in the service of Jesus Christ, you know that this must be the work of the Holy Spirit in his soul, for nothing else could have changed his nature but the same Omnipotence which first of all created him. God's hand is in that conversion, which is proved by the holiness of the man's outward character.

Besides this, while the sinner is disinclined to everything that is holy, we know that he especially despises the Savior, and thinks little of his people. Consequently, when a man is brought to serve the Savior and to be willing to do good to the children of God for Christ's sake, there is a sure mark that a miracle has been worked in him which has touched the secret springs of his being, and altogether transformed him. The woman's rising up to minister to our Lord was a sure sign of returned health, and the change of outward character which leads a man to devote himself to the service of Christ is even more infallibly a proof of true salvation.

I want you to note however, dear friends, for a moment, the nature of the acts which this restored woman performed, because they are symbolic of the best form of actions by which to judge a person's being renewed. Her duties were humble ones. She was probably the head of the household, and she began at once to discharge the duties of a housewife: duties unostentatious and commonplace. Many persons who profess to be converted aspire at once to preaching; a pulpit for them is the main thing, and a large congregation is their ambition. They must do some great thing, and occupy the chief seat in the synagogue. But this good woman did not think of preaching; women are always best when they don't; but she thought of washing Christ's feet and preparing him necessary food, which was her proper business. To these kind but simple actions she devoted herself. Attention to humble duties is a better sign of grace than an ambition for lofty and elevated works. There is probably far more grace in the loving service of a mother towards Christ in bringing up her children in the fear of God, than there might be if she were well known as taking a leading part in great public movements.

There may be more service for Christ done by a workman in discharging his duties as such, and trying to do good to his fellow workmen, than if he aspired to become a great leader of the minds and thoughts of others.

Of course there are exceptions, for glorious was Deborah and great shall be her name in Israel, and those who are sent of God to lead his church shall not be without their reward; but even then when they have to look for personal evidences of grace, they never dare say, "We know that we are passed from death unto life because we preach the gospel," for they remember that Judas did the same. They never say, "We are confident of salvation because God has worked wonders by us," for they remember that the son of perdition had the same distinction. But they fall back upon the same evidences which prove the truth of the religion of humbler people; they rejoice in testimonies common to all the elect. "We know that we have passed from death unto life because we love the brethren." The humbler graces and duties are the best tests. Hypocrites mimic all public duties, but the private and concealed life of true godliness they cannot counterfeit; and because they cannot "do so with their enchantments," we feel like the men of Egypt, that *"this is the finger of God."*

Remember, too, that this good woman attended to home duties. She did not go down the street a hundred yards off to glorify Christ; she, I dare say, did that afterwards, but she began at home: charity begins there and so should devotion. That is the best religion which is most at home, at home. Grace which smiles around the family hearth is grace indeed. If your own household cannot see that you are godly, depend upon it that nobody else can; and if your parents or children have grave doubts about the sincerity of your religion, I am afraid you ought to have grave doubts about it yourself. Peter's mother-in-law ministered to Christ at home, and that was clear evidence of her being restored to health; and in your case it will be the best witness to your conversion if you serve Jesus in the bosom of your family and make your house the dwelling place of all that is kind and good and holy.

She attended to suitable duties, duties consistent with her sex and condition. She did not try to be what God had not made her, but she did what she could. She attended to natural duties, duties which suggested themselves in a moment, and were not far-fetched and fanciful.

She set about doing present duties required there and then, and did not wait to serve the Lord in a year's time. In a quiet, natural manner, she pursued her calling as if it never occurred to her to do otherwise. If somebody had thought it wonderful that she ministered to Christ, she would have been surprised at them. It seemed to her the most natural thing for her to do.

Dear soul, I dare say while lying in bed sick there were fifty things she would have liked to have done – what housewife would not in such a case see many grievous obligations of work all around her – but Jesus being there, no sooner did she feel her health returned than she at once arose to discharge the offices of grateful hospitality as a matter of course. How could she do otherwise but wait upon Jesus and his friends? Now observe, that those good works which prove a man to be a Christian are not such as he could boast of; he does them as a matter of course. He feels he could not do otherwise, and wonders that anybody else can. Is he born of God? He yearns to teach others about the Savior, he cannot help it; his tongue wants to be talking about Jesus. Then he begins to give of his substance to the poor. It does not strike him as being at all a remarkable or extraordinary thing; he wonders that anyone can help being generous to real need. Now he begins to inquire about the little children in the neighborhood; can he get them into the Sunday school? Or he occupies himself with some other form of Christian work, and he does it because he feels it to be inevitable for him to do so; it is one of the instincts of the new nature which God the Holy Spirit has implanted in him. Those natural, commonplace duties which grow out of holy instincts within, are the best evidence of a work of grace: the more genuinely natural and unstrained, the better.

Vain is the religion which aims at unnatural conditions and makes much of distinctions of a needless kind. What is there in a peculiar garb, or affectation of speech, or separation of residence? These minister to our own pride; true godliness aims not at her own honor, but is content to labor among the many, to be a man among men, yet differing in nothing but character. Ours it is, as the true salt, to mingle with the masses, not to seek a proud isolation. We are men, not monks; and our sisters are women, not nuns. All that interests men interests us; we only differ from our race by being conformed to the image of

Jesus, while they wear the image of the fallen Adam. May God grant us grace to exhibit the Christianity of common life, the real and practical Christianity of every day. Christianity is not with hermits in their cells, nor nuns in their convents, nor priests in their cloisters; those are all cowardly soldiers who shun the battle of life. But the true faith is the joy and strength of all who love the Lord and fight his battles on the broad plains of life.

True religion must be manifested in your workshops, in your houses, in the streets, in the fields, in the nursery, and in the parlor. This celestial flower reveals its richest perfume not in the conservatories of unnatural seclusion, but under the clear sky of human life, for *as a flower of the field, so [it] flourishes* where God has planted it.

One other point before leaving this: these things become a conclusive proof of grace in the heart when they are voluntarily rendered as this good woman's ministry was. I do not read that she was asked to do anything for Christ, but it suggested itself to her at once, without command or request. Her work was done promptly, for *she immediately got up* and did it. She no sooner had power to work than the occasion was seized without delay. Promptness is the soul of obedience: *I hastened and did not delay to keep your commandments.* I doubt not that she did her ministering cheerfully. There is all the air of cheerfulness about the words *she immediately got up;* it reads as if with willingness, vigor, sprightliness, and eagerness she entered into the service. That is the best service for God that is done promptly, without delay; voluntarily, without pressing; generously, without grudging; heartily, without complaining. With us it is not "This you should do, and this you must do," but we serve Jesus because we love to do so, and labor for him is to us a joy and a delight.

> The true faith is the joy and strength of all who love the Lord and fight his battles on the broad plains of life.

I have thus brought before you the first point of our discourse; now notice the second one, which is most interesting. This woman's ministry for Christ and his disciples showed, secondly, the perfection of her cure. It may not strike you for a moment, but just think. She was sick with a fever. Suppose a prophet should visit your house and restore your friend from a great fever; yet the person healed would not be able to rise from the bed for some time. Fever leaves extreme weakness behind, and when the fever itself is entirely gone, it needs some two or three weeks, and sometimes more, before the person who has been prostrated by it will be able to go about his daily work. But this healing was obviously from God, a divine work emphatically, because the woman was so healed that all her weakness vanished, and she was able to proceed to her work without difficulty.

And, beloved, it is one mark of a work of grace in the soul when the converted man becomes at once a servant of Christ. The human theory of moral reformations makes time a great element in its operations. If you are to reclaim a great offender, you must win him from one vice first, and then from another; you must put him through a process of education by which he gradually perceives that what he has been accustomed to doing is bad for him, and he wakes up to the conviction that honesty and sobriety will be the best for his own profit. Time is required by the moral reformer, or he cannot develop his plans. He ridicules the idea of accomplishing anything in an hour or two. Man, the creature of time, must have time for the accomplishment of his very imperfect works, but to the eternal God time is nothing. His miracles annihilate time. A man who is converted is cured at once of his sins; the taproot of his sins is cut away then and there, and though some of his sins linger, yet every one of them has received the stroke which will prove its death blow.

Once for all, in a moment, when a man believes and is born again, the axe is laid at the root of all the evil trees within him; sin is there and then condemned to die. And what is more, all graces are in a moment implanted in the soul, not in perfection – they will have to grow – but they are all sown in the man in a moment in embryo, so that the renewed sinner, though he has only been born again for five minutes, has within him the embryo of the perfect saint who shall stand before the throne of God; and this is one of the marvels which certify the work to be divine.

For note, beloved, that those who have just been converted to God can worship God, can praise God, can pray to God, and can love God, though they were strangers to these things up to then; and some of the sweetest worship that God himself ever hears comes from the hearts of the newly regenerate. Of all the prayers that strike the Christian's ear like music, surely among the sweetest are the broken pleadings of those who have just found the Savior. I delight in the expressions of faith of elderly and full-grown Christians – they are exceedingly instructive and precious; but, oh! that first grip of the hand, that first flash of the eye, that first tear of joy when a soul has seen Christ for the first time, and stands astonished at the matchless vision of incarnate love! Why, there is no worship sweeter beneath the sun! The woman arises at once and ministers to Christ, and the sinner arises at once and begins to adore Christ.

Did not I say that the newly converted sinner can love, and does love his Lord as soon as ever he is born to God? I must correct myself. He not only can and does love, but he also loves beyond most others, for very seldom does man's after-love exceed in fervency the love of their espousals, which is also called their first love. This standard love is implanted in us at once, all blooming and full of perfume. Hating Christ one minute, hearts have been brought to be ravished with his love the next; the men were enemies to God an hour ago, and now they could die to defend his gospel, so changed are their natures. This must be a divine work. If that which was waterflood, quenching every spark of fire, should suddenly blaze and glow like Nebuchadnezzar's furnace, God alone could have worked the change. Say, Who has turned the waters of raging hatred into the flame of holy love? Who has done it but the mighty God himself. If the iceberg suddenly becomes a flaming beacon, who could have worked this marvel but the Miracle Worker who alone does great wonders? Glory be to God we often see it, and he shall have the praise of it!

How pure some men's lives become at conversion – pure at once, though before they were polluted with every vice. Certain sins we may have to fight with all our lives, but a renewed man usually has no difficulty whatever with the grosser sins. For instance, I have known a man habituated to blasphemy, who probably never did since he was a boy speak a dozen sentences without a curse word, and yet, after he was converted, the profane habit has never molested him. We have known some who have been troubled with a ferocious temper which made them like demons, but from the moment of conversion they have been remarkable for their singular gentleness and meekness. We have known misers who instantly display the freest generosity, and thieves who become scrupulously honest. Though the temptation to old sin may return, yet for the most part those who have been saved from gross vices have been the greatest despisers of the very mention or name of their former abominations.

Such is the work of God in the soul, that these evils are driven out at once and sent right away, and then the man who before had been an expert in all manner of evil work becomes as much an expert in all manner of holy labor. He may not at once have picked up the technicalities of religion – perhaps it would be as well if he never did – but he gets to the bottom of it, the secret of it, and goes to work for Jesus Christ in his own fashion and way, with wonderful wisdom and extraordinary skill from the very first. Some of the best evangelists we have ever seen have been those who learned at once to evangelize, who seemed to have known it from the first hour in which they were converted to God, taking to it from inward love as the young swans take to the stream. Some of the best persons who speak to others about their souls privately began to do so immediately after they found the Savior, and attained to the sacred art – and a blessed art it is – as though they were in a moment touched by the hand of God and inspired for the service he meant them to render.

> If you love Jesus, do not wait till you have been ten years a Christian; serve him now.

Now, what is the practical drift of this second remark but this. As it proved the real divinity of this woman's cure that she was able immediately to go to work for Christ, so you young converts should hold the honor of Christ in great esteem, and prove the reality of his grace in your souls by bringing forth immediate fruit to his honor. See if you cannot at once rise and minister to him. Be as zealous as the dying thief; he had no sooner known Christ than he confessed him, and he did the only thing he could do for his dying Lord: he rebuked the other wrongdoer who had reviled the Savior. Oh, if you love Jesus, do not wait till you have been ten years a Christian; serve him now. If you are healed from sin, do not wait for experience; with your inexperience of everything except the new birth, go and seek the good of others. Do not suppose you must be trained for this war through a long process of spiritual drill, but march forward at once with all your heart and soul, in the freshness of your newly given life. It may be that you will achieve greater triumphs than some of the older ones, for, alas! some of them are dry and sapless, and have long forgotten their early days of enthusiasm.

In too many Christians the peach has lost its bloom, the flower has withered from the stem; they are not now loving and earnest, but they have declined into the dry and yellow leaf of religion. Go with the dew of the morning still upon your spirit, and I know not what great and gracious works the Lord may do by you.

Now we pass on to a third head briefly. Peter's mother-in-law, in ministering to Christ, proved her own gratitude. Her acts of hospitality were an exhibition of her thankfulness. Brethren, if we want to evidence our gratitude to Christ, we had better do it in the same way as she did. There is no record of her having fallen at Jesus' feet and saying, "Blessed be your name," although she may have done so; the Bible has not room for many holy expressions, though it finds space for gracious acts. I do not know that she sat down and sang a hymn, but perhaps she did; good women before her have done so, and I hope they will after her, but the hymn is not recorded. Holy Scripture has not room for all the hymns which good people sing, but it finds a corner for the actions which they perform. We have the Acts of the Apostles, though we have not the devotional emotions, the hymns, or the loyal resolutions of the apostles. This good woman proved her gratitude by tangible deeds. Did she not say to herself, "The Lord has served me; I will serve him!" It never strikes an awakened person that mere words are a suitable return for the grace of God. Can you give for the Lord's healing fruit a handful of mere leaves from the tree of talk? It looks like mockery. Give him the leaves, but wrap the fruit up within them. Let him have true action – consecrated service – for this is the fittest fruit of a grateful heart.

Observe that it is not said that she waited upon Christ before she was healed. The fevered patient is first restored, and then she begins to minister. I am far from exhorting any of you to serve Christ in your lives if your inner life be not first of all renewed by him. There must be a regenerated heart through his blessed touch, or else a renewed life may be imitated but cannot be truly possessed. First the healing, then the serving. The healing is first, but note well that the serving follows close at its heels. If you are saved, arise and *work out your salvation with fear and trembling; for it is God who is at work in you, both to will and to work for His good pleasure.* Since the light is now kindled, let it shine forth from you; since Christ has opened in your soul a well of living waters, let it flow out of the midst of you, as a river of water, for his service and the benefit of your fellow men.

This good soul knew to what end she had been raised up. She knew *from whom* she had received the healing: it was from the Lord alone. She knew *from what* she was restored, namely, from the very jaws of death. She knew *to what* she was restored, for she felt that health and strength had returned to her, and, therefore, she guessed rightly *for what* she was restored, namely, that she might wait upon the Lord. You, my brother, are saved from hell, you are lifted up into spiritual life and acceptance, you are ennobled and made an heir of heaven; what was this done for but that you might minister to your Lord here, and glorify him hereafter? Our gratitude ought to teach us the divine object of grace, and we ought to take care that it be attained. The Lord cannot have saved us at such an expense as the death of his own Son for any reason less than that we should live unto him. What is the reckoning of all our grateful hearts about this? Is it not this: that if we are bought with a price, we are not our own; that if the Holy Spirit has given us a new nature, it must be that we should lead a new life, and that our new life must be consecrated to him who is the author of it?

Beloved, true gratitude always leads us to serve, and it distinctly makes our healing Lord the object of our service; it puts him in the forefront. *She immediately got up and waited on them.* To him first, and to his disciples next – to the Head, and for the Head's sake to all the members; to the Redeemer, and because of him to all the redeemed. I put to each one here present who has been healed from sin and saved from spiritual death by Christ, this question: What are you rendering unto your Lord? What are you doing for him? Begin with him; do it as unto him; do what you do in his presence, and present it at his dear feet. Then I know you will be doing something for his people too. His poor you will befriend, his backsliding ones you will seek to gather in, his sick ones you will visit, his comfortless ones you will console, his wandering ones – as yet uncalled – you will seek after them; his lost sheep, your anxieties will go out for them; you will minister to him and to his chosen, to all the members of his body. What are you doing, brother? What are you doing, sister? I do not ask you now in my own name, for I am no master of yours, neither are you accountable to me, but I ask it in the name of him whose hands were pierced for you, and whose heart was set astir by the soldier's spear for your redemption. Oh, what are you doing for him? Do you love him? If you love him, feed his lambs and his sheep. If you love, serve; and if you serve, serve *him* first, and serve his children and his people next, and you will prove your gratitude.

But now, lastly, this woman's ministering to Christ proved in the fourth place the condescension of the Great Physician. He who healed her of the fever did not need her to minister to him; he who had power to heal diseases certainly had power to subsist without human ministry. If Christ could raise her up, he must be omnipotent and divine, so what need then had he of a woman's service? Might he not have used the grand style of the Old Testament and said, "If I were hungry I would not tell you, for the cattle on a thousand hills are mine"? But instead of this, the mighty Master of all angels condescended to be waited upon by a poor female. It was great condescension on Christ's part that he needed ministry, and great gentleness that he so often chose woman's ministry. He came to earth and the first garments of his infancy were wrapped around him by a woman's hands, and here he dwelt till at last he died, and holy women bound him up in the shrouded cloths of the tomb and laid him in the sepulcher. Matchless marvel was this of condescension, that he who is almighty and ever blessed should stoop from heaven to need the ministry of human beings. He has ministered to us by humbling himself to accept mortal ministry.

Peter's mother-in-law was one of the despised poor, but Jesus honored her. What was she but a fisherman's wife, at any rate the mother of a fisherman's wife, a poor, obscure, illiterate woman, yet Christ allowed her to wait upon him, an honor which Herodias the royal princess never had. So the Lord today should be beloved of us for his humility in allowing us to wait upon him, in allowing me, in allowing you, to do anything for his dear name's sake. I do not wonder that Christ allowed Paul and Peter and John to serve him, but that he should permit *me* to do it! I am overwhelmed with astonishment at it! Do not you marvel also? It seems easy enough to believe that the blessed Virgin and Mary Magdalene and other holy women were honored of God; but that you, dear sister, should be allowed to take a part in his service, is not this marvelous? Will you not bless him, and minister with the utmost cheerfulness because you feel it to be so great a grace?

Is it not gracious on our Lord's part to leave room in his church for ministry? Suppose, now, that the Lord had made all his people rich; then there would be no room for the generosity of his people to help his poor saints, and you would not have had the opportunity of proving your love for him as now you can. Suppose he had converted all his elect by the secret working of his Spirit without any teaching; then he would not have wanted you in the Sunday school, nor you with your tracts, nor me with my sermons, and we should have had nothing to do for Christ; we should have been sighing and crying, "The good Master has not permitted us to give him anything." Why, on our birthdays our little children love to give their father something, if it is only a bunch of flowers out of the garden, or a fourpenny piece with a hole in it; they like to do it to show their love, and wise parents will be sure to let their children do such things for them. So it is with our great Father in heaven. What are our Sunday school teachings and our preachings, and all that, but these cracked fourpenny pieces? Just nothing at all; but the Lord allows us to do his work for his own love's sake. His love for us finds a sweetness in our love for him. I am most thankful that in the church there is room for such a variety of ministries.

> The Lord allows us to do his work for his own love's sake.

Some brethren are so strangely constituted that I cannot tell what they were made for; but I believe if they are God's people there is a place for them in his spiritual temple. A man who was accustomed to buying timber and working it up, on one occasion found a very crooked stick of wood in his bargain, and he said to his son as he put it aside, "I cannot tell, John, whatever I shall do with it; it is the ugliest-shaped piece I ever bought in my life." But it so happened while building a barn that he needed a timber exactly of that shape, and it fit in so thoroughly well that he said, "It really seems as if that tree grew on purpose for that corner." So our gracious Lord has arranged his church so that every crooked stick will fit in somewhere or other, if it be only a tree of his own right-hand planting; he has made it with a purpose, and knows when it will answer that purpose. How this ought to rebuke any who say, "I do not see what I can do." Dear friend, there is a peculiar work for you; find it out, and I think it will not be far off. The exercise of a little reflection will soon enable you to discover it.

Be grateful that this is a certain fact, without exception, that every child of God who has been healed has some ministry which he can render to Christ, and which he ought to render at once. May the Lord give to every one of you to show your gratitude in this way, and while you do it, let it always be in an adoring spirit, saying, "Lord, I thank you I am allowed to go to my Sunday school class." Do not look at your work as a burden; instead say, "Lord, I thank you I am permitted to do it." "O God, I bless you that I am allowed to go around that little district and call at the houses." You Bible-women, bless God that he has let you be Bible-women; and you city missionaries, thank God that you are allowed to be city missionaries. "Oh," says one, "I can hardly do that because I suffer so much abuse and so much ill treatment." Bless God, dear brother, that he counts you worthy to suffer for his name's sake.

You know the old story of Sir Walter Raleigh. When Queen Elizabeth one day came to a miry place in the road, he took off his cloak for her to walk upon. Did he regret it? No, he delighted in it, and half the court wished for another muddy place that they might be able to do the same. Oh, you that love your Lord, be willing to lie down for Christ's sake, and pave the miry parts of the way by being despised for his name's sake. This honor you should desire and should not shun. Arise and minister, you healed ones; and as for you who are not healed, may you believe in him who is able to restore you with his touch. He is mighty to save. Believe in him and you shall live. Amen.

Chapter 11

With the Disciples on the Sea of Galilee

The men were amazed, and said, "What kind of a man is this, that even the winds and the sea obey Him?" (Matthew 8:27)

They became very much afraid and said to one another, "Who then is this, that even the wind and the sea obey Him?" (Mark 4:41)

This story of the storm upon the sea is wonderfully full of spiritual interest. Not only does it, literally, show to us the divine power of our blessed Master in lulling the storm, rendered the more conspicuous by being placed side by side with the human weakness which made him sleep in the ship upon a pillow, but also, spiritually, it is a kind of ecclesiastical history, a miniature outline of the story of the church in all ages. No, the teaching does not end when you have read the incident in that light; it also contains a suggestive forecast of the story of every man who is making the spiritual voyage in company with Jesus.

Notice, first, how it is a kind of ecclesiastical history. There is Christ in the vessel with his disciples. What is that but a church with its pastor? We see in the church a vessel bearing a rich cargo, steering for a desired haven, and fitted out for fishing on the road, should fair opportunity occur. Her being upon a sea shows her to be here below, subject to trial, suffering, labor, and peril. I scarcely know of any more suitable picture of a church than a ship upon the treacherous Galilean sea with Jesus and his disciples sailing in it. After a while comes a storm; this we may safely reckon upon. Whatever ship makes a fair voyage, with a favoring wind, the ship of the church never will. She has her calms, but these do not last forever; her sail is sure to be weather-beaten at one time or another, and the occasions are seldom far apart. The vessel which has Jesus for its captain is destined to feel the storm. Christ has not come to send peace on earth, but a sword: this is his own declaration, and he knows his own intent. Every sail of the good ship which bears the flag of the Lord High Admiral of our fleet must be beaten with the wind, and every plank in her must be tested by the waves.

To Christ's church there are many storms, and some of them of the most terrible character. Of heresy – ah, how near to wrecking has she been with the false doctrines of Gnosticism, Arianism, Roman Catholicism, and rationalism! Of persecution she has constant experience, but sometimes exceedingly vehement has the tornado been. In the early stages of church history, the pagan persecutions of Rome followed thick and fast upon each other; and when Giant Pagan had emptied out all his fury there came a worse tyrant, whose magical arts raised hurricanes of wind against the good ship. There sat at Rome a harlot who persecuted the saints exceedingly, being drunken with their blood. Then there raged a cyclone which almost drove the boat out of the water, and drenched and almost drowned her crew: a fierce Euraquilo beat upon the royal vessel, so that the waves threatened to swallow her up quickly. Tears and blood covered the saints as with a salt and crimson spray: hers was no pleasure trip; she went forth like the lifeboat, fashioned for the purpose of outriding the storm. The true ship of the Lord was, and is, and will be in a storm until the Lord shall come; and then there shall be for it no further wave of trial, but the sea of glass forever.

Note, again, that while this tempest was roaring worse and worse, the Lord was in the ship, but he seemed to be asleep. So has it often been. No Providence delivered the persecuted; no marvelous manifestations of the Spirit scattered the heresy. The Christ was in the church, but he was in the rearward part, with his head upon a pillow, asleep. You all know the portions of church history which this illustrates. Then came distress: the people in the vessel began to be alarmed; they were afraid that they would utterly perish. And do you wonder at it when the peril was so great? That distress led to prayer. Mighty prayer has often been produced by mighty trial. Oh, how slack has the church been in the presentation of her spiritual offering until the Lord has sent fire upon her, and that fire has seemed to kindle her frankincense, so that it has begun to smoke towards heaven.

Prayer was produced by distress, and prayer brought distress to an end. Then up rose the Master who displayed his power and Godhead. You know how he has done so in reformations and revivals time after time. He has chided the unbelief of his trembling saints, and then he has hushed the winds and the waves, and there has been a time of quiet peace for his poor, weather-beaten church – a period free from bloodshed and heresy, an era of progress and peace. The church has a history which has many a time repeated itself. If you take an interest in the navigation of that wondrous vessel which carries Christ and all his chosen, you will never have to complain of a lack of incidents.

> Mighty prayer has often been produced by mighty trial.

But I think I said that the story of the storm upon the sea is an admirable emblem of the spiritual voyage of every man who is bound for the fair havens in company with Jesus. We are with Christ, happy with him, and sailing pleasantly; will this last? Right speedily comes a storm; the ship rocks and reels; she is covered with the waves. It looks as if our poor flimsy boat would sink to the bottom. Yet Jesus is in our hearts, and that is our safety. We are not saved by seamanship, but by having on board the Lord Paramount, who rules all winds and waves, and never yet lost a vessel that bore the cross at its masthead. Sometimes within our hearts he seems to be asleep. We hear not his voice, we see but little of his face, his eyes are closed, and he himself is hidden away out of sight. He has not altogether left us, blessed be his name; but he appears to be asleep. Ah, then the ship rocks again, and we reel again, and we wonder that he still can sleep; then are we driven in great alarm to prayer, to which we ought to have committed ourselves long before.

It may be that we have been busy with ropes and tackle, strengthening the mast, furling the sail, doing all kinds of necessary work, and therefore leaving undone the most necessary work of all, namely, seeking out the Master and telling him the story of our peril. We pray not till we are forced to our knees, sad sinners that we are. The boat will go down! She will go down! And now it is that we also go down to the cabin and begin to wake him up with, *"Save us, Lord; we are perishing!"* Then you know what happens: how the gentle rebuke passes over our spirit and we are humbled; but the grander rebuke is heard by winds and waves, and they are quieted and sleep at the Master's feet, and in us and around us there is a great calm. Oh, how profound the peace! How blessed the stillness! We were about to say, "Would God it would last forever"; but as yet tranquility cannot be perpetual. Our perils of waters will be sure to repeat themselves. Often we go down to the sea in ships, and do business in great waters, so that we see the works of the Lord and his wonders in the deep. Hear how a poet sings the story:

> Fierce was the wild billow;
>   Dark was the night;
> Oars labor'd heavily;
>   Foam glimmer'd white;
>
> Trembled the mariners;
>   Peril was nigh;
> Then said the God of God,
>   "Peace! It is I!"
>
> Ridge of the mountain-wave,
>   Lower thy crest!
> Wail of Euroclydon,
>   Be thou at rest!
>
> Sorrow can never be,
>   Darkness must fly,
> Where saith the Light of Light,
>   "Peace! It is I!"

> Jesus, Deliverer!
> Come thou to me:
> Soothe thou my voyaging
> Over life's sea!
>
> Thou, when the storm of death
> Roars sweeping by,
> Whisper, O Truth of Truth!
> "Peace! It is I!"

On this occasion I will not further call your attention to the storm, or to the calm, but I beg you to observe the feelings of the disciples about the whole matter. The text says that *the men were amazed, and said, "What kind of a man is this, that even the winds and the sea obey Him?"*

God evidently thinks much of his people's inward feelings, for they are recorded here and in many other cases. The report of what these poor fishermen felt is as carefully made as the record of what their Lord and Master said, since this was needful to set forth the intent and purpose of their Lord's utterances. God often regards the external action as a mere husk, but the feelings of his people is the innermost kernel of their life story, and he prizes it. Some men practice introspection so much that they grow at last to make a kind of fetish of their inward feelings. This is wrong. Yet there is an error on the other side in which we cease to make conscience of our feelings, and think them to be a matter of no consequence, as if there could be real life without feelings. I will cry up faith as much as anyone, but there is no need to depreciate all the other graces, and especially all the emotions, in order to do honor to faith: we may honor the heir, and yet see no reason for slaying all the rest of the royal seed. We must both feel right and believe right, and it is sometimes good for us to have a lesson about how to feel towards our Lord Jesus Christ. Though feeling must be secondary to faith, yet it is far from being unimportant.

At this time we shall principally talk about three feelings towards Christ. First, the men marveled. We will dwell upon that – *marveling at Christ's work*. Secondly, if you will turn to Mark chapter 4 and the forty-first verse, you will see that Mark describes the feeling of the men as *very much afraid.* That shall be our second head – *awestruck at his presence.* Thirdly, we see them in our text *admiring his person,* for they said, *What kind of a man is this,* or, more correctly, "What kind of person is this, *that even the winds and the sea obey Him?*"

First, then, is marveling at Christ's work. May I ask you to indulge for a little while the feeling of wonder. You believe in Jesus Christ and you are saved. Salvation comes not by wondering, but by believing; but now, having been saved, having passed from death unto life, and having been preserved for years upon the sea of life in the midst of many storms, and at this moment enjoying a great calm and restfulness of spirit, I invite you to marvel. What wonderful things Jesus has done for me! It is in my power, if I choose, to waste my time in reading romances, but I care nothing for them, for my own life is to me more romantic than romance; the story of God's goodness to me is more thrilling than any work of fiction could possibly be. I am speaking to some here whom I am sure will join with me in owning that there is a freshness, a novelty, a surprise power about the dealings of God with us which we do not meet with anywhere else. Well do we sing in our hymn:

> I need not go abroad for joys:
> > I have a feast at home,

And we can also add that we need not go abroad for wonders, for we have a perfect museum at home in our own experience. John Bunyan, when he was describing the experience of his pilgrim, said, "Oh, world of wonders! I can say no less." And so it is. The life of the godly man on the God side of it, as he receives grace from Jesus, is a gallery of heavenly art, an exhibition of divine skill and power, a wonderland of mercy.

> Still has my life new wonders seen
> > Of lovingkindness rare;
> A monument of grace I stand,
> > Thy goodness to declare.

Let us think for a minute or two of the parallel between us and these disciples as to wonderment. Consider first, that the instantaneous and profound calm was *contrary to nature*. The Galilean sea lies in a deep hollow, much below the level of the ocean; and in the sides of the cliffs and hills which shut it in there are valleys and openings which act as funnels, down which blasts of cold air from the mountains often rush upon, all of a sudden. When the time of a storm is really on, the Sea of Galilee is not tossed about like an ordinary open sea, but is ripped, and torn, and upheaved, and almost hurled out of its bed by down-driving hurricanes and twisting whirlwinds. No sailor knows which way the wind does blow except that it blows all ways at once, and particularly downwards; as if with a direct downdraft from heaven, it blows the vessel into the water, and immediately, changing its course, lifts it into the air. Any mariner who is not used to that strange, wild sea would soon lose his head, and despair of life. It is like a boiling cauldron; the spirits of the vast deep stir it to its bottom. Yet this billowy sea in a moment was turned to glass by the word of Jesus: a fact far more wonderful to witness than to read about. Such a change in the uproarious elements was altogether contrary to nature, and therefore *the men were amazed*.

Now, beloved, look back upon what your life has been. I do not know exactly where you begin your life story. Some commence in the slime pits of Sodom, in vice and drunkenness; others begin with wandering on the dark mountains of infidelity, or among the bogs and swamps of pharisaism and formality. However, it is a miracle that you should have been made to fall at Jesus's feet and cry out for mercy through his precious blood. That you should give up all trust and confidence in self, and at the same time should turn away from favorite lusts which you once reveled in, is such a wonder that nobody would have believed it had it been prophesied to them. Certainly you never would have believed it yourself, and yet it has taken place, and other unlooked-for changes have followed it. Why, you have lived since then in a way that would have been once condemned by yourself as utterly absurd. Had an oracle informed you of it you would have ridiculed its forecast. "No," you would have said, "*I* shall never be *that; I* shall never feel *that; I* shall never do *that*." And yet, so it has been with you. The boiling cauldron of your nature has been cooled down and quieted, and an obedient calm has succeeded rebellious rage. Is it not so?

I can only say that if your religion has never produced a wonder, I wonder that you believe in it. If there is not something about you through divine grace which quite surprises your own self, I should not be amazed if one of these days you wake up and find that you have been self-deceived. Far above nature are the ways of grace in men, and if you know them, they have produced in you what your natural temperament and your worldly surroundings never could have produced. There has been fire where you looked for snow, and cool streams where you expected flames. A growth of good wheat has been seen where nature would have produced nothing but thorns and briars. Where sin abounded, grace has much more abounded, and your life has become the theater of miracles, and the home of wonder.

These men marveled, next, because the calm was so *unexpected by reason*. The ship was near going to pieces. A gust of wind threatened to lift her right out of the water, and the next one threatened to plunge her to the bottom of the sea. The weary fishermen certainly did not look for a calm; there were no signs of such a help. When they said, *"Save us, Lord; we are perishing,"* I do not know what they thought their Lord would do, but they assuredly never dreamed that he would stand up in the rearward part of the ship, and say, "Winds and waves, what do you mean? Your Master is here. Be still." That was beyond their nautical experience, and their fathers had never seen such wonders in their day. They could not hope that in a moment they would be in a profound calm.

Now, may I ask you to wonder a little at what the Lord has done for you? Has he not done for you what you never expected? To speak for myself, I never reckoned upon standing here to preach to thousands of God's people. When I was first brought to Jesus I had no such hope. Why should I be taken from the school and from the desk to lead a part of his flock? I wonder more and more that by his grace I am what I am. Some of you, when you sit at the communion table, may well feel that the most wonderful thing about it is that *you* should find a welcome place at the Lord's own festival. Did some of you expect, a year ago, that you would be here now, listening to a talk about Jesus Christ? Why, you hardly know how you did get here. You can scarcely tell the way by which the Lord has led you to be a lover of the gospel.

Look at your inner feelings, as well as your outward position: are you not often made the subject of desires, of longings, of groanings, and, on the other hand, of enjoyments, of sweet and precious endearments, of high and gracious expectations, which utterly surprise you as you remember what you used to be? Are you not *like those who dream* when you think about the Lord's loving-kindness? And if others say that *the Lord has done great things for [you]*, does not your heart chime in with all its bells, and ring out the joyful notes, *The Lord has done great things for us; we are glad*? Come, indulge your wonder. Admire and marvel at the exceeding grace of God towards you in working contrary to nature, and contrary to all reasonable expectations, and bringing you to be his dear and favored child. Marvels of mercy, wonders of grace, belong unto God Most High.

Besides this, the idea of a storm which should immediately be followed by a great calm was *strikingly new to experience*. These fishermen of the Galilean sea had never seen it after this fashion before. We read in the Old Testament of some to whom it was said, *"You have not passed this way before"*; and certainly the same might have been said to these disciples. "You have been in a storm, but you never in your lives before were one minute in a storm and the next in a calm." It must have been enough to make them weep for joy, or, at least, it must have led them to hold up their hands in glad astonishment. The deliverance brought about by their Lord was so fresh, so altogether new, that marveling was natural.

Well now, brothers and sisters, to come back to ourselves again – have you not often experienced that which has astounded you by its novelty? Are not God's mercies new every morning? I address some of you who have been forty or fifty years in the ways of God: do you not find a continual freshness in the manifestations of God's goodness to you both in providence and in grace? Let me ask you, Has religious life been to you like mounting a treadmill – monotonous, wearisome, uniform? If so, there is something wrong about you; for while we live near to God, we dwell under new heavens and walk upon a new earth.

When a man travels through the Alps on a bright, sunshiny day, all things are new, as though born that morning: that drop of dew on the grass he never saw before, that drifting cloud has newly arrived on the scene. Never before has the traveler seen the face of nature radiant with the same smile as that which now delights him. Has it not been so with you in the journey of life? Have not all things become new and remained new since you were born anew? Has not grace been heaped upon grace, so that each new experience has excelled its predecessor? Still have I beheld fresh beauties in my Master's face, fresh glories in my Master's Word, fresh assurance of his faithfulness in his providence, fresh power in my Master's Spirit as he has dealt graciously with my soul. I know that it is so with you; and I want you to marvel at it that God should take so much trouble to manifest himself to poor creatures that are not worth his treading on, and that he should devise a thousand things most rare and new for such insignificant insects of a day as we are. Glory be to his blessed name, it may well be said of us, *The men were amazed, and said, "What kind of a man is this, who deals so with his people?" Who is a God like You? What is man that You take thought of him, and the son of man that You care for him?* These three things made the disciples wonder.

> **Man travels with weary foot; the Lord rides upon a cherub and does fly.**

There was another. I should think that it was a great marvel to them that a calm was sent *so soon* after the storm. Man needs time, but God's word runs very quickly. Man travels with weary foot; the Lord rides upon a cherub and does fly, yes, he flies upon the wings of the wind. The particles of air and the drops of water were all in confusion through the tempest, rushing as if chaos had come again, rising in whirlwinds and falling in floods; yet they did but see the face of their Maker, and they were still. In one single instant there was a calm.

Have not you and I experienced instantaneous workings of divine grace upon our spirits? It may not be so with all, but some of us at the first instant of our faith lost the burden of sin in a moment. Our load was all gone before we knew where we were. The change from sorrow to joy was not worked in us by degrees, but in a moment the sun leaped above the horizon, and the night of our soul was over. Has it not been so since? We have been in the midst of God's people as heavy as lead, and without power to enjoy a truth, or to perform a holy act. The hymns seemed a mockery and the prayer an empty form; and yet in a single moment the rod of the Lord has touched the rock and the waters have flowed forth, and by the very means of grace which seemed so dull and powerless, we have been enlivened and comforted. We have blessed the Lord that ever we came to the place. I do not know how it is that we undergo such sudden changes. Yes I do. It is because God works all good things in us, and he is able to accomplish in an instant that which we could not effect in a year. He can in a moment change our prison into a palace, and our ashes into beauty; he can tell us to put off our sackcloth and put on the wedding garments of delight. As in the twinkling of an eye this corruptible shall put on incorruption, so in an instant our spiritual death can blossom into heavenly life. This is a great wonder. Go and marvel at what the Lord has so speedily done for you.

And then to think that it should have been *so perfect*. When a storm subsides, the sea is generally angry for hours, if not for days. A great wind at Dover yesterday would make the channel rough for some time. But when our Lord Jesus makes a calm, the sea forgets her raging and smiles at once; in fact, *He caused the storm to be still, so that the waves of the sea were hushed.* The winds hush all their fury and are quiet in an instant when he bids them rest. And oh, when the Lord gives joy and peace and blessedness to his people, he does not do it by halves. *When He keeps quiet, who then can condemn?* There is no such thing as a half blessing for a child of God. The Lord gives him fullness of peace – *the peace of God, which surpasses all comprehension.* He causes him to enjoy quiet through believing, and he enables him to rejoice in tribulation also, for tribulation works blessing to the souls of men.

I feel that I cannot speak as I could wish, but I shall finish this division of the discourse by saying that one point of wonder was that the calm was *brought about so evidently by the Master's word.* He spoke and it was done. He poured no oil upon the waters; his will was revealed in a word, and that will was law. Not an atom of matter dares to move if the divine decree forbids; the sovereignty of Jesus is supreme, and his word is with power.

Now, dear friend, I know that there must have been very much that is wonderful in your life as a Christian, but do not think yourself the only partaker of such wonderment. Let us all sit down, and inquire each one of us, "What is this to me? Why me, Lord? How can such great grace be shown to me; and how can the Son of God stoop to look at me and take me into marriage union with himself, and promise that I shall live because he lives, that I shall reign because he reigns?" Sit down, I say, and believingly marvel, and marvel, and marvel, and never leave off marveling.

And let me drop one little word into your ear. Is there something that you want from God concerning which unbelief has said that it is too wonderful to be expected? Let that be the reason why you shall expect it. There is nothing to a Christian so probable as the unexpected, and there is nothing which God is so likely to do for us as that which is above all we ask or even think. God is at home in wonderland. If what you want is a commonplace thing, perhaps it may not come; but if it strikes you as a marvel, you are in a right state of heart to honor God for it, and you are likely to receive it. Do not think that because between you and heaven, if you reach it, there will be a giant's causeway of marvels, therefore you will never get there; but, on the contrary, conclude that the God who began to save you by so great a miracle as the gift and death of his own dear Son, will go on to perfect your salvation even if he has to fling into the sea a thousand heavens to make stepping-stones for you to tread upon before you can reach his presence. *He who did not spare His own Son, but delivered Him over for us all, how will He not also with Him freely give us all things?* Therefore expect wonders. These men marveled: expect to keep on marveling till you get to heaven, and to keep on marveling when you are in heaven, and throughout eternity. Wonder will be a principal ingredient of our adoration in heaven: we

> Shall sing with wonder and surprise
> His lovingkindness in the skies.

I have been somewhat long on this first head, so I will therefore give you a little, and only a little, upon the second.

Let us now see how the disciples were awestricken at our Lord's presence. Mark says that *they became very much afraid.* They were very afraid because they found themselves in the presence of one who had stilled the winds and the waves. Brothers and sisters, it is well to cultivate that holy familiarity which comes from nearness to Jesus, and yet we ought always to be humbled by a sense of that nearness. Permit me to remind the boldest believer that our loving Lord is still God over all. He is to be honored and reverenced, worshiped and adored, by all who draw near to him. However much he is our brother, he says, *"You call Me Teacher and Lord; and you are right, for so I am."* He is all the greater because of his condescension to us, and we are bound to recognize this.

Whenever Jesus is near, the feeling of holy awe and solemn dread will steal over true disciples. I am afraid of that way of being so familiar with Christ as to talk of him as "dear Jesus," and "dear Lord," as if he were some Jack or Harry that we might pat on the back whenever we liked. No, no. This will never do. It is not such language as men would use to their prince, so let them not thus address the King of Kings. However favored we may be, we are but dust and ashes, and our spirit must be chastened with reverence.

When Jesus is near us we ought to be very afraid *because we have doubted him.* If you had been suspicious of a dear friend, and had indulged hard thoughts about him, and on a sudden you found yourself sitting in the same room with him, you would feel awkward, especially if you understood that he knew what you had said and thought. Oh, you will feel ashamed of yourself, my brother, if Jesus shall draw near to you. The wisest thing you can do in such a case is to say, "My Master, my Lord, since you do favor me with your presence, I will first fall at your feet, and confess that I did doubt you, that I did think that the stormy wind would swallow up the vessel, and that the waves would devour both you and me. Forgive me, Master. Forgive me for having thought so ill of you." Whenever we are near to Christ, one of the first feelings should be that of great humiliation. Let us fall at his feet, and confess how sternly we have thought of him.

Brethren, *we have been so foolish as to fear his creatures,* paying to them a sort of worship of fear, as if they had more power to harm than Jesus had to help. We clothe wind and sea with attributes which belong to God only, and look upon our trials as if they tested the Lord too, and vanquished him because they vanquish us. Are we not because of this struck with dread in the presence of the Christ?

And then the next feeling should be – since he has come to me, this

Mighty One who has worked such marvels for me, *let me try to order myself correctly in his presence.* I notice whenever the Lord Jesus Christ is very present in this congregation how carefully everybody sings. I notice about tune, time, and tone a difference from the singing which is usual, and even from that singing which comes of having an acquired skill in music. Though it may seem a trifle, yet I cannot help observing that when people come to the Communion table as a matter of routine they frequently behave roughly, walking noisily and looking about, or else they sit like statues, with a chill propriety of posture and vacancy of countenance; but you will notice that fellowship with Jesus affects the glance of the eye, the thoughts of the soul, and consequently the movements of the body.

When a man is truly conscious that Jesus, the Wonder-worker, is near, he is very afraid. If ever you say to Jesus, *"You know that I love You,"* mind you, put "Lord" before it – *"Lord, You know all things";* for he is your Lord still. Where Jesus is, there is godly fear, which is by no means the same as slave-like fear. Every true child has a reverence for his father. Every true daughter has a loving respect for her mother. So it is with us towards our Lord Jesus. We owe so much to him, and he is so great and so good, and we are so little and so sinful, that there must be a blessed sense of holy awe whenever we come before him. Indulge it. Indulge it now. You know how John puts it: *When I saw Him, I fell at His feet like a dead man.* Why, that is the man who leaned his head on the bosom of Christ. Yes, that is the man who fell at his feet *like a dead man.* If your head has never leaned upon the bosom of the Lord, I should not wonder if you can hold it up in his presence; but when it has once lain there in confiding love, resting upon boundless mercy, then that head of yours will lie in the dust uncrowned if God has honored it; for it will be your delight to cast your crown at his feet, and give him all the glory.

O, reign forever, King of Kings and Lord of Lords! Conquer me, my Lord; subdue me perfectly. Make dust of me beneath your feet, if you shall be but the tenth of an inch the higher for my downcastness. Oh, my Master and my Lord, with joy I would shrink to nothing before you, that you may be all in all. May this be your feeling and mine. The men were very afraid; let us be afraid also, with a believing sort of fear.

Now to close; the third thing is admiring the person of Jesus, for these men who marveled, and who were very afraid, admired the person of him who had set them free from the storm, saying, *"Who then is this, that even the wind and the sea obey Him?"* Come, let us admire and adore the nature of Christ which is altogether beyond our comprehension. The winds and the sea obeyed him, though he had slept like other men. When his head was that of an infant, the crown of the universe was about his brow. When he was in the carpenter's shop he was still the Creator of all worlds. When he went to die upon the tree, a myriad of angels would have come to rescue him if he had but willed it. Even in his humiliation he was still the Son of the Highest, God over all, blessed forever. Now that he is exalted in heaven, do not forget the other side of the question; believe that he is just as much man now as when he was here – as truly a brother of our race as he is God over all, blessed forevermore.

Let us now give our hearts to admiration of him in *his complex nature which is beyond comprehension*. He is my next of kin, and yet my God, at once my Redeemer and my Lord. We may each one cry with Job, *"I know that my Redeemer lives, and at the last He will take His stand on the earth. Even after my skin is destroyed, yet from my flesh I shall see God."* Because he lives as my Redeemer – there is the sweetness of it; and because he is my God – there is the glory of it; he is both tenderly compassionate for my infirmities, and gloriously able to overcome them. He is a complete Savior because he is both human and divine. Come, my soul, bow down in wonder that ever God should send such a Savior as this to you. A person asked me the other day whether I had seen a book entitled *Sixteen Saviors*. I answered, "No, I have not, and I do not want to know of sixteen saviors; I am perfectly satisfied with one." If all who dwell in heaven and earth could be made into saviors, and the whole were put together, you might blow them away as a child blows away thistledown; but there is this one Savior, the Son of Man and yet the mighty God, and he cannot be moved. Joy then, my brethren, and rejoice in the nature of your blessed Lord.

Next, rejoice in *his power which has no limit,* so that even the winds and the waves obey him. The winds – can they have a master? The waves that cast their spray upon the face of princes, can they own a sovereign? Yes, the most fickle of elements, the most unruly of forces, are all under the power of Jesus. Joy and rejoice in this. Little as well as great – yonder Atlantic that divides the world, and that little drop in the basin of Gennesaret – are alike in the hand of Jesus. The power of God is seen in a falling mountain when it crushes a village; but it is as truly present when the seeds are scattered from the pod of the gorse shrub, or a rose leaf falls upon the garden walk. God is seen when an angel flashes from heaven to earth, and is he not seen when a bee flits from flower to flower? Jesus is the master of the little as well as of the great, yes, King of all things; and I joy this moment to think that even the wicked actions of ungodly men, though they are not deprived of their sinfulness so as to make the men the less responsible, are, nevertheless, overruled by that great Lord of ours who works all things according to the counsel of his will. In the front I see Jesus leading the van of providence. Behind, he guards the rear. On the heights I see Jesus reigning King of Kings and Lord of Lords. In the deeps I mark the terror of his justice as he binds the dragon with his chain. Let the universal cry of "Hallelujah" rise unto the Son of God, world without end.

Sit down and admire and adore his unlimited power, and then conclude by paying homage to *that sovereignty of his which tolerates no question*; for the winds and waves did not only perform his will, but, as if they were waking into life and rising into intelligent knowledge of him, they are also said to have *obeyed* him; from this I gather that Christ is not only the forceful master of unintelligent agencies, but that he is also the sovereign master of things that can obey him, and he will be obeyed. Ah, you may bite at him, and hiss at him; but as the viper broke his teeth against the file, yet hurt it not, so shall the ungodly exercise all their craft and all their strength, and the end shall be shame and confusion of face to them.

The kingdom of our Lord and Master is by some thought to be a long way off, and his cause is half despaired of by fainthearted men; but he that sits in the heavens laughs at the impatience of saints as well as at the defilement of sinners, for he knows that all is well. Out of seeming evil he produces good, and from that good something better still, and better still in infinite progression. All things move towards his eternal coronation. As once every atom of history converged to his cross, so does it today project itself towards his crown; the Lord Jesus comes to his well-earned throne as surely as he came to the shameful cross. He comes, and when he comes it shall be as when he rose in the ship and rebuked the winds, and the men marveled; for all storms of raging passion, conflicting opinion, and fierce warfare shall be hushed, and he shall be admired in his saints, and glorified in all them that believe, while even unbelievers shall marvel at him and say, "What manner of person is this, that even earth and hell obey him, and all things are subject to his sovereign power!"

> All is safe because of his presence, and all shall end gloriously because of his manifestation.

Happy are the eyes that shall see him in that day with joy. Happy are the men who shall sit at the right hand of the Coming One. Oh beloved, your eyes and mine shall see it if we have first looked to the Redeemer upon the cross and found salvation in him. Courage, brethren; let the waves dash and the winds howl. *The Lord of Hosts is with us; the God of Jacob is our stronghold.* All is safe because of his presence, and all shall end gloriously because of his manifestation. The Lord bless you, in storm and in calm, for Christ's sake. Amen.

Chapter 12

Christ Asleep in the Vessel

"Teacher, do You not care that we are perishing?"
(Mark 4:38)

The day had been a very illustrious one. Our Lord had remarkably displayed his teaching and healing powers. Great crowds had been attracted, and he had both delivered to them most precious parables and worked among them most marvelous cures. Grand as the day was, it could not come to a close without a storm. After the same manner you will find it in the history of the church of God, that intermingled with great successes will be great afflictions. Pentecost is followed by persecution: Peter's sermon by Peter's imprisonment. Though today a church may flourish abundantly, in a very short time it may be visited with stern adversities; it may be tested nonetheless, but all the more because God is in its midst and is blessing it.

When our Lord took ship, the weather appears to have been very fair, and many little boats which scarce would have tempted the sea had its surface been ruffled, put out upon the sea under the convoy of the great Teacher's vessel. His was the admiral's flagship, and they were the happy fleet. They made a lively flotilla sailing softly like seabirds when the ocean is in a gentle mood. All hearts were happy, all spirits were serene, and the sleep of the Master was but a type of the general peace. Nature rested; the sea was as a molten looking glass, everything was quiet; and yet all of a sudden, as is the custom with these deep-lying inland seas, the storm-fiend rushed from his haunt among the mountains, sweeping everything before it. The little vessel was thrust hard into it; she was almost filled with water, and ready to sink through the force of the driving hurricane. Thus may our loveliest calms be succeeded by overwhelming storms. A Christian man is seldom long at ease. Our life, like April weather, is made up of sunshine and showers.

> We should suspect some danger nigh
>   When we perceive too much delight.

Nothing beneath the moon can be depended upon, all things are invariably variable. *"Do not boast about tomorrow,"* says the wise man; and he might have added, "Do not boast about today, for you know not how the evening may close, however brightly the morning may have opened." Let us learn this lesson at the outset. Let us not reckon upon the continuance of present ease, nor fix our happiness upon the fickle weather of this world; but let us be ready for changes, so that, come when they may, we shall not be afraid of evil tidings, our heart being fixed, trusting in the Lord.

It would seem that when the storm began the disciples did not at first arouse the Master. They had some consideration for his extreme weariness, for he had spent the whole day in very severe toil, and his human strength was exhausted. They thought, perhaps, that the hurly-burly of the storm would wake him. How could he sleep amid the howling winds and roaring waves? They little knew how deeply calm his heart was, so that amid the storm he could sleep very well, for the storm came not near his soul.

When at last they found that they were in great jeopardy, for their ship would surely sink, they began to judge their Lord, and to think of him unbelievingly and unkindly. They thought they would perish, and they wondered how he could allow them to do so; and therefore they went to him, crying, as Luke says, *"Master, Master, we are perishing!"* or as Mark gives it, *"Teacher, do You not care that we are perishing?"* Many of them cried out; one said one thing and one another, but their general spirit was one of complaint against their Lord. They knew he loved them, and yet half-thought him cruel. They trusted him, and yet had grievous doubts. They called him Master, and yet they were in a sort of semi-rebellion against him; they retained his influence, but were ready to mutiny against him because he did not exercise his power for their rescue.

We shall take the text as the keynote of our subject, and first we shall think upon *the apparent indifference of the Lord to his people;* but we shall note, secondly, that *it is only apparent;* thirdly, *that he has a real care for them at times when he seems indifferent;* and, fourthly, *they shall see this to be the case by and by.*

First, then, we, as well as the disciples on the Galilean sea, sometimes complain of the indifference of the Lord to us. It is but an apparent indifference.

Sometimes the complaint takes this shape: God permits natural laws to proceed in their prescribed course, even when his own children will be crushed by them. There is a vessel out at sea. It is enveloped in dense fog. Prayers are offered up by godly men on board for the right guidance of the vessel, but if it continues to be steered as it now is, it will come upon a rock, and on a rock it does come, notwithstanding the prayers. Does not God care that a vessel should perish with people on board it who are praying for direction and deliverance? At another time the rough winds are out, and the vessel flies before them. She will soon sink, she cannot long live in the storm; many supplications and pleadings are sent up to God, yet the storm does not abate one jot of its fury. The laws of nature at such times appear to be as grim and heartless as if they were managed by the prince of the power of the air.

As God has ordained, so does nature move; for us the floods do not stand upright as a heap, neither do the waters refuse to drown. Whether it be martyr or murderer, the fire devours with equal fury, and the sword falls with an equally deadly blow. *There is one fate for the righteous and for the wicked.* From this fact arises many a complaint, and we cry, *"Teacher, do You not care that we are perishing?"* Our dear one, whom Jesus loves, is sick; day and night we plead for his recovery, but the fever takes its course, or the broken limb requires its full time to heal. God does not often alter the physical laws of the body for the convenience of his chosen; to them poison is poison, and disease is disease. Often the Lord permits those whom we love to suffer long, and he does not seem to pay attention to our prayers and pleadings; no, instead, the case grows worse and worse. We are very apt, when we are under a trying dispensation, to judge the laws of nature to be very pitiless ordinances without bowels of mercy, and we say, *"Teacher, do You not care that we are perishing?"*

It is well to remember, however, what we may all too easily forget, that the present complaint is based upon an error, for the laws of nature do nothing whatever, and are no more to be blamed than the commandments on the church wall. There is no such power as a law of nature acting by itself; all power lies in God, and a law of nature is neither more nor less than a description of the way in which the Lord usually works. The vessel, badly steered, strikes upon the rock, because usually God causes ships to obey their helms, and rocks to retain their hardness; and the man who dies of sickness does not die because of some ungovernable force in nature, but because God continues to give energy to destructive agencies.

The laws of nature are but a powerless letter; God works all things. What has he himself said but that he is *the One forming light and creating darkness.* Not a seed swells beneath the soil, not a bud bursts into beauty, not an ear of corn ripens for the harvest, without God; he is in the dew and the sunshine, and the light and the warmth, which nourish and perfect the plant. Happy is he who in all things beholds a present Deity. I see laws of nature, and I know that God acts according to them, but I see best the God who is behind the law. Law, what force has that? It is God working by the law; he does it all. This truth sets matters in another light, for if the Lord brings the trial upon us, we open not our mouth, but yield to his will. His ways of action must be right, and if they cause us grief, we nevertheless feel that he is not afflicting us willingly, or grieving us without design. When we perceive his hand we kiss the rod. Instead of saying, *"Teacher, do You not care that we are perishing?"* we cry out in surrender, *"It is the Lord; let Him do what seems good to Him."*

Sometimes our lament assumes another shape. We view the troubles which come upon us as the result of the stern decrees of fate, and shudder because it seems to our unbelief that God has made small account of us, and arranged affairs with slight reference to the weakness, sorrow, and infirmity of his people. Brethren, most of us now present believe in predestination, and are persuaded that the Lord works everything according to the counsel of his will: we believe that all things, great and small, are fixed in the eternal purpose, and will surely be as they are ordained. This doctrine becomes the lurking place of a temptation. We gaze upon the tedious wheels of predestination in their awful revolutions, and fear that they will grind us to powder. In the forebodings of our trouble, we fear that we may be entangled in the terrible machinery, and that since it will not pause for our crying, it will tear us to pieces.

Like the prophet, only with far greater dread, we cry, "O wheel!" But we ought to reflect that there is no such thing as blind fate – predestination is a far different thing. Fate is a blind man who rushes madly on because he must; predestination is full of eyes, and proceeds in one line, because it is the best path which could be taken. Fate is a tyrant declaring that such a thing shall be, because he wills it; predestination is a father ordering all things for his good household. God has his purpose and his way, and his purposes are both for his own glory and for the good of his people. Who among us would wish the Lord to turn aside from his holy and gracious designs? He has ordained the best; would we have him vary? He has determined all things wisely; would we have him determine otherwise? That which happens to us occurs because in the judgment of infinite wisdom and goodness it is on the whole best that it should be so; would we wish the Lord to arrange otherwise? Will you tempt the Holy One of Israel? Will you ask him to do other than that which is wise and just, and good and holy, and for his own glory? Instead of crying out against destiny, let us cheerfully accept it, because the Lord is in it. Do not say, *"Teacher, do You not care that we are perishing?"* but believe that instead of perishing your complete salvation will be promoted by all the events of Providence.

It may be that we are in a different state of heart, and are worrying ourselves today because it seems to us that affliction is sent upon men altogether irrespective of their character, and the godly were made to suffer even more than the wicked. If you read the apostles' question with an emphasis, *"Teacher, do You not care that **we** are perishing?"*

(emphasis added), it will show you my meaning. They did as much as say, "We are your apostles. We love you, we spend our lives for you; do you not care that we are perishing? We could understand that the vessel which carries a load of publicans and sinners should go to the bottom, but do you not care that we are perishing?"

Sometimes under trouble we have wondered why we are so afflicted, for we have felt that the Lord has kept us from known sin, and led us in the way of holiness; and therefore we have seen no special cause for his scourging. Our cry has been, *"Let me know why You contend with me"*; and if any have been cruel enough, like Job's comforters, to say that we were suffering because of special sin, we have held fast our integrity, and declared that we were not wicked in the sense in which they accused us. Now let us look one minute at this, and we shall discover that God does send affliction according to character, after all, but not according to the rule which flesh and blood would prescribe. It is not written, "As many as I hate I chasten" – far from it. He permits the wicked to spring as the grass, and allows them to flourish like a green bay tree. As oxen they are well fed, that they may be prepared for the slaughter; they are pampered, but their end is near.

But it is written, ***Those whom I love, I reprove and discipline*** (emphasis added). The favorites of heaven are inheritors of the rod. It is not said, "The branches which bring forth no fruit shall be pruned." No, they shall be utterly taken away in due season, and cast into the fire. But it is written, *Every branch **that bears fruit,** He prunes it so that it may bear more fruit* (emphasis added). And, therefore, when affliction comes upon our beloved relative who has lived a most exemplary life, or when a painful death happens to an unusually gracious man, we must not judge the Lord unkindly, as though he were unjust, but we must see his loving hand in it all, and bless him that he deals with our beloved ones as he is accustomed to dealing with sons, *for what son is there whom his father does not discipline? "He scourges every son whom He receives."*

The gold is put into the furnace because it is gold; it would have been of no use to put mere stones and rubbish there. The corn is threshed because it is corn; had it been weeds it would have been untouched by the hand-threshing instrument. The great Owner of heaven's jewels thinks it worth his while to use a more elaborate and sharp cutting machine upon the most valuable stones. A diamond of the greatest brilliance is sure to undergo more cutting than an inferior one, because the King desires that it may have many facets, which may throughout eternity, with greater splendor, reflect the light of the glory of his name.

Perhaps, dear brethren, we have thought that Jesus did not care for us because he has not worked a miracle for our deliverance, and has not interceded in any remarkable way to help us. You are at this time in such sore distress that you would willingly cry, "O that he would tear the heavens and descend for my deliverance!" But he has not torn the heavens. You have read in biographies of holy men the details of very extraordinary Providences, but no extraordinary Providence has come to your rescue. You are getting gradually poorer and poorer, or you are becoming more and more afflicted in body, and you had hoped that God would have taken some extraordinary method with you, but he has done nothing of the sort.

My dear brother, do you know that sometimes God works a greater wonder when he sustains his people in trouble than he would do if he brought them out of it? For him to let the bush burn on and yet not to be consumed is a grander thing than for him to quench the flame and so save the bush. God is being glorified in your troubles, and if you realize this you will be ready to say, "Lord, heap on the loads, if it be for your glory; give me but strength equal to my day, and then pile on the burdens. I shall not be crashed beneath them, but I shall be made to illustrate your power. My weakness shall glorify your might."

Possibly the hard suspicion that Jesus does not care for you takes another form. "I do not ask the Lord to work a miracle, but I do ask him to cheer my heart. I want him to apply the promises to my soul. I want his Spirit to visit me, as I know he does some for good people, so that my pain may be forgotten in the delight of the Lord's presence. I want to feel such a full assurance of the Savior's presence that the present trial shall, as it were, be swallowed up in a far more exceeding weight of joy. But, alas, the Lord hides his face from me, and this makes my trial all the heavier." Beloved, can you not believe in a silent God? Do you always want tokens from God? Must you be petted like a spoiled child? Is your God of such a character that you must mistrust him if his face be veiled? Can you trust him no further than you can see him?

Besides, you are losing what you have while pining for what you have not. You say, "I want promises," and I ask you,

> What more can he say than to you he hath said,
>   You who unto Jesus for refuge have fled?

You say you need a token for good – what greater tokens do you require than he has already given you in your past experience, or than he has presented to you in the flowing wounds of a dying Savior? The tokens for good which Jesus gave on the cross ought to be enough and more than enough to spare.

"Still," says one, "if he does not come to me and break the darkness with some light from his presence, I wish he would mitigate the pain I bear. If he will not take it away altogether, yet surely he will not let me utterly perish through its severity." Ah, "perish" – there is the point, and I pray you observe the distinction: that he may test us we can understand, but that he should let us perish we cannot comprehend? No, my dear brother, you are not asked to understand it, for you have not perished yet. Bad as your case is, it could be worse. You are brought very low, but you could be lower; you could be in the dungeons of hell. What a mercy it is that you never can sink lower than the grave, you shall never make your bed in hell; thank God for that. When you come to the lowest, God intercedes. The tide turns when you reach the full point of ebb, and the darkest part of the night is that which preludes the rising of the sun. Be of good courage, you have not perished yet, and let this be a wonder to you –

> Lord, and am I yet alive,
>   Not in torment, not in hell!

Why should a living man complain? Should he not still have hope, and expect that in his extremity God will appear for him?

Thus we have mentioned various forms in which the temptation to charge the Lord foolishly presents itself to the soul.

But now, secondly, the indifference of God to his people at any time must be apparent that it cannot be real. Meditate a little. Consider the character of the triune God of whom we are speaking. The Father – can he be unkind? *His lovingkindness is everlasting;* his name, his essence, is love. It is said of him that he *delights in unchanging love,* and we know that he is an unchangeable God, and therefore we are not consumed. Can you, O heir of heaven, believe that he is indifferent to you, his child? You, being evil, are careful for your children, so how much more shall your Father who is in heaven pity his own? Can you stand by and see your child tortured with pain, and not wish to relieve him? Have you not sometimes felt, O mothers, that you would take your children's pangs upon yourselves right joyfully if you could set your dear ones free? And have you, poor fallen creatures, such bowels of compassion, and has your heavenly Father none? O judge him not so. Say not to him, *"Do You not care that we are perishing?"*

Think of Jesus, the Son of God, your brother as well as God's dear Son – can he forget his people? Has he not taken upon himself your nature? Was he not tempted in all points like as you are? Has he not graven your name upon the palms of his hand, and written the dear memorials of his love on his side nearest to his heart? Can you look into the face of the Crucified One and believe that he is indifferent to you? O, there was a time in the love of your betrothals when his left hand was under your head and his right hand did embrace you, when you would not have thought so sternly of him. When he has kissed you with the kisses of his mouth, and you have known his love to be better than wine, you could not have said such a barbarous thing concerning your Well-Beloved. No, it cannot be that Jesus should ever be indifferent to his people's woes.

Consider next, beloved, the ancient deeds of divine love, of which the Scriptures speak expressly, and you will see that the Lord cannot be careless as to your welfare. Know you not that the eternal God loved you before the earth ever was? Have you forgotten that the mountains, with their ancient heads, are but newborn babes compared with his love for you? He chose you. He might have passed you by, but he chose you to be his own. *"The Lord appeared to [me] from afar,"* says the prophet, *"saying, 'I have loved you with an everlasting love; therefore I have drawn you with lovingkindness'";* and has he loved you these myriads of ages to be indifferent to your groans now? Can it be? If he had meant to cast you away, he would have done so long ago. If he wanted reasons for rejecting you, he had reasons from all eternity, for he knew what you would be. No sin in you has been a surprise to him. He foresaw the hardness of your heart and the waywardness of your disposition, and if he could now reject you, he would never have chosen you, he would never have taken you to himself at all. O, then, let eternal love forbid you to dream that he can ever be careless as to whether you perish or not.

Next, I pray you think of what he has done for you. I will only put it in brief. Do you think that Christ came from heaven to earth to save you, and now is indifferent about you? Do you think that he lived here thirty years of toil and weariness for your redemption, and will now cast you away? And do you believe that he went up to the cross for you, having endured Gethsemane's terrible garden, and its bloody sweat for you, and yet has no concern about you? Do you think he bore all the wrath of God on your behalf, and now thinks your salvation such a trifling thing that he cares not whether you perish or not? Do you believe that he slept in the grave for you, and rose again for you, and is gone within the veil for you, and pleads before God for you, and is, after all, a hypocrite, and has no real love for you? Man, if what Christ has done does not convince you, what can? Many waters could not quench his love, neither could the floods drown it. Will you not confide in him for the present, and the future, after what he has done for you?

Consider, yet again, what he has worked upon you personally, and what you have known and felt within yourself. Years ago you were his enemy, and he saved you and made you his friend. Do you remember when, in the agony of your soul, you cried to him as from the lowest pit, and he came to your rescue? Will he leave you now? Remember how our poet makes a plea out of his past history and urges it with God – do you do the same?

> Once a sinner near despair
>   Sought thy mercy seat by prayer;
> Mercy heard and set him free;
>   Lord, that mercy came to me.

> Many days have passed since then,
>   Many changes I have seen;
> Yet have been upheld till now;
>   Who could hold me up but thou?
>
> Thou hast helped in every need,
>   This emboldens me to plead;
> After so much goodness past,
>   Wilt thou let me sink at last?

There is the point. If God had not done so much for us already, we might question his intentions concerning us; but after the goodness and the mercy he has manifested, surely he will go through with it, and perfect the work which he has begun. He has spent too much upon his work to relinquish it now.

Recollect, too, beloved – and this is a sweet refreshment to the spirit – recollect the relationship which exists between you and your God. Fatherhood and sonship are full of comfort. Can the Lord be an untender Father? Will the Lord cast away his own children? *"Can a woman forget her nursing child and have no compassion on the son of her womb? Even these may forget, but I will not forget you."* Remember, also, that between you and Christ, O believer, there is the relationship of husband and of spouse. *I am married unto you,* says the Lord; and the prophet tells us that the Lord, the God of Israel, says, *For I hate divorce. Where is the certificate of divorce?* says he, as if he defied any to prove that he had ever put away his beloved. *"I will betroth you to Me forever"* is the language of our immutable God. The Lord has not cast away his people whom he foreknew. Why then mistrust him? Oh, by the fond relationship which exists between our hearts and God, let us not suspect him of indifference.

Remember also the divine promises. Will he be a liar, and let us perish? Remember his oath! It is base profanity to think that he can ever forego his oath! Remember the solemn seal of the blood of reconciliation; how can the Lord treat the blood of Jesus with indifference, or renounce the covenant which was made sure and ratified by the death of his own Son? Let a believer perish? Be indifferent to whether his redeemed be saved or not? Impossible! It cannot be. Far from it, horrible thought! Let the storm rage as it may, and let Christ sleep as he may; he must feel for his people, his indifference is but imaginary.

Thirdly and briefly, there is in our Lord a real care for his people in the midst of his apparent indifference. It was certainly so on the Galilean sea. Observe in the narrative that though Christ was asleep, he was in the ship. He had not left his disciples; and however God may seem to deal with his people, he is still with them. *"Do not fear,"* he says, *"for I am with you."* If there be nothing more, the presence of the Lord ought to be enough to cheer us. Our heavenly Father knows our need. To be banished from the presence of God would be hell; but however tossed with storms our vessel may be, we cannot despair as long as the Lord is our companion.

Remember, again, that although Christ was asleep, he was tossed about as much as the disciples were, and was in the same peril. They might well say, *"Do You not care that we are perishing?"* putting him with themselves, for they would have gone down together, both he and they. If we are persecuted, Jesus is persecuted. If we suffer, the Head suffers in the members. Our cause is his cause. This should encourage us. When Caesar said to the frightened captain, "Fear not, you carry Caesar and all his fortunes," he did but afford us an earthly type of the great heavenly truth that the vessel of salvation carries Christ and his honor in it, as well as his people.

Remember, too, that our Lord was benefiting his people when he was asleep, for he was setting them a good example, an example of sacred restfulness in times of trouble. He slept not merely because of his fatigue as a man, but also because he felt safe in his Father's hands. When the Master put his foot on board that vessel he knew there would be a storm. The tossing did not take him by surprise, and yet he went to sleep because he knew that all was right. No one could have slept with such foreknowledge except one whose heart was full of confidence in God. The Lord would have his people be restful and not fretful, *for He gives to His beloved even in his sleep.* We have never read of our Lord's sleeping except on this occasion, this majestic occasion, when he was asleep in a storm-tossed ship, with his head on a pillow, because his heart was on the bosom of God. He did as good as say to all his servants, "Rest in troublesome times, and leave all in the hands of him who cares for you." His sleeping was an acted-out sermon upon *"Do not let your heart be troubled."*

Moreover, he was testing them and revealing themselves to themselves. Perhaps many of them were in the same state as Peter, and thought they could bear anything, that they would never mistrust the Lord. He let the storm blow till they got into a doubting frame of mind, so that they might see the evil heart of unbelief which lurked within them still. By this trial he was strengthening them. They were to be fishers of men all their lives, and fishermen must encounter storms. This was one of the storms of their apprenticeship, when their captain was with them, so that when they came to be captains themselves, no strange thing might happen to them if a storm overtook them. If they had enjoyed all fair weather when Christ was with them, hurricanes would have startled them afterwards when he was gone, but now they will say one to the other in the time of persecution and trial, "Did he not formerly show us this, on that very day when he took us to Gennesaret? He was in the vessel with us, and yet we were in a storm."

Best of all, Christ was caring for them, because he was making their danger an opportunity for the display of himself. He wanted to show them his omnipotence, but how could he do so if there were no difficulties for his divine power to encounter? He had shown them how he could baffle devils and overcome disease; but now he desires them to see how winds and waves are subservient to his will, and so he lets loose the raging storms. For a man to confront a chained lion is little, but let the monster loose, and then only a hero will encounter him. The hurricane is loosed, the waves are raging, they devour the ship; now shall you see how great the Master is as he stands at the bow of the ship and cries, *"Hush, be still,"* and all is hushed beneath him. Without the storm they could not have seen the glory of the Peacemaker, and so the trial was absolutely necessary so that they might learn his deity to the full.

We come now to our last thought, which is this: in due time all those who trust shall see that God does care about them. When Jesus was awakened he was not angry. He might have walked away from his disciples if he had pleased. It was quite in his power to cross the billows, and to have left them in disgust; and after the hard things we have said and thought of God, he might leave us to perish if he would, but he will do no such thing. Jesus did not reject the unworthy prayers of his feeble followers. He might have taken offense, and have said, "Is that what you think of me? Is this the way in which you speak of me?" But not thus did he rebuke them. He did restrain them gently, out of love for them, but there was no anger. He accepted their prayers, and he awoke, and what an awakening it was! How mighty were his works! There was no trace of a storm another moment after he had been aroused. The most blustering of the conflicting winds slept like a babe in its mother's bosom. The waves were as marble.

Troubled one, you will enjoy calm yet. Poor tested and tempted child of God, you will see days in which you will wonder where your troubles are; you will say to yourself, "They are quite gone, I have nothing left to be troubled with; Christ has chased my griefs away." Perhaps you will henceforth enjoy a long, unbroken calm – not an ordinary one, but such a calm so deep and so profound that you will say to yourself, "It is worthwhile to have gone through a storm to enter upon a peace like this." After crossing the wilderness you will enter Canaan; the angels will visit you when the devils have ended their temptation. You will leave the battlefield for the land of Beulah, where you shall hear the choirs of heaven sing, and the angels will bring you spices from the gardens of the blessed. Only have courage! Stand to your post, trust in your Lord, think well of him, and rest in him; for as the Lord lives, no vessel that has Christ on board shall suffer shipwreck. He who has faith is insured against destruction. Wait on the Lord, even if the vision delays, and fair sunlight and smooth sailing shall be your reward.

I shall leave the subject when I have hinted at its application in two ways.

The first is this. I think this is very applicable to the state of the church at this present time. There is great trouble in some minds about the church, for everything is going badly, all things are in commotion. The signs of the times are dark. To me the worst trouble is that Jesus seems to be asleep; there is nothing doing, no great revival of religion, and but little power with the ministry. I am, however, comforted by the reflection that Jesus sleeps, but he never oversleeps. When we fall asleep we do not know how to awake, but Jesus Christ does – he sleeps, but he does not oversleep. Glory be to his name, he sleeps, but he is not dead; and as long as he is alive, our joy is alive. While there is a living Christ there will always be a living church. There may be both a sleeping Christ and a sleeping church, but neither Christ nor his church can perish. If our Lord be asleep, he is asleep near the helm – he has only to put his hand out and steer the vessel at once. He is asleep, but he only sleeps until we cry more loudly to him. When we get into such trouble that we cannot help ourselves, and feel our entire dependence on him, then he will reveal his power.

> While there is a living Christ there will always be a living church.

Perhaps during the next twenty years the state of religion in England will grow worse, and worse, and worse. Very possibly for another twenty years infidelity will abound, and superstition will abound, and then his church will be in a desperate state, and she will cry, "O God, the candle is all but quenched; the light is nearly withdrawn!" and then there will go up such an exceedingly great and bitter cry that Christ will hear it and come and revive his work right gloriously. It may be he will let the battle go against us for many a day yet, and our slender strength will be broken into utter weakness, and we shall almost despair of the fight. Then will he send his trumpeter to us; then will his Spirit come, and the clarion call shall be heard: "Be of good courage; when you are weak then are you strong!"

Then, on a sudden, in our utter impotence, we shall rush upon the foe once more, and, like Gideon's barley loaf which struck the tents of Midian and made them lie along, so shall the Lord's people do great exploits because the Lord has awakened as a mighty man out of his sleep. A sudden and glorious victory shall make heaven and earth ring with his praise. Be not discouraged nor discomforted. The storm is not at its worst yet, the vessel is not filled with the waves yet, the water is not up to her bulwarks yet; she floats still. When she can scarcely keep from sinking, and is almost going down by the head, then the captain will stand in the front of the vessel and calm the seas. When the roaring waves nearly overwhelm her, he will say to them, *"Hush, be still."*

The calm, the long millennial calm, it may be, is close ahead – we know not how near it may be, but let us hope on.

The other application is to the sinner. It may be that there is someone here who is in a desperate plight; he feels his sins, like hungry waves, ready to devour him, and he does not know how to escape. But he has been praying, and I am glad of it. Dear friend, never give up praying! The poor soul has been crying, *"Lord, help me!"* It is the right prayer. Brother, keep on at it. But it seems to him that Jesus is asleep, and he says, "Does he not care for a poor sinner? Will he let me go down to hell and think nothing of it?" What do you say, friend? Would you let a praying sinner go to hell if you could save him? "Oh no!" you say. "If he cried to me I would help him." Do you think you are kinder than Christ? I tell you that

> His heart is made of tenderness,
>   His bowels melt with love.

Believe in his love, cast yourself upon his grace, and when you believe in him you are saved. Do not think hard thoughts of him. Touch the hem of his garment, and you shall be made whole! Trust your guilty soul with him, and it is well with you now and forever. May God give you his blessing, for Jesus' sake. Amen.

Chapter 13

Why Is Faith So Feeble?

And He said to them, "Why are you afraid? Do you still have no faith?" (Mark 4:40)

Last Lord's Day morning our music was pitched upon a high key. We sought after great faith in the Master's name. It struck me that I might, perhaps, have discouraged some of the feebler sort, and that, therefore, it would be fitting today to follow up that sermon by endeavoring to encourage those of weak faith to exercise it until it becomes stronger, and also to invite those who as yet have no faith to venture in the direction of childlike trust.

With this brief introduction, let us come at once to our subject.

I should not wonder if the disciples considered that they had much faith in Jesus, their Master and Lord. They had been with him all day listening to his teaching, believing it even when they did not understand it. They had afterwards gathered around him in private to listen to his fuller explanations, and they were thankful to be favored with those expositions in which their Lord became their private tutor. I do not question that each one of them esteemed himself a firm believer in Jesus. How could he tolerate a doubt? But, my brethren, none of us have any idea how meager our faith really is. When trial comes, the heap from the threshing floor becomes very small beneath the influence of the winnowing fan. After a day of calm service with Jesus a storm came on, and that storm tested their faith, and left so little of it, that Jesus said to them, *"Why are you afraid? Do you still have no faith?"* Remember that we have no more faith at any time than we have in the hour of trial. All that which will not bear to be tested is mere carnal confidence. Fair-weather faith is no faith; only that is real faith in Jesus Christ which can trust him when it cannot trace him, and believe him when it cannot see him.

This storm was a special trial to the disciples, because it was so exceedingly severe. They had often been tossed upon that sea before, but this time the elements were moved to an excessive tumult: the winds poured down in all their force and fury. The war of nature raged around their devoted ship. When tribulation is heavier than usual, it is a serious test to faith. When we appear to be tested above the common measure of men, the weak ones are full of trembling, and even the strong fall upon their knees and cry, "Lord, *I do believe; help my unbelief."*

The storm was the more harsh because it came upon them when they were in the path of duty. Their Master had bidden them cross the sea; they were not on a holiday trip. They had not even followed the suggestion of a brother who had said, *"I am going fishing"*; but they were steering under their great Captain's orders. They were doing right, and suffering trouble as a consequence. This has often perplexed good men. I have heard a believer say, "I prospered more before I was a Christian than I have done since. Things went smoothly with me before I knew the Lord. How can these things be? The very fact of my endeavoring to do what is right, and laboring to maintain my integrity, has become the cause of my severest trial." This is no new thing upon the earth. The living child of God will have to swim against the stream. Not without fighting will he win his crown.

Moreover, it was an item which helped to test their faith, that the storm attacked them when Jesus was in the ship. Had the Lord been absent, they could have understood it; but he was in the vessel with them! How could the sea be so boisterous with Christ in the vessel? If I am out of communion with Christ, I can understand why I am chastened; but if I am walking in conscious nearness and fellowship with him, and I am even then tested and perplexed, how can I account for it? Herein is the test of faith. *"For those whom the Lord loves He disciplines, and He scourges every son whom He receives."* This we forget, and imagine that trials must mean anger, when, indeed, they may be tokens and tests of love.

It may have seemed to them also, that the storm was very untimely, since there were with Jesus and his disciples many other little ships, and all those boats were caught in the same storm. We are always anxious for those who come to hear the gospel, lest anything should prejudice them against it. The disciples may have feared that such ill weather would drive away from Christ those hearers who might otherwise have become converts. If they met with a storm so soon after rowing close to Jesus, they might judge him to be another Jonah, and resolve to give the Galilean preacher a wide berth next time. I know how I like to see fine weather at an open-air service, and a continuance of it till the country people can get home, and I suspect that the disciples felt much the same. They did not wish their Lord to be looked upon as a storm petrel, or a man of evil omen; and you know that superstition was strong in those days. Had you and I been there, we should have said, "Gracious Lord, let us have a calm, that those who have come to you in their boats may get home in comfort. Cause this wonderful service by the sea to end pleasantly, so that the next time you come this way the people may gather in still larger numbers to hear you." Sometimes the strange occasion of the trial makes it the harder to bear. Trial is never welcome, but sometimes it is peculiarly disagreeable.

See, my brethren, how these disciples came out of the tempest! They went into the trial well enough, but they were in an evil plight before long. We have seen a bird of glossy plumage, bearing half the colors of the rainbow on its breast, glorifying itself in the sunlight, and we have admired its beauty; but immediately the heavens have poured down pitiless showers, and we have seen our brave bird in quite another form. Dripping and draggled, he has sought dishonorable shelter. You would hardly have known him to be the same creature whose crowing challenged all his fellows; truly his glory has departed. Such are we, as a rule, after severe trial. We make a fair show in the flesh till we are tested, and then our feathers cling around us, and we droop and hide away, till our Master has to say to us, *"Why are you afraid? Do you still have no faith?"*

These two questions of the Master we will use today with a view to spiritual profit. May the Spirit of God make it so! First, we shall view the text as *the exclamation of pity:* "*Why are you afraid?*" Secondly, we shall regard it as *the rebuke of love:* "*Do you still have no faith?*" And, thirdly, we shall consider it as *the inquiry of wisdom:* "*Why are you afraid? Do you still have no faith?*" May our threefold meditation richly profit us all!

We will first use the questions as the exclamation of pity. The dear Master waking up from his sleep, calm as if it were a bright summer's morning, though it was the dead of night and the midst of a storm, looks upon them with wonder, finding them so strangely different from himself, and he asks, in all the calmness of his own brave spirit, "*Why are you afraid?*" He pitied them; and he pitied them, I think, for several reasons.

First, that *their fears had made them so unlike himself.* They were his servants, and they should have been as their Master; they were learning of him, and they should have put in practice the lessons of his example. He was delightfully quiet, and the contagious influence of his peace ought to have affected them. He was ever restful in himself, and therefore he gave rest to those who came to him; yet these were missing the blessing, and so he compassionately cried, "*Why are you afraid?*" He marveled not that they were afraid in such a hurricane, but he was sorry that they were *so* afraid as to act as if they had no faith. They were little like him as yet, although the great design of all his teaching was to make them like himself.

> Jesus marveled not that they were afraid, but he was sorry that they were so afraid as to act as if they had no faith.

Our blessed Master must often look upon us, dear friends, with much pity, and grieve over us, that after being with him so long – for some of us are getting gray in his service – we still fall so far short of his glory. We are predestinated to be conformed to his image, but the process is a slow one. After copying his handwriting, our own writing is still greatly marred with crooks and turns. Each page of the copybook of life is marred with errors and blots; therefore, the great Teacher pities his poor scholars. How is it that we are so afraid when Christ is so calm? Is this our imitation of Jesus? Our doubts, fears, alarms, mistrusts of God – are these such as a follower of Jesus should exhibit?

He pitied them, next, because *it made them so unlike themselves.* They were men, but their fears unmanned them. They were fishermen, but you would have thought them mere landsmen if you observed their fears. Like frightened children they cried, *"Teacher, do You not care that we are perishing?"* They were by no means overwise, but now they were at their wits' end. When you and I get fearful, how foolishly we think and speak and act! We could have done well enough if faith had steadied us; but unbelief makes us stagger and reel to and fro. We could have weathered the storm had we not given way upon the point of confidence in God; but, failing there, we became weak as water. How are the mighty fallen! Alas, the children of Ephraim, being armed and carrying bows, turn back in the day of battle! Those who once were patterns of courage become cowards when faith fails. Fathers in Israel act like babes in grace when faith ebbs out! Our Lord is grieved for us when he sees us fall so low that instead of being like himself, we are not even like ourselves.

Jesus pitied them again, because *their fears made them so unhappy.* Terror was depicted on their countenances. They were as white as a sheet when they saw that the boat could not be baled, but was evidently filling and sinking. What caused their terror? Were they afraid of death? Their fears were causing them more pain than death itself could have cost them. We "feel a thousand deaths in fearing one." To die is nothing compared with fearing to die. All the agony of death lies in the foresight of it; death itself is the end of all agony! Death is not the storm, but the *quietus* of the disturbing elements. Through death souls enter into rest. The apostles were made wretched by their fears.

I know some Christian people who suffer greatly from the same cause. I know a man who lives where I live, and stands in this pulpit where I stand, who has to confess his own faults this day; for he might enjoy unbroken peace were it not that in the care and labor of this great church, and all its various agencies, he looks to the difficulties and the necessities of the case, and to his own weakness, and then fears rush in. Beloved, we must not forever be thus childishly fearful. Let us strive after a courageous bearing. Let us crush the eggs of our woes while they lie in the nest of our unbelief. Our sorrows are mostly manufactured at home, beaten out upon the anvil of unbelief with the hammer of our foreboding. The Lord pardon us! Jesus pities us that we should lacerate ourselves by our needless fears, and miss the joy of a restful faith.

Again, the Master felt pity for them because *their fears made them so unkind.* Does unbelief make the timid unkind? I am sure it does. The disciples were ungenerous to their sleeping Master. If they had only considered a little, they would have said, "No, do not wake him! He has had so weary a day. The cares of the world rest on him; he is a man of sorrows, and acquainted with grief; if he can sleep, let him sleep. Let us sooner suffer than disturb him." If they needed to wake him, might they not have addressed him in fitter words? To say, *"Teacher, do You not care that we are perishing?"* was fretful and wicked. It was enough to wound their Lord's tender heart to be thus spoken to. Our unbelief has a tendency to make *us* unkind also. We are not tender toward others when we are disturbed about ourselves.

Here let me digress to teach a lesson of pitying love. It is well to recognize that sour speeches often proceed from a sad heart. It is wise to view ungenerous language as one of the symptoms of disease, and rather pity the sufferer than become irritated with the offensive speech. It is a pity to take much notice of what some sufferers say, for they will be sorry for it soon. If we knew the real reason for many a harsh word, our sympathy would prevent even momentary anger. Our Lord did overlook the grumpiness of the apostles; for he did not say, "Why are you so unkind?" but he inquired, *"Why are you afraid?"* In every case let us cure unkindness with double love.

I heard yesterday of a wise old Welsh minister of a generous spirit who was afflicted with a horrible deacon, and if a deacon is unkind, he can wound terribly. This deacon was most perverse and cruel, and he tormented the old gentleman in all sorts of ways. At last he fell sick, after having said certain dreadful things which were more bitter than even his usual gall and bitterness. The patient pastor soon went to see him, and on the road he bought some of the best oranges and took them with him. "Brother Jones," he said, "I am sorry you are so ill. I have come to see you, and I have brought you a few oranges." Brother Jones was very much astonished at this kind act, and had not much to say on the matter. The minister gently talked on, and said, "I think it would refresh you to eat one of these. I will peel you one." So he went on with peeling the orange, and talked with him pleasantly. Then he divided the fruit very neatly, and handed the sick man a nice piece in the gentlest possible manner. The bitter-spirited man ate it, and began to melt a little; the conversation became hearty, and the prayer was pleasant. Brother Jones was getting better in more ways than one. An outsider, who knew all about brother Jones and his ill temperament, could hardly believe that the minister had acted thus to one who had opposed him constantly and slandered him foully, and so he asked, "Did you really go and see that cruel old Jones?" "Oh yes," he said, "I went to see him; I was bound to do so." "And did you take him some oranges?" "Oh yes, I took him some oranges; I was glad to do so." "And did you sit down by his bedside, and peel him an orange?" "Yes, I peeled him an orange, and I was pleased to see him enjoy it; for I have learned, brother, that when a man is afflicted with a very bad temper, an orange is a good thing for him to take. At any rate, it is a good thing for me to give." The lesson is – if you wish to cure a man of ill feeling, be kind to him. View unkind and irritable speeches as symptoms of a disease for which the best medicine is not a dose of bitters, but an orange. Yet, beloved, if you have used such speeches yourself, do not repeat them. Cease from being so fearful, that you may cease from being so ill-tempered.

Our blessed Master did not find fault with the unkindness of his disciples, but he went to the root of the evil by silencing their fears. He said to them, *"Why are you afraid? Do you still have no faith?"*

Here you perceive our Lord's pity. I wish I could speak the words as he spoke them, and you would wonder at their surprising tenderness.

But now, secondly, these words were spoken also as the reprimand of love. They were intended to convey a measure of gentle rebuke to their mistrustful hearts.

Their unbelief was grievous to the Lord Jesus. They ought to have believed him, and it was an injury to his perfect love that they should so readily mistrust him, or even mistrust him at all. How could they think that he would let them sink? He was in the vessel with them. Did they suppose that, after all, he was a mere pretender to deity, and that the ship would go down with him on board? Beloved, let us strike upon our breasts to think that we should ever have caused a pang of heart to that dear Lord who yielded up his life for our salvation. He must not be doubted anymore; it is malicious cruelty. What if I call it "an excess of naughtiness" to doubt him whose life and death are crowded with infallible proofs of his unchanging love for us?

Our Lord questioned his apostles thus, not only because their unbelief grieved him, but also because *it was most unreasonable.* The most unreasonable thing in the world is to doubt God. Faith is pure reason. That may seem a strange paradox, but it is literally true: nothing is so reasonable as to believe the word of God, who cannot err or lie.

The fears of the tempest-tossed disciples were unreasonable because they were contrary to their own belief. They did believe that Jesus was sent of God upon a glorious mission; how could that mission be accomplished if he drowned? If they sank in the sea, he must sink too, for they were embarked in the same bottom. Ought not the faith they had in his divine mission to have kept them hopeful even in the worst moment of the storm? My brethren, be not inconsistent with what you do believe. Do not deny your own creed, however meager it may be, for that is irrational.

Moreover, their fears were opposed to their own experience: they had seen their Lord work miracles, and miracles for them, too. They had already beheld abundant proofs of his power and Godhead, and of his care on their behalf. Is not this true of us also? Has the Lord ever failed us? Has he not helped us to this day? Are you going to fly in the teeth of all your past experience? Is all that you have ever believed of God a fiction? Have you been under a gross delusion up to this day? You who are advanced in years, how can you doubt? With so many Ebenezers to look back upon, you ought to rise above all fear.

Their fears were altogether inconsistent with their observation. They had seen Jesus heal the sick and feed the multitudes. I am not quite sure how many of his miracles had already been worked before them, but certainly enough for their observation to compel them to believe that he was able to save them from death. How, then, could they doubt? But have not we also seen enough of the finger of God to be confident in the day of trouble? If we believe not, we dare not lay the blame upon the lack of evidence. To mistrust is irrational, because it is contrary to all the experience of our hearts and the observation of our eyes.

Moreover, their unbelief was contrary to their common sense. Some people make a great deal of common sense; and well they may, for it is the most uncommon of all the senses. Was it reasonable for these men to think that he, who could foresee the future, would take them on board a ship when he foreknew that a storm would wreck them? Would so kind a leader have taken them to sea to drown them? Was it reasonable to think that he who was so favored of God would be left to perish? Would he have gone to sleep if they had really been in danger? Was it reasonable to believe that the King of Israel was about to be drowned, even he whom they knew to be the Light of the World? Our unbelief, my brethren, seldom deserves to be reasoned with. Our fears are often intensely silly, and when we get over them, and look back upon them, we are full of shame that we should have been so foolish. Our Lord kindly rebuked their unbelief because it was unreasonable.

In very truth their unbelief deserved rebuke because *it sprang from low views of the Lord Jesus.* When they afterwards saw what wonders he worked upon the deep, they said one to another, *"What kind of a man is this, that even the winds and the sea obey Him?"* Should they not have known that beforehand? If they had remembered it, could they have been so overwhelmed with fear? Oh, that we thought more of Jesus! We cannot think too much of him. If we took him to be what he really is, if we regarded him as most truly God, we should rest in him and say farewell to suspicions and complaints. If Jesus were greater in our esteem, our lives would be grander by far.

Jesus rebuked his friends because *he foresaw that such unbelief as theirs would unfit them for their future lives.* That ship was the symbol of the church of Christ, and the crew of the ship were the apostles of Christ. The storm represented in parable the persecutions which the church would have to endure; and they, if they were cast down as cowards in a storm on the inferior Sea of Galilee, would be proving themselves altogether unfit for those more tremendous spiritual storms which in later years tossed the church, and mingled earth and hell in dire confusion. Peter and James and John and the rest of them were to steer the ship of the church of God through seas of blood, and to stand at the helm in the midst of hurricanes of error; and therefore fearfulness was a sad evil, because it would render them unfit for their solemn task. Jesus might have said to them, "If you have run with the footmen, and they have wearied you, what will you do when you contend with horses? If these winds and waves have been too much for you, what will you do when you wrestle with principalities and powers, and spiritual wickedness in high places? If natural causes destroy your peace, how will spiritual influences distract you?"

Brethren, our present trials may be a training ground for more serious conflicts. We do not know what we have yet to endure; the adversities of today are a preparatory school for the higher learning. If we do not play the man now, what shall we do by-and-by? If because of some little domestic discomfort we are ready to give up, what shall we do in the swellings of Jordan? If a little toil oppresses us, what shall we do when the death sweat trickles from our brow? My Christian brethren, let us attentively hear our Lord as he lovingly rebukes us; let us shake off our fears, and resolve that by his grace we will have no more of them, but will trust, and not be afraid. Oh, for calm hope, and a childlike rest on the love which cannot fail! I have hurried over ground where I might profitably have waited, because I want to have an earnest word with you upon the third point.

We may now regard these words as an inquiry of wisdom. It is always good to probe a sorrow to the bottom, if there is any hope of finding out its cause, and putting it away. If you are in fear, you may rise above it by removing its cause. If there be clearly no reason for fear, you will cease to fear; and if there be a cause of fearfulness, you can deal with it. My utterances will be as short as telegrams; please enlarge on them at your leisure.

"Do you still have no faith?" This is the question.

Is it a lack of knowledge? If the disciples had known Jesus better they would have had no fear, but would have exhibited firm faith. Is it so with any of you? Are you badly taught in the gospel? Do you as yet know only half the doctrines? Have you a cloudy view of the covenant of grace, and of the great salvation which is wrapped up in the person of your Lord? If it be so, your quickest way to faith will be to read your Bible more, to study it with greater attention, and to hear the gospel more often. Come out to weeknight services, and commune more with Christ in private. Spend three, four, five times the amount of time you now do in devotion, and so draw nearer to your Lord, begging the Holy Spirit to lead you into all truth. If you kill your fears and strengthen your faith, you will have invested your time admirably in acquiring more knowledge. Remember the word – *Yield now and be at peace with Him; thereby good will come to you.* Learn more of Jesus, and when you know him better, the main causes of your fear will be removed.

Next, *is it a lack of thought?* Did these good people know and yet forget? Did they fail to consider? Were they superficial in their thinking? Is that the reason why you also are so fearful and have so little faith? Are you a skimmer and not a digger? Are you content with the surface soil when nuggets of gold lie just below? Is it so? Do you think too little of the invisible and the eternal? Are your thoughts incessantly occupied with business, and is God thus shut out? Are you always using the muckrake of greed, and never using the telescope of faith? Are the abiding treasures covered up and buried amid the seeming and shadowy things of time and sense? If so, mend your ways, my brethren. Mend them at once. Have more thought, more prayer – much more prayer, more praise – much more praise, more meditation, more calm investigation of your own heart, and more acquaintance with the things of God. Do you not think that often you might find the remedy for your fears in the direction of holy intimacy with unseen realities? Let these be more true to you, and the troubles of this life will sink into their proper places as light afflictions which are but for a moment.

The question as to why we are so fearful may be helped by another question: *Is it that our trials take us by surprise?* Perhaps the disciples reckoned that everything must be right, since they had Christ on board. Let us not indulge such a notion. Never let any affliction surprise you, for your Lord has told you, "In the world you have tribulation." If your children die, do not be surprised; shall mortal parents bring forth immortal offspring? If your riches disappear, do not be surprised – they always had wings; what wonder if they fly! If any other adversity happens to you, be not surprised; *for man is born for trouble, as sparks fly upward.* The Lord has told you before it comes to pass, that when it is come to pass you may believe. Count on tribulation, and then you will not be overtaken by surprise, nor fret as though some strange thing had happened unto you.

Why were they so full of fear? *Was it a lack of simplicity of confidence?* Did they trust in their good ship, or feel that they were safe because of their seamanship? Perhaps not, but I am sure that we too often mingle reliance upon self, or upon some other arm of flesh, with our reliance upon our Lord. Good, easy men, we whisper to ourselves, "We can manage." Oh yes, we have had trouble before, and we are persons of experience and shrewdness, and therefore we can see our way. Brethren, we are never so weak as when we feel strongest, and never so foolish as when we dream that we are wise. When you are "up to the mark" you will soon be down to the mark. When our confidence is partly in God and partly in ourselves, our overthrow is not far off. That angel who stood with one foot upon the sea and the other upon the earth would have been drowned if he had not been an angel. Since you are not an angel, take care that you put both feet upon the *terra firma* of divine strength and truth. If you trust in yourself in the least degree, one link of the chain is too weak to bear you, and it is of no avail that the other links are strong. Is this the reason why you are so fearful, that your faith is diluted with self-confidence?

Again, *was it absorption in their trial* which led to their excessive fearfulness? If they had described their case, they would, no doubt, have dwelt upon the darkness, the hideous *"darkness which may be felt."* They would have bidden us hearken to the howling of the winds, and their terrific screams, like the neighing of wild horses maddened in fight. Mark how the wind descends in downpours from the hills and forces the boat under water! And this, again, is resented by the sea, which hurls the frail vessel aloft, and tosses it to and fro with watery hands, as though it were a juggler's ball. The storm was very fierce, and the boat was very frail. See how it is spun around and around in the whirlwind! Suppose we had urged them to be trustful and quiet; might they not have answered that we were not in their situation, or we would not find it quite so easy to be calm? "Ah!" says one, "I have a wife and family at home who depend upon my fishing. How can I be calm when I think of them as a widow and orphans? A man cannot afford to be drowned who has a household depending on him. It is all very well for you to talk, but you do not know what it is to be drenched to the skin and near to death."

Well, brother, perhaps we do not; but this we do know, that when we fix our thoughts solely and alone on the winds and the waves and the wives and all that, it is then that we are troubled. If we could put the master-thought first, it would be different. The thought which covers all is that Jesus is with us. The winds blow, but Jesus is on board! The waves rage, but Jesus is on board! These poor sailors will not perish, for Jesus is on board! If they could have kept this cheering fact to the front, they would have banished their alarms, and, like their Lord, they would have been grandly calm. Instead of that, their brooding upon the present trial was too much for their faith, and they became childishly fearful.

Have I yet hit the nail on the head? If you have not found out the cause of your fearfulness, I must leave you to look for it yourselves, and I trust you may discover it and destroy it at once. We must not continue to be of little faith. We must glorify our Lord by a believing confidence in him, such as neither storm of sorrow nor tempest of temptation can shake.

I shall conclude by carrying this inquiry into another region for another purpose. In this congregation there are a considerable number of friends who are not yet believers in Jesus Christ, and I want to know from them why they have no faith. I implore them to help me in the question of why it is that they are still so fearful, still so undecided. My dear friend, you will want faith soon, for you will have to die. Whether you live in Christ or not, you will have to die; and dying is hard work to those who have no Savior. Perhaps before another Sabbath day you may be in the swellings of Jordan, and what will you do if you have no faith in Christ? Do you say that you desire to have faith? I am glad to hear it, but I would like to press this matter home, and to ascertain whether this desire is earnest, thorough, and hearty.

Do you know what it is that you desire? Are you in earnest to be saved? I do not mean, are you in earnest to escape from hell. That I should think is very likely, if you are in your senses; but are you in earnest to escape from *sin*? Do you want to be saved from the power of evil? Do you desire to be made good, and obedient, and true, and pure in life? If you do, then I would remind you that faith in Jesus is the only way of salvation; and I would press upon you eagerly to desire immediate faith. Yes, I would urge you now to believe in the Lord Jesus Christ with all your heart.

"I want to believe," say you. Well, then, what is to hinder this? If you cannot sit still in your seat, and make yourself believe all at once, there are ways to that end. If I were told that the king of Tartary was dead, and it was a matter of interest to me, I do not know whether I would be able to believe it or not, because I do not know anything about the king of Tartary, nor even whether there is such a person. If I wanted to believe the news, I would get the newspaper and read about it; and I dare say I would either believe it or disbelieve it within the next ten minutes.

Knowledge and evidence lead up to faith. It is just the same with faith in the Lord Jesus Christ. Faith is the gift of God and the work of the Holy Spirit, but it comes to us in a certain manner. Consider a minute. *Consider who the Savior is.* He is God and man. He came down to earth on purpose to save sinners. Do you not think that this Divine Person can save you? Is he not able? Do you not think that this loving Man will receive you? Is he not willing to save? Well then, trust him. Next, *consider what Jesus did.* He lived on earth a life of labor and sorrow, and he died on the cross to make atonement for sin. Stand and look at him as crucified for men. *He Himself bore our sins in His body on the cross.* The greatest source of faith is the contemplation of the cross of Christ. Look to his agonies, and say to yourself, "I can believe that by the merit of such a wondrous death, endured by such a person as this, God can justly forgive sin." Believe, then, for yourself, and see your own sins put away by the death of Christ. Will you also *consider what Jesus Christ is doing now?* He has risen from the dead; he has gone up into heaven; he is making intercession for transgressors – even for such persons as you are. Trust him, then. Trust Jesus because of who he is, what he has done, and what he is doing for sinners.

Remember that this is the whole of the business, as far as you are concerned. You are to accept what the Lord Jesus presents to you. Accept him. Yes, take him to be your own. Look you here. I turn to this friend behind me, and I say, "Will you take my hand?"¹ See? He takes it freely. Jesus Christ is as free to every sinner that feels his need of him as my hand was to my friend. He took my hand at once without question – will you not take Jesus? Take him now. If you take him, he is yours forever. Take his hand, and he will not withdraw it from your grasp. Oh, that you would cry out, "Lord, I accept you!"

Have you any doubts about the truth of the gospel? If so, I want to know what you think of us who preach to you. Do we deceive you? What do you think of your mother's confidence in Christ – is she also deceived? Those dear friends of yours who died so happy in the Lord, were they all deceivers or deceived? No. You know that the Word of God is true. Then believe it. Believe it for yourselves, and it will be as true to you as it has been true to us. You cannot, I am sure, deny the Scriptures; you dare not say that the gospel is a forgery, for it bears its own proof upon its forefront. Salvation by the substitution of our Lord is so grand an idea that no one could have invented it. It is self-evidently a divine fact. That God can be just, and yet pass by our sins, is a marvel past the conception of men; it could only have come from the heart of God. Believe it then, accept it as being true, and trust yourself to it. May the Spirit of God lead you to do so!

If you are not believing in Christ, I would like to know why not. Is it that you are believing in yourself? If so, give up such folly. You cannot trust yourself and trust Christ too; away with all notion of such a conjoining. Hang up self-confidence on a gallows as high as that on which Haman was suspended, for it is an abominable thing.

Perhaps it is your great sin that leads you to despair of pardon. There is no occasion for such unbelief, for God is abundant in mercy, and the blood of Jesus cleanses us from all sin. If you have great sin, remember that there is a great Savior. He who came to save us is the Son of God, and he laid down his life for us, and, therefore, he can save to the uttermost. Instead of doubting, I pray you to glorify God by believing in the greatness of his salvation.

---

1   The preacher suited the action to the word, and his hand was readily grasped by one of the deacons.

It was a pleasure to me in years past to enjoy the friendship of Mr. Brownlow North. Before conversion he was a thorough man of the world, and, I suppose, about as frivolous and corrupt as men of his position and character often are. After his conversion he began to preach the gospel with great fervor, and certain of his old companions were full of spite against him, probably considering him to be a hypocrite. One day when he was about to address a large congregation, a stranger passed him a letter, saying, "Read that before you preach." This letter contained a statement of certain irregularities of conduct committed by Brownlow North, and it ended with words to this effect: "How dare you, being conscious of the truth of all the above, pray and speak to the people this evening, when you are such a vile sinner?" The preacher put the letter into his pocket, entered the pulpit, and after prayer and praise, commenced his address to a very crowded congregation. But before speaking on his text, he produced the letter, and informed the people of its contents, and then added, "All that is said here is true, and it is a correct picture of the degraded sinner that I once was; and oh! how wonderful must the grace be that could revive and raise me up from such a death in trespasses and sins, and make me what I appear before you today: a vessel of mercy, one who knows that all his past sins have been cleansed away through the atoning blood of the Lamb of God! It is of his redeeming love that I have now to tell you, and to plead with any here who are not yet reconciled to God, to come this night in faith to Jesus, that he may take your sins away and heal them."

Thus, instead of closing the preacher's mouth by this letter, the Enemy's attempt only opened the hearts of the people, and the word was with power. Oh, that you, my dear hearers, would believe the Lord Jesus to be a real Savior of real sinners, and come to him with all your sins around you! Do not hope because you think yourselves pure; but come to Jesus because you are impure, and need to be cleansed by him. Cast yourselves at his dear feet at once. Take the Sinner's Friend to be your friend, because you are a sinner. Let the Savior be your Savior, because you need saving. God bless you, for Christ's sake! Amen.

Charles H. Spurgeon – A Brief Biography

Charles Haddon Spurgeon was born on June 19, 1834, in Kelvedon, Essex, England. He was one of seventeen children in his family (nine of whom died in infancy). His father and grandfather were Nonconformist ministers in England. Due to economic difficulties, eighteen-month-old Charles was sent to live with his grandfather, who helped teach Charles the ways of God. Later in life, Charles remembered looking at the pictures in *Pilgrim's Progress* and in *Foxe's Book of Martyrs* as a young boy.

Charles did not have much of a formal education and never went to college. He read much throughout his life though, especially books by Puritan authors.

Even with godly parents and grandparents, young Charles resisted giving in to God. It was not until he was fifteen years old that he was born again. He was on his way to his usual church, but when a heavy snowstorm prevented him from getting there, he turned in at a little Primitive Methodist chapel. Though there were only about fifteen people in attendance, the preacher spoke from Isaiah 45:22: *Look unto me, and be ye saved, all the ends of the earth.* Charles Spurgeon's eyes were opened and the Lord converted his soul.

He began attending a Baptist church and teaching Sunday school. He soon preached his first sermon, and then when he was sixteen years old, he became the pastor of a small Baptist church in Cambridge. The church soon grew to over four hundred people, and Charles Spurgeon, at the age of nineteen, moved on to become the pastor of the New Park Street Church in London. The church grew from a few hundred attenders to a few thousand. They built an addition to the church, but still needed more room to accommodate the congregation. The Metropolitan Tabernacle was built in London in 1861, seating more than 5,000 people. Pastor Spurgeon preached the simple message of the cross, and thereby attracted many people who wanted to hear God's Word preached in the power of the Holy Spirit.

On January 9, 1856, Charles married Susannah Thompson. They had twin boys, Charles and Thomas. Charles and Susannah loved each other deeply, even amidst the difficulties and troubles that they faced in life, including health problems. They helped each other spiritually, and often together read the writings of Jonathan Edwards, Richard Baxter, and other Puritan writers.

Charles Spurgeon was a friend of all Christians, but he stood firmly on the Scriptures, and it didn't please all who heard him. Spurgeon believed in and preached on the sovereignty of God, heaven and hell, repentance, revival, holiness, salvation through Jesus Christ alone, and the infallibility and necessity of the Word of God. He spoke against worldliness and hypocrisy among Christians, and against Roman Catholicism, ritualism, and modernism.

One of the biggest controversies in his life was known as the "Down-Grade Controversy." Charles Spurgeon believed that some pastors of his time were "down-grading" the faith by compromising with the world or the new ideas of the age. He said that some pastors were denying the inspiration of the Bible, salvation by faith alone, and the truth of the Bible in other areas, such as creation. Many pastors who believed what Spurgeon condemned were not happy about this, and Spurgeon eventually resigned from the Baptist Union.

Despite some difficulties, Spurgeon became known as the "Prince of Preachers." He opposed slavery, started a pastors' college, opened an orphanage, led in helping feed and clothe the poor, had a book fund for pastors who could not afford books, and more.

Charles Spurgeon remains one of the most published preachers in history. His sermons were printed each week (even in the newspapers), and then the sermons for the year were re-issued as a book at the end of the year. The first six volumes, from 1855-1860, are known as *The Park Street Pulpit*, while the next fifty-seven volumes, from 1861-1917 (his sermons continued to be published long after his death), are known as *The Metropolitan Tabernacle Pulpit*. He also oversaw a monthly magazine-type publication called *The Sword and the Trowel*, and Spurgeon wrote many books, including *Lectures to My Students, All of Grace, Around the Wicket Gate, Advice for Seekers, John Ploughman's Talks, The Soul Winner, Words of Counsel for Christian Workers, Cheque Book of the Bank of Faith, Morning and Evening*, his autobiography, and more, including some commentaries, such as his twenty-year study on the Psalms – *The Treasury of David*.

Charles Spurgeon often preached ten times a week, preaching to an estimated ten million people during his lifetime. He usually preached from only one page of notes, and often from just an outline. He read about six books each week. During his lifetime, he had read *The Pilgrim's Progress* through more than one hundred times. When he died, his personal library consisted of more than 12,000 books. However, the Bible always remained the most important book to him.

Spurgeon was able to do what he did in the power of God's Holy Spirit because he followed his own advice – he met with God every morning before meeting with others, and he continued in communion with God throughout the day.

Charles Spurgeon suffered from gout, rheumatism, and some depression, among other health problems. He often went to Menton, France, to recuperate and rest. He preached his final sermon at the Metropolitan Tabernacle on June 7, 1891, and died in France on January 31, 1892, at the age of fifty-seven. He was buried in Norwood Cemetery in London.

Charles Haddon Spurgeon lived a life devoted to God. His sermons and writings continue to influence Christians all over the world.

Other Similar Titles

***Life in Christ (Vol. 1, 2 & 3),*
by Charles H. Spurgeon**

Men who were led by the hand or groped their way along the wall to reach Jesus were touched by his finger and went home without a guide, rejoicing that Jesus Christ had opened their eyes. Jesus is still able to perform such miracles. And, with the power of the Holy Spirit, his Word will be expounded and we'll watch for the signs to follow, expecting to see them at once. Why shouldn't those who read this be blessed with the light of heaven? This is my heart's inmost desire.
 – Charles H. Spurgeon

Available where books are sold.

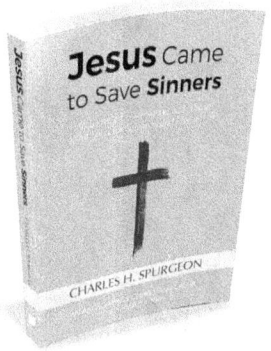

Jesus Came to Save Sinners, **by Charles H. Spurgeon**

This is a heart-level conversation with you, the reader. Every excuse, reason, and roadblock for not coming to Christ is examined and duly dealt with. If you think you may be too bad, or if perhaps you really are bad and you sin either openly or behind closed doors, you will discover that life in Christ is for you too. You can reject the message of salvation by faith, or you can choose to live a life of sin after professing faith in Christ, but you cannot change the truth as it is, either for yourself or for others. As such, it behooves you and your family to embrace truth, claim it for your own, and be genuinely set free for now and eternity. Come and embrace this free gift of God, and live a victorious life for Him.

Available where books are sold.

***Words of Warning*,**
by Charles H. Spurgeon

This book, *Words of Warning*, is an analysis of people and the gospel of Christ. Under inspiration of the Holy Spirit, Charles H. Spurgeon sheds light on the many ways people may refuse to come to Christ, but he also shines a brilliant light on how we can be saved. Unsaved or wavering individuals will be convicted, and if they allow it, they will be led to Christ. Sincere Christians will be happy and blessed as they consider the great salvation with which they have been saved.

Available where books are sold.

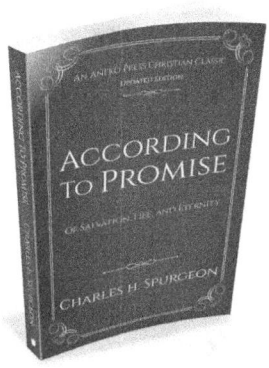

According to Promise,
by Charles H. Spurgeon

The first part of this book is meant to be a sieve to separate the chaff from the wheat. Use it on your own soul. It may be the most profitable and beneficial work you have ever done. He who looked into his accounts and found that his business was losing money was saved from bankruptcy.

The second part of this book examines God's promises to His children. The promises of God not only exceed all precedent, but they also exceed all imitation. No one has been able to compete with God in the language of liberality. The promises of God are as much above all other promises as the heavens are above the earth.

Available where books are sold.

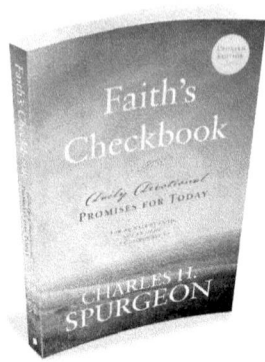

Faith's Checkbook, by Charles H. Spurgeon

Faith's Checkbook is a one-year devotional meant to encourage you to take God at His Word – to take hold of God's promises by faith. Each day you will be presented with a specific promise from the Bible, along with accompanying exhortation by Charles Spurgeon.

This is your "spiritual checkbook," if you will. God's bank account of provision is ample, and it cannot be overdrawn. Every situation you might face is equally met with a promise that, if accepted, will sufficiently see you through.

"God has given no promise that He will not redeem. He does not offer hope that He will not fulfill. To help my brethren believe this, I have prepared this little volume." – Charles H. Spurgeon

Available where books are sold.

***Morning by Morning,* by Charles H. Spurgeon**

Charles H. Spurgeon's devotionals *Morning by Morning* and *Evening by Evening* have inspired, encouraged, and challenged Christians for generations. Spurgeon, with his masterful hand, carefully selected his text from throughout the Bible and covered a broad range of topics, in order to present a well-balanced and fruitful daily devotional for readers both young and old.

Now updated into more-modern English for today's readers, and again separated into two volumes as originally published, with morning devotionals in one volume and evening devotionals in the second. We chose a 11-point font for the sake of legibility, and formatted the devotionals so each fits on a single page.

Available where books are sold.

Faithful to Christ, by Charles H. Spurgeon

I believe that many Christians get into a lot of trouble by not being honest in their convictions. For instance, if a person goes into a workshop, or a soldier into a barracks, and if he does not fly his flag from the beginning, it will be very difficult for him to run it up afterwards. But if he immediately and boldly lets them know, "I am a Christian, and there are certain things that I cannot do to please you, and certain other things that I cannot help doing even though they might displease you" – when that is clearly understood, after a while the peculiarity of the thing will be gone, and the person will be let alone.

However, if he is a little dishonest and thinks that he is going to please the world and please Christ too, he can depend on it that he is in for a rough time. If he tries the way of compromise, his life will be like that of a toad under a harrow or a fox in a dog kennel. That will never do. Come out. Show your colors. Let it be known who you are and what you are. Although your course will not be smooth, it will certainly not be half as rough as if you tried to run with the hare and hunt with the hounds, which is a very difficult piece of business.

Available where books are sold.

Following Christ, **by Charles H. Spurgeon**

You cannot have Christ if you will not serve Him. If you take Christ, you must take Him in all His qualities. You must not simply take Him as a Friend, but you must also take Him as your Master. If you are to become His disciple, you must also become His servant. God-forbid that anyone fights against that truth. It is certainly one of our greatest delights on earth to serve our Lord, and this is to be our joyful vocation even in heaven itself: *His servants shall serve Him: and they shall see His face* (Revelation 22:3-4).

Available where books are sold.

www.ingramcontent.com/pod-product-compliance
Lightning Source LLC
Chambersburg PA
CBHW070133080526
44586CB00015B/1672